The Competition Horse
Breeding, Production and Management

Susan McBane

with

Gillian McCarthy BSc (Hons)

New York

Maxwell Macmillan Canada
Toronto

Maxwell Macmillan International
New York • Oxford • Singapore • Sydney

Published in Great Britain by BSP Professional Books, an
imprint of Blackwell Scientific Publications Ltd
Osney Mead, Oxford OX2 0EL
First published 1991

Howell Book House
Macmillan Publishing Company
866 Third Avenue
New York, NY 10022

Maxwell Macmillan Canada, Inc.
1200 Eglinton Avenue East, Suite 200
Don Mills, Ontario M3C 3N1

Library of Congress Cataloging-in-Publication Data

McBane, Susan
    The competition horse: breeding, production and management/
Susan McBane with Gillian McCarthy.—1st American ed.
        p.   cm.
    Includes bibliographical references and index.
    ISBN 0-87605-831-4.
    I. Competition horses.   I. McCarthy, Gillian.   II. Title.
SF294.3. M36   1991
636.1′088′8—dc20   91-8390
                                                  CIP

Macmillan books are available at special discounts for bulk purchases for sales
promotions, premiums, fund-raising, or educational use. For details, contact:

                    Special Sales Director
                    Macmillan Publishing Company
                    866 Third Avenue
                    New York, NY 10022

First American Edition 1991

10 9 8 7 6 5 4 3 2 1

Printed in Great Britain

This book is dedicated to all those who put their horses first when competing and training, ahead of any potential prizes and kudos.

Contents

Preface   ix
Acknowledgements   x
Introduction   xi

 1   Market Forces: The Horse for the Job   1
 2   Conformation, Action and Temperament   46
 3   Heredity and Selective Breeding   60
 4   Breeding Practices   67
 5   Environmental Considerations   78
 6   Selecting Breeding Stock   108
 7   Dietary Management   119
 8   Prohibited Substances   175
 9   Management Topics   184
10   Marketing   212

Bibliography   230
Index   231

Preface

Competitive equestrianism and the requirement for horses capable of taking part has never been greater. Demand increases yearly as does the all round interest and involvement in the equestrian industry as a whole, by 5 per cent annually it was claimed at one conference.

Some breeders seem to have it all taped; they regularly produce winners and have carved their own niches in the market. Others go about the process of producing a competition horse in a much more haphazard fashion and are often disappointed in their results. Yet more people would like to breed a competition horse, or set up a stud, but have little knowledge of how to go about it, not only the practical skill and technical expertise involved in stud management but also the more theoretical, intangible aspects such as what to mate with what.

This book cannot help with practical stud management. There are several excellent manuals on that topic. I hope that what it *will* help with is the second aspect – that of specifically producing horses for competition work with a fair chance of success. A quick glance down the contents page will reveal the topics covered in these pages.

The book is not intended for existing professionals or notably successful amateurs but for those wishing to get in on the competition scene at the production end and wanting an overview of the aspects involved – what type to breed, what discipline(s) to concentrate on, an understanding of heredity, modern developments such as artificial insemination and embryo transfer, breed characteristics, management, selection, marketing and so on.

It is also intended for those wishing to buy a competition horse either for breeding or performance and who wish to know generally more about the competition horse milieu.

For all those people, I hope the book will act as a significant help and encouragement at the start of a fascinating enterprise – the satisfaction, both spiritual and practical, of producing a world-beater of your very own making!

Susan McBane

Acknowledgements

I should like to thank my fellow author, Gillian McCarthy, who has written the sections on pasture management, dietary management of the competition horse, prohibited substances and physiotherapy. Her contribution has brought an authoritative, scientific accuracy which I could not have provided and the subjects she has covered are of primary importance to competition horse owners, breeders, trainers and riders, not to mention their managers and grooms.

We would like to thank the following for their help in the preparation of the section on prohibited substances:

M.A. Atock, MRCVS, head of the Veterinary Department, FEI, Berne, Switzerland.

R.B. Williams, BVSc, MPhil, MRCVS, Horseracing Forensic Laboratory Ltd, Newmarket, England.

Charles Frank, MRCVS, veterinary adviser, the UK National Trainers Federation.

Henry Leach, MSc, independent analyst, Bangor, North Wales.

Thanks are also due to Joy Claxton who has illustrated several of my books and who is not only a competent equestrian artist but also very helpful and easy to work with.

Finally I wish to thank all those who helped provide photographs to illustrate various points in the book and which helped bring it to life and make it easy on the eye.

Susan McBane

Cover illustration
The front cover illustration is the famous British show jumper, Henderson Milton, one of the most popular and successful horses of recent years. By Marius out of Aston Answer (a Grade A show jumper), his breeding is a mixture of Dutch warmblood and Thoroughbred with performance ability on both sides of his pedigree. He was bred by Mr John Harding Rolls. (*Photo:* Howard Kingsnorth, kindly supplied by Henderson Unit Trust Management Limited.)

Introduction

The competition horse is a comparatively new phenomenon, the expression itself being probably less than ten years old, and the use of horses for competition as we mainly know it today is certainly a development of this century and particularly of the past 30 years.

Probably the oldest equestrian sport is polo (allowing for the fact that chariot racing as such is no longer carried on), so the actual use of horses for competition is not new but several thousand years old. However, it is only since the end of World War II that riding for leisure and competition has become a sizeable recreation, industry even, and the breeding of competition horses taken with a serious professionalism.

The three Olympic equestrian disciplines, at the time of writing, are show jumping, eventing and dressage and these are the ones most people think of when we speak of competition horses. However, significant numbers of people are interested in competition carriage driving, endurance riding and harness racing. These six disciplines are the ones with which this book is most concerned. There is also polo, point-to-point racing, showing in all its many forms and, of course, the bloodstock racing industry comprising both flat racing and hurdling and steeplechasing. Team chasing, at least here in Britain, is increasingly popular, demanding high class horses; hunter trials also continue to attract no shortage of entries, and rodeo, vaulting (*voltige*), gymkhana, Western sports such as roping and barrel racing and other more obscure equestrian pastimes such as jousting all have their devotees.

The demand for horses bred for competition and capable of acquitting themselves well has never been greater. Unfortunately, very many people have jumped on to the bandwagon of competition horse breeding and production. As in nearly every field, more nearly always means worse, and the quality and true potential of some of the animals put forward as the proverbial 'potential competition horse' have no hope of reaching even regional standard let alone being likely to hold their own in national or international competition. Potential is exactly that – crystal-ball gazing. 'Will go far in the right hands' is a convenient get-out for the seller of just about any animal with a remote chance of filling the bill. When the horse *does not* go far, obviously yours weren't the right hands!

But there are certain standards we can look for when seeking a competition horse, standards which, if adhered to, give us a reasonable, even good, chance of acquiring or breeding a horse which genuinely *will* go far – in the right hands, of course! Despite the vast amount of instruction, management advice and general help available, there are still, and will always be, good, bad and indifferent riders, trainers, managers and grooms. It has always been the case, and probably always will be, that a truly good horse will succeed in spite of, not because of, his human connections.

It is not false modesty (well, not always!) that causes some of the best competitors, in any discipline, to say they could never have succeeded without their horse, that the horse got them out of trouble or knew better than the human element of the team what to do in a sticky spot. It is a salutary experience to be put in your place by your horse – they truly are great levellers – and this extra quality, far and above physical conformation, constitution and temperament, often divides the winners from the also-rans in equestrian competition.

It is, however, a quality that can be recognised and bred for, just like all the others. The science of genetics (heredity) may sound esoteric and off-putting to the 'ordinary', non-scientific horse breeder, but a basic understanding of it is a great practical help and not difficult to grasp, as I hope Chapter 3 in this book will show. The other essential facets of competition horse breeding, management (especially feeding) and production (although not specific training for individual disciplines) are also covered, and I hope that, compact though it is, the book will give sound basic guidelines to those wishing to become involved in this aspect of the equestrian world.

International production

The book, although written by a British author, is not, I hope, too jingoistic. It is specifically intended to appeal to an international readership, having regard to the obvious international nature of equestrian competition today. The competition horse market may not yet be quite so integrally international as the racing and bloodstock industries, but as prices for these horses rise and international equine travel becomes, one hopes, easier, this may well happen.

In Britain and Ireland, at least, a common complaint is that breeders cannot make a decent living, or even a living at all, out of breeding competition horses. Most studs only survive because of their stallion fees, not the prices they obtain for youngstock when they reach saleable age. On the other hand, British and Irish buyers often complain that they cannot find the right sort of animals 'at home' and when they do they are far too expensive, yet so many of these same buyers seem to think little of going abroad, usually to the rest of Europe from the UK, and paying much larger sums for foreign bred animals which do not seem to have any more of that magic potential than home-bred horses. Is there something about locally-produced stock which buyers see as automatically inferior, or is it simply another of the many whims and fashions to which the horse world seems heir?

It works the other way, too. Foreign buyers very often come here and pay large sums for British and Irish bred horses which were turned down by those very buyers who paid similar sums for foreign bred and produced animals! Not being a psychologist, I cannot explain that. Some people will always think that the grass is greener on the other side and take some sort of masochistic delight in paying out huge sums to the detriment of their bank balances, those of home breeders and the country's trade deficit, to procure animals which, to them, have something a little bit extra special because they are foreign. This happens, it seems, in all countries, not just Britain, which simply reinforces the international nature of the competition horse market.

Every equestrian country today has the stock to produce international-quality horses. The level of import/export exchanges and purchases has now reached the point where so many breeds are related to each other, and have so much common blood, or rather blood in common, that national boundaries and identities, as far as bloodlines and breeds' genetic pools are concerned, are melting away. It is reaching the point where national reputations are made not only because of the various qualities of a country's indigeneous stock, but also because of the abilities of a country's human inhabitants and horse breeders to blend together animals of varying qualities to produce their idea of the perfect competition horse, no matter where the foundation stock originated.

The current vogue in competition horse breeding is for what are known as Warmblood horses, and there is nothing wrong with that. Warmbloods are normally a blend of indigenous stock from various European countries, in other words not Britain and Ireland, with Thoroughbred blood. The Thoroughbred, of course, is undoubtedly a British breed, having been created here largely in the eighteenth century for the purpose of racing. European breeders who wanted to change or 'improve' their indigenous stock did so initially with oriental, usually Arabian, horses, and later imported Thoroughbreds from England.

The Thoroughbred itself is similarly the result of blending indigenous stock with oriental blood, again mainly Arabian, with the latter being allowed to predominate as the breed was developed for more and more speed and earlier and earlier maturity for the purposes of racing. Barb and Turkmene blood were also used and, as the varying appearances of individual Thoroughbreds today shows, the indigenous foundation stock probably varied widely too, from native ponies to larger, heavier stock.

Strictly speaking, any breed comprising Thoroughbred with non-Thoroughbred blood could be described as a Warmblood. The term simply denotes a mixture of 'hot' blood (meaning the more sensitive, fiery temperament of the Thoroughbred and Arab) with 'cold' blood (meaning the more phlegmatic, dull temperamental characteristics of coarser, heavier breeds and types). In practice, however, the breed description Warmblood means the breeds developed by mixing the Thoroughbred and sometimes the Arab (or the Anglo-Arab – a cross between the two) with the continental European indigenous horses of cold blood type. It does not, for example, refer to the cross between a Thoroughbred and a Shire, to use two extreme examples, or an Arab and an Irish Draught. The description Warmblood always denotes continental European origin, even though many other countries such as Britain and America are now developing their own Warmbloods based on such stock.

Those who decry the current popularity of Warmbloods (which are without doubt making an indelible mark on the competition horse scene) might do well to really look into their pedigrees. Most of them are largely Thoroughbred these days – and where did the Thoroughbred as a breed originate? In Britain, of course. But where did we British acquire the bulk of the stock making up Thoroughbred blood and genes? From the Orient, notably Arabia, so we certainly cannot claim to have created the breed on our own from purely our own natural resources. We used other countries' stock, with the characteristics we were looking for, on our native animals (many of which already contained some oriental blood due to low-level imports of such blood from Roman times onwards), to create the breed we wanted. That is exactly what Warmblood breeders on the continent of Europe have done.

A cross which has proved singularly successful in both hunting and competitive sports is the Thoroughbred/Irish Draught cross – technically a warmblooded horse but in practice not regarded in the same context as European-based Warmbloods as described above. Although Britain has a thriving Irish Draught Horse Society of its own, the Irish Draught is patently not a British horse. And what Welsh Cob breeders would say if anyone described their stock as English does not bear thinking about!

Whatever you want

The purpose of this preamble is to stress the truly world-wide, international nature of competition horse breeding today and in the past. It is fine to be patriotic but perhaps what we all should be patriotic about is our individual national skills at blending characteristics to produce what we want. In fact, if any country could claim to have played the foundation role in the development of the horse as a species it is America, since the horse's primeval ancestors developed there and spread to much of the rest of the world before dying out in its native continent – but that is splitting hairs. The horse did not 'return home' until the time of the Spanish Conquistadores, and America has been re-importing coals to Newcastle ever since, creating many breeds of its own. It has taken our own British Thoroughbred and moulded it in recent years to the extend that a recognizably American type of Thoroughbred has emerged, with heavier muscling in the hind-quarters and legs and with a longer hind leg, too, due to the almost blanket demand for pure speed in the US. They have done this with existing, General Stud Book-registered stock of course – within the breed, not by using outcrosses, which would not have been permissible anyway – by selecting individuals with the characteristics they wanted and mating them together, the most required characteristic obviously being speed, which brings with it the necessary conformation, in extremes, described above.

Within the Arab breed, to take another example, there are instantly recognizable types from country to country, often from stud to stud within the same country. With the judicious use of stock that shows, or is known to produce in its progeny, the characteristics you are looking for, there is, it seems, almost no end to what you can produce.

It is a well-known fact that no horse is perfect; there is something wrong, however slight, with them all but by careful selection you can produce horses which are, as they say, extremely hard to fault. Often, selecting for one or more good, desirable characteristics such as particularly good feet or a strong, medium-length back, means that you have to accept faults as well, such as a suspect temperament or a slightly bent hind leg, or whatever. However, handsome is as handsome does. In the world of the competition horse, performance is almost everything – in the racing world performance *is* everything; looks do not matter at all. For dressage, whether ridden or driven, an attractive appearance and markings (white socks) which, if present, are even and do not detract from good paces, are highly desirable.

The racing world produced its superb breed, the Thoroughbred, purely by mating for performance, in other words mainly speed with varying degrees of stamina depending on what racing distances were in fashion at the time. Within the breed, there are sprinters bred to gallop full out for comparatively short distances (starting at five furlongs), middle distance horses bred for the English Classics and those bred to race at longer distances.

America has produced what is said to be the fastest horse in the world over a quarter of a mile – the Quarter Horse – whereas the Arab is known particularly for stamina with fair speed over very long distances such as 100 mile races.

The point is that the type of performance required and the equestrian discipline involved often dictate the appearance of the horse, its morphology, rather than the other way round. The racehorse evolved to have a long, low, ground-devouring stride because that type of stride proved to be the fastest in practice. It gradually dawned that the winning individuals conformed basically to a particular type.

Today, in the competitive dressage arena, the type of horse favoured has more knee-action, less daisy-cutting, than the Thoroughbred, more 'flexible' hocks and more swing and elasticity in its stride. This type of action adds activity and athleticism to the movement and general

Plate 1 An Andalusian stallion of an ideal type for high school work and true classical equitation. His name is Pedro and he belongs to Mary Chipperfield who has used him for years for high school acts in the circus ring. He spent much time with Miss Sylvia Stanier, LVO, who gave high school demonstrations with him on long reins as well as under saddle. (Photograph by Peter Sweet.)

impression in the arena, and impressing the judges with these qualities is just as important today as performing the movements and figures correctly. In fact, often the actual movements are not well performed but the horse receives good marks purely, it seems, because he or she created a favourable overall impression, which was more pleasing than the specific failings and inaccuracies were *dis*pleasing!

Plate 2 The Andalusian stallion Pedro ridden in *passage* by his owner, Mary Chipperfield. He shows the 'lift' and bearing needed for this type of advanced movement and performs both *passage* and *piaffe* to a much higher standard than the vast majority of competitive dressage horses, most of which do not have ideal conformation for such airs. With the current requirement for almost spectacular extension as well as collection in the advanced and Grand Prix dressage arena, they have to be jacks of all trades within their discipline, and be conformed accordingly. (Photograph by Peter Sweet.)

A case in point is the movement *piaffe*. It is *very* rare to see even a top-level competitive dressage horse perform a classically correct *piaffe*; many of them barely leave the ground, particularly behind, yet if the ordinary paces and the horse's overall appearance are favourable it will usually receive good marks.

Talking of classical matters, the old masters' idea of a suitable horse for classical equitation was certainly not today's competition horse, not because it did not exist as a type in their day but because the type required for classical airs requires more spring, lift and extravagance in collection than today's competitive dressage horses have, not least because of our present-day emphasis on extension as well as collection. The type of horse considered ideal for classical equitation, because its proud bearing and natural paces lend themselves ideally to it, is the Iberian type – the Andalusian and Lusitano and also the Alter-Real. Although the Spanish Riding School in Vienna use Lipizzaners (based on the Andalusian) and most modern schools of equitation claim to base their methods on the Spanish Riding School's methods (which do differ from the classical French, Spanish and Portugese (Latin) schools), Lipizzaners do not normally excel in today's competitive arenas, again because of the inability to extend sufficiently for today's competitive requirements.

Few people would consider a 'classical' type of horse when it came to breeding jumpers, yet the Lusitano stallion Novilhero, with John Whitaker here in England, was of international class when it came to show jumping. Here was a horse who could really perform and he was an entire! Yet when he was put to stud here with a view to breeding jumpers he received a miserly ten mares – illogicality exemplified!

Jumpers come in so many different shapes, types and sizes that some otherwise sensible people have said that they cannot be bred, despite hard evidence to the contrary. This is patent nonsense. The tragedy is that so many performance horses are gelded before even having a chance to show what they can do. It is not always possible to go back to their sire and dam, who may be dead or retired. However, there *are* proven guidelines as to the conformation most likely to produce capable jumpers, given in Chapter 2. These plus the performance abilities of near relatives can take much of the guesswork out of breeding show jumpers, although many people, surely, would welcome seeing more entires performing, in the mould of Galoubet and Marius.

1
Market Forces:
The Horse for the Job

Whatever equestrian discipline is your particular preference, your likelihood of success, or at least enjoyment, is probably increased 75 per cent by buying the right horse for the job and for you personally. Many horses are multi-disciplinary and effective in more than one field, but it is a rare animal which succeeds at the top level in more than one, although they are certainly not unknown.

Chapter 2 is concerned with conformation, action and temperament in general and with some emphasis on particular disciplines. Let us look here generally at the sort of horse called for today in the main competitive disciplines.

Competitive disciplines

Show jumping

Rather obviously, a potential show jumper must be able to jump with more than average ability. Although show jumpers are notorious for failing to conform to any particularly recognisable type, coming in all shapes and sizes, the horse itself must be harmoniously made and in proportion. Workmanlike rather than showy action is preferred, with a calm, intelligent temperament which does not hot up against the clock, and athletic use of the limbs, naturally inclined to fold the front legs right up and lift the knees at the same time; the hocks too must be noticeably flexed to help get the back end over without dragging a toe and collecting faults. Although training plays a great part in performance, the horse should show a natural bascule over fences – a type of action which helps provide those vital extra inches when it counts.

The walk, as in all horses, is indicative of the other paces. The show jumper must have an active, smooth pace, with the hind end, the propulsive force, strong and the hind hooves over-tracking the fore. The front end, too, should move freely and the shoulders must be mobile to help provide the agility needed; in other words, the horse must move from the shoulder and not just the elbow.

When tried over a pole, the horse must look where he is going and approach his fence calmly, with purpose and intent but not treating the whole event as if some extra special effort were required. His quarters should thrust the horse seemingly effortlessly upwards with the shoulders lifting easily and the legs flexing neatly. The head and neck should be used naturally to balance during the bascule and the whole performance appear strong and fluid.

The top show jumper must be able to stand pressure of a regular sort, because he does not get anything like so much time off as, say, an event horse, but may be jumping several days a week for several months, depending on his rider's policies. He should not panic under pressure or direction from his rider, which can result in his jumping 'flat' or rushing fences.

Eventing (horse trials)

The event horse has rather unkindly been called a jack of all trades, but in fact it requires a special kind of horse to excel in three major disciplines – dressage, cross-country and show jumping – and also be able to tackle a steeplechase course alone and in cold blood at racing pace, perform calmly in the dressage phase when fighting fit and, after the cross-country, come out again the next day, when he must be feeling tired and somewhat stiff no matter how fit he is, and perform a creditable show jumping round with accuracy, precision and obedience.

Probably the ideal three-day event horse is the same type as a class steeplechase horse: about 16 hands and over but not much above 17 hands, Thoroughbred or, more probably, seven-eighths Thoroughbred, with strength, scope, power and speed – an all-round athlete, in fact. Stamina (most important), the ability to combine their jumping ability with speed so as not to waste time on the critical cross-country phase, and conformation as 'correct' as possible, are three points which typify the top event horses. Substance is essential not only to withstand the rigours of the sport but the training involved, and a willing, calm but not phlegmatic temperament is advantageous.

The action must be straight and economical, as anything else uses up vital energy and inclines the horse to self-inflicted injury and difficulty in getting himself out of trouble over tricky obstacles. A Thoroughbred-type gait, with fairly low, sweeping strides, is far preferable to a high, more rounded action, since it creates speed.

Courage is a much-discussed topic when considering horses, and is difficult to define in a species which is by nature a prey animal evolved to be nervous and to run away from trouble. However, the quality of courage as we humans define it is certainly to be looked for in both

Plate 3 Welton Apollo, the only stallion currently standing at stud to have completed and been placed in the gruelling Badminton three-day event. He is pictured here with his rider, Leslie Law, with whom he formed a well-known and successful partnership in advanced event classes. Welton Apollo is a Thoroughbred by the Limbury Stud's prolific event horse stallion, Welton Gameful, out of Water Rights (by Game Rights), herself an intermediate event mare. (Photograph kindly supplied by Mr Sam Barr of the Limbury Stud, Hartpury, Gloucestershire.)

show jumpers and event horses faced with high, wide and often awkwardly-placed obstacles with, in the case of the eventers, often no clue as to what lies on the other side. Many horses, thankfully, do seem to possess courage, although more than one top trainer has publicly said that we mistake it for stupidity and a lack of a sense of self-preservation!

Probably the most important physical qualities are good legs and feet to stand up to this tough sport, and the agility to use them nimbly and quickly to avert a fall and to jump economically but at speed.

Carriage driving

Carriage driving, too, is a tough sport needing a tough horse, or rather five of them if the human element of the team wishes to go in for the ultimate in this discipline – four-in-hand competition work – the fifth horse, obviously, being a reserve who must still be given his full quota of training, management care and competition experience if he is to be 'fully qualified'.

Driving horses need to be strong and compact with plenty of substance and particularly good legs and feet. The best height is somewhere between 15 and 16 hands. Driving horses need a slightly more upright shoulder than pure riding horses as this makes it more comfortable for them to lean into the collar and really push.

There is a very common misconception that the horses actually *pull* the vehicle. This is physically impossible – the only way you can get a horse to pull anything is by tying it to his tail. The horses push into their collars, or breast harness where this is preferred, in the same way a man might get his shoulder behind a heavy piece of furniture and push it along. For this reason, the driving horse's quarters are just as important as those of a riding horse, and could perhaps receive more attention than they seem to at present.

They must be strong and muscled, not too short, and the thighs should similarly be well-muscled. The horse must certainly not be cut-up behind (in other words, the muscles between the thighs must meet) and the quarters must show an even hip height and a strong, squarish appearance from behind, with plenty of width throughout this vital engine.

The horse should have a shortish back, although not so short that he habitually overreaches, a good front with a longish shoulder and a slightly (or even markedly) sloping croup to enable him more easily to get his hind legs under him to provide that pushing power. However, there is a fine line between a quarter which is sloping and one which slopes *too* much! Perhaps it is safer to look for hind quarters which are not, at least, flat, and have that vital element, good muscling, along with size and strength.

The horse's paces and pushing power will be assisted if he has a well set-on head and neck – no upside-down necks, angular jaws or 'chopped about' withers. He should present a flowing, rounded outline and be big, rounded and muscled up even when very fit. His training will assist this type of development.

As for action, driving horses need a particularly good, ground-covering walk with loose, swinging strides and the ability to lengthen and shorten naturally. The trot, too, needs long, free strides with a certain showiness and elegance without over-extravagance, for the dressage phase. The horses do not work at the canter, of course, with the exception of a few strides now and then to make up time.

The horse is, obviously, under much less human control than the ridden horse. He must have a willing, obedient temperament in order to work largely from vocal command and also to get on well with his neighbour, if in a team. Again, as in any competition horse, a courageous, calm temperament is looked for.

Dressage

Today more than ever the charismatic quality called 'presence' is essential in the competitive dressage horse, plus, at present, a certain

Plate 4 Jennie Loriston-Clarke MBE, FBHS riding Dutch Gold, a son of Dutch Courage, at the Hermès International Dressage event.

amount of size – 16 and 17 hand animals being quite the norm now. The horse must, probably above all others, present a smooth, flowing outline/shape and preferably be handsome rather than flashy, pretty or beautiful, although, as ever, there are exceptions.

The dressage horse is an athlete, a gymnast, and unlike showing dressage is not largely a 'beauty competition'. Today, swinging, elastic, straight paces are essential, with the ability to both collect and extend, particularly in the higher echelons of the sport. Although a very great deal of improvement can be made in the horse's appearance by correct work and, therefore, muscular development, this should be done with a view to improving the horse's natural attributes rather than attempting to turn a sow's ear into a silk purse, as it were. Naturally harmonious and symmetrical conformation, presence, confidence and free, straight paces with the natural inclination to flex, but not over-flex, the joints, are what to look for.

The set of the neck and head are also important. In the higher levels of the sport, collection is, of course, essential, and this will be easier to

Fig. 1 The natural 'long and low' type of conformation common in many Thoroughbreds and their crosses, evolved unintentionally for speed during the development of the flat racehorse. Such horses will always find difficult the more collected paces in, for example, the higher levels of competitive dressage, because they are simply not conformed to naturally achieve *and maintain* the type of outline or carriage necessary.

Fig. 2 A warmblood-type horse with a naturally higher head carriage which will enable collected paces to be achieved more easily. Care should be taken, though, when selecting a horse to ensure that the head can flex comfortably at the poll and the horse has good natural back conformation, not a naturally stiff, hollow back sometimes found in such horses.

achieve if the horse has a natural set of head and neck which facilitates this, rather than having the neck set low on the shoulders and an angular or thick jowl which will make it uncomfortable and difficult for the horse to 'bridle', i.e. carry the front line of his face 5° in front of the vertical.

If the rider has no ambitions to progress beyond the lower levels of the sport, this type of neck and head carriage is less important due to the longer, lower outline required in the earlier stages. However, if the horse is being selected with a view to Advanced or even Grand Prix work, a *natural* long, low outline will be a decided disadvantage as the horse will subsequently be struggling to achieve and maintain the higher and more flexed/collected carriage required in advanced competition.

Typical riding conformation is required, with plenty of front and a well-laid back or sloping shoulder. The back should be of medium

Fig. 3 A horse which is croup-high will never be able to work physically up to the standards required in top-level competition without significant discomfort to both himself and his rider, who will have a permanent 'going downhill' sensation. Such a conformation also causes the saddle to constantly press into the backs of the shoulder blades causing muscle damage, soreness and sometimes permanent thickening of soft tissues. Being in more or less constant discomfort will also cause the horse's action to be adversely affected, not to mention his temper and willingness.

length or even very slightly on the long side and the quarters must *not* be higher than the withers or be too flat, both of which will make it very difficult for the horse to lower his quarters and get his hind legs under him for the propulsion and, later, collection, necessary. A flat or lumpy wither not only detracts from the appearance and 'quarters low' conformation but affords insufficient attachment for the muscles of the shoulder and forearm so, while a noticeably prominent wither is equally undesirable if for different reasons (a break in the outline and saddle-fitting problems) it must, if anything, be preferable to a flat one. However, a 'good' wither somewhere between the two is what to look for.

The rider will also be helping himself or herself if a horse with naturally free, straight paces is chosen, obvious though it may sound. Crooked action is anathema in a dressage horse. The horse, as already stated, needs elastic, swinging strides with an ability to flex easily all the joints if it is to respond to training and also catch the judges' eyes. A smart mover rather than an easy-going one is needed, and over-long strides can create problems later on when collection is sought. Most horses extend more easily and willingly than they collect. The gaits should be rounded and smooth, not long and low nor high and choppy, and the horse should appear to move on top of the ground, not go down into it. The horse should, particularly at canter, look as though he would find it easy to sit down if requested as this makes for an impressive canter with lift in the forehand.

Long distance/endurance riding

This is the sport which can truly claim to be the closest to the horse's natural inclinations to wander and for which his natural stamina is best fitted. Of course, man's demands in this extremely demanding sport do tax the horse much further than he would tax himself in nature, even if

Plate 5 Hourane, an Arab stallion who enjoys high school work and jumping alike, here shown by his owner, Miss Sylvia Stanier, LVO, on long reins. The Arabian breed has been used for centuries to improve very many other breeds and is even found in heavy horse breeds. It is the source, in good measure, of toughness, gaiety and panache in most of today's competition breeds including the Thoroughbred. (Photograph by Peter Sweet.)

being pursued by a predator, but the standards of horsemastership and equine fitness which generally prevail in the sport today, thanks to international control and policies, normally ensure that accidents and 'over-riding' occur no more often than in other equestrian disciplines.

Not all horses, however, are suited to this sport, which can range from casual competitive trail rides or training rides of 25 miles or less with moderate speed limits, to races of 100 miles in 24 hours which obviously demand the very highest standards of constitution, stamina and acquired physical fitness in both horse and rider. Any sound, fit horse should be able to complete successfully rides at the lower to medium levels but at the top end of the sport, temperament, way of going, constitution and, usually, size are the main points to consider, assuming the horse is healthy and sound anyway, of course.

In temperament, the horse must be biddable and willing to go at the pace he and the rider mutually agree, on a loose rein, largely finding his own way and looking where he is going. He must look after the rider to a large extent and, whether by training or natural inclination, must not be prone to leaning on the bit which is impossibly tiring when you are going mile after mile.

He must have a ground-covering stride at all paces, the trot being of the utmost importance, and next the canter, depending on the type of events the horse is aimed at and the consequent average speeds to be aimed at. His action must be straight and neat so he is not in danger of hitting himself nor of using up too much energy with unnecessary flamboyance. His paces must obviously be comfortable to sit. A tough constitution and tip-top, all-round good health are most important. Heart and lungs, feet and legs come to mind firstly, but every bodily system must work at peak efficiency. There is no room for a weak link in this sport.

Conformation should meet the classical ideal described in the next chapter, as far as possible, but once again individual harmony and symmetry are what to look for first. Good muscling, straight limbs, powerful quarters, deep girth, hard, flinty hooves and plenty of room for the windpipe in the jowl area are the most important points to check. Long backs are out for endurance horses. Medium to short backs denote the strength to carry a rider for many miles at sometimes a tough pace. Such a conformation will almost always result in the horse being close-coupled, not slack in the loins.

Sizes of successful horses do vary, but generally it is found that the smaller horses, and often ponies, are consistent winners. Generally, an animal around 15 hands high, and compact with it, will fill the bill.

Incidentally, it is often found that animals with all or much Arab blood succeed above others in this sport. The breed's stamina and keenness to go on without hotting up, as might a Thoroughbred, are legendary, and the fact that they often fill the winner's place in long distance and endurance rides confirms their general overall suitability for the sport. Other breeds and types do succeed, of course, but the Arab's qualities fit him so well for the sport that it has been said that your battle is half won before you even start if you have an Arab.

Harness racing

Britain, for some reason no one seems able to explain, has never really taken to harness racing and is virtually alone among the equestrain/ racing countries to have no significant harness racing industry. It takes place sporadically in Wales, the midlands and the north-west mainly, but attracts nothing like the crowds that mounted racing attracts. In other European countries, North America and Australasia, it is very big business indeed for the participants and extremely popular with spectators and punters.

The American Standardbred is probably the harness racer *par excellence* today, although other breeds have been developed and used extensively in the past. Harness racers either trot or pace, the trot being the normal if almost 'flying' diagonal gait and the pace being a lateral gait, in which the legs move in lateral pairs, the fore and hind on one side both moving forward together, and so on. This pace is natural to many horses and is popular with harness racing enthusiasts because pacers are slightly faster than trotters as their period of suspension in the air is longer due to their bodies rising slightly higher off the ground with each stride. The ground, obviously, acts as a brake or obstacle when the hooves make impact, so the less time a horse spends touching it, flying through the air instead, the faster he will be.

Harness racers, whether trotting or pacing, reach speeds almost as fast as ridden Thoroughbreds, averaging speeds of 30 mph to 32 mph, some faster. This sport is very much more standardised than Thoroughbred racing, most races taking place over about a mile. Training methods are similarly more standardised and the outcome of races, many say, much easier to predict – perhaps one reason why it is so popular with the punters.

The sport *is* very stressful on the horses and, without wishing to repeat myself *ad nauseam*, again a very tough, sound horse is required. Easily flared nostrils and windpipe room in the jowl are essential for a horse working at peak effort. A well-defined wither and a shoulder sloped at the almost universally-desired 45° are looked for, together with well-muscled forearms, straight forelegs and symmetrical, hard feet. Short cannons are another classical feature required, but interestingly longer, more sloping pasterns than are usually considered desirable are no drawback in a harness racer.

In fact, many trainers look more to the hind legs for absolute perfection, noticeably well-let-down hocks with the consequent long thigh and short cannon being particularly important. The hind end, as previously described, provides the thrust, but in trotting and pacing, the hind feet hit the ground a fraction of a second before the fore, and take the main weight of the horse's body at that moment, rather than the foreleg as in other disciplines. Particularly well-muscled, slightly sloping, powerful and harmonious quarters and thighs are especially important, with large, clean hocks. As ever in an athletic horse, a smooth, ground covering stride is wanted, with great extension and thrust for this sport.

In temperament, the horse must be 'controllably excitable', as was described to me by one trainer. Phlegmatic horses are an advantage in that they do not worry themselves into a lather before a race, but they must be able to be 'ignited' when it matters.

The natural inclination to pace has been reinforced by line- and inbreeding, and pacers also wear hobbles in training and during a race to prevent diagonal movement. Those unfamiliar with harness racing may have wondered why these horses wear the overhead check (similar to a bearing rein) which looks so uncomfortable. In practice, it is finely adjusted so as to leave the horse comfortable but prevent him lowering his head enough to facilitate a break into canter, which is not allowed. As for the horse's natural head carriage, surprisingly trainers do not particularly look for a high head carriage, but a low one would count against a horse.

Polo

In polo, the horses used are always called ponies no matter how big they are (and the favoured height for handiness is between 14.3 and 15.3 hands high today) just as Arabs are always called horses no matter how small they -may be. The main requirements are a placid temperament so the animal will not hot up during this very exciting game, physical agility and handiness for the constant starts, stops and turns, speed, and particularly acceleration plus strength.

Although obviously a riding horse, polo ponies are preferred with slightly different requirements from other riding horses. A rather short back, which is not generally synonymous with armchair comfort, is preferred as this feature does facilitate agility on the field. As polo is very much a contact sport, a stocky build without coarseness is an advantage so that the horse can withstand bumps, knocks and being ridden off, or riding off an opponent himself. Again, to make the trainer's and rider's job easier, it is best to choose a horse whose physical attributes make the necessary movements and manoeuvres easier; as far as head carriage is concerned, this means a well balanced body with a head and neck set on well, not too low on the front and not with a nose-poking carriage or a natural inclination to go behind the bit, as both these make control and manoeuvreability difficult.

As polo consists of twists and turns as well as sudden starts and stops, a good wither to help keep the saddle in place and a well-defined girth groove help considerably, although the ponies invariably wear breast girths. The nature of their work also makes long, sloping pasterns undesirable. Indeed, shorter more upright pasterns than normal are looked for, as these are less prone to tendon strain although increasing slightly the possibility of concussion injuries.

A well-sprung barrel with plenty of lung room is needed, with well-muscled quarters – over-all, a sprinter's conformation rather than a stayer's longer, leaner physique. In addition, good natural balance is a definite advantage.

The specific breed most likely to fulfil these requirements is the American Quarter Horse but relatively few of these animals are seen on the polo field, even in the United States. The Argentinian polo pony, a carefully bred type, not a breed, still seems to be most players' ideal mount. It was developed out of indigenous Argentinian Criollo ponies crossed with judiciously selected Thoroughbred lines and has been exported wherever polo is popular.

Animals of other breeds, of course, can be used provided they comply with type requirements. Arabs used to be very popular with British army personnel playing in India and other Asian countries but are less used now. It has to be said that in polo the welfare of the ponies comes second to the game itself and the ponies have to submit to being knocked about somewhat during the game. Apart from the fact that most Arabs, although having substance within their type, are more lightly-built than the modern idea of a good polo pony, temperamentally they resent rough treatment which they appear to regard, understandably, as an injustice and do not suffer what they consider to be fools gladly. Always willing to please, they do nevertheless expect personal consideration and a mutual partnership, when they will try their hearts out. Domination and assaults on their person create resentment and lack of co-operation.

Some pure Thoroughbreds are used in polo, but problems can occur with those retired from the racecourse as sometimes extended training and re-schooling is needed to persuade them that they are no longer expected to gallop all the time but are required to stop quickly, whip round, develop ball sense and be handy as well as performing their familiar standing starts into a flat-out, albeit now short, gallop.

Point-to-point racing

Basically the physical conformation of a point-to-pointer coincides fairly exactly with that of a good three-day event horse or steeplechaser, to which latter pursuit, of course, point-to-pointing is very similar if not so fast. The point-to-point field is often, it is said, where 'chasers 'proper' start and finish – they are either on the way up or on the way down – but this is by no means always the case, of course.

Point-to-pointing is a very popular amateur sport in its own right with a short spring season, and many of its participants have no desire to hurdle or steeplechase. They still want a tough, well-conformed racehorse with the ability to jump fences at speed, who is also controllable with hounds during the essential qualifying period, even though many 'pointers still do not do much more than simply see hounds, particularly after Christmas when their training intensifies ready for the season's start.

Showing

This book is not intended to cover the many aspects of showing, with its very varied classes for horses and ponies of all breeds and types. Mention can certainly be made, however, of its place in forming part of the groundwork of most competition horses. It is invaluable for accustoming horses to 'an occasion' – the crowds, the music, the loudspeaker, the sense of something different and special, the patience required in the ring itself to stand, often for long periods, waiting to be judged and then having to pull out of line and give your all; all these things provide valuable mental education.

Popular now are the potential competition horse classes of various kinds, begun with the aim of not only giving such animals suitable showing classes to enter but also of helping market potentiality and giving owners a public opportunity of receiving expert opinions on their animals. 'Ordinary' showing classes are frequently not suitable for very athletic animals such as the type of competition horse we are considering in this book, and there has long been discussion in the equestrian press over why youngstock in particular, despite winning in hand, never seem to go on to 'do' anything later.

Traditional showring standards, at least in Britain, do not coincide often with the physical requirements of a potential athlete. Horses who are successful in the ring often seem to have a slightly 'stuffier' conformation than is desirable for a competition horse. They are almost without exception shown too fat, which is damaging to their physique and therefore lowers their potential for athletic work later.

The American Green Hunter classes are marvellous spawning

grounds for potential competition horses and in our classes specifically for the latter here in Britain, we are at last concentrating more along those lines. The horses are judged not as 'showpieces' but as athletes and are asked to go in a manner which befits that, showing flow, athleticism and willingness. Our traditional show hunter classes do not feature jumping, incredible though it may seem to overseas spectators. Only our Working Hunter classes have done that until recently. Even there, the animals were judged as potential hunters which were 'not good enough' or 'rather off type' to be 'proper show hunters' – poor relations, in other words.

There will undoubtedly be more potential competition horse classes at our shows and in conjunction with major specialist events within the individual disciplines – ideal venues for them so that would-be purchasers can see what animals are likely to be available in future, and breeders and producers can display their wares to the right kind of audience.

Breeds for competition

Arabian

The Arab horse is without doubt the fountain-head of all competition horses today, at least of the type and in the disciplines being considered in this book. Not only was the Arab the founding father of the Thoroughbred, but it is still used to infuse its qualities of hardiness, stamina, intelligence, courage and speed into many breeds today.

Arabians are united by the World Arab Horse Organization. They have their own competitions apart from showing and still excel in long-distance riding and endurance racing. There is no doubt that, were they available, pure Arabians of greater size than is average today (mostly around 15 hands) would be much in demand as competition horses despite there being much prejudice against them by those who, it must be said, either do not understand them or prefer horses who are more submissive and will tolerate a measure of domination.

The Arab is unique and will continue to be an indispensible element in the production of quality horses worldwide.

Thoroughbred

The Thoroughbred was developed purely for speed, and this requirement gradually moulded a horse with not only that facility but courage and boldness, scope, size and, some say, a competitive spirit, although the latter is certainly doubtful. When quality and refinement combined

Plate 6 Ben Faerie, sire of Priceless, Night Cap and many other successful event horses and surely one of the most successful event horse sires of all time. A Thoroughbred stallion, he was purchased as a youngster by his owners, Mr and Mrs M.R. Scott of Brendon Hill Farm, because of his limbs and quality. (Photograph by Kit Houghton.)

with size are wanted in a breed it is often the Thoroughbred which is used to introduce or heighten it.

Thoroughbreds are nowhere as near to a standardised ideal as some of the continental Warmbloods. There is considerable variation because they have been mainly bred for one quality only – speed. Not all individuals, therefore, possess the 'traditional' Thoroughbred qualities. Thoroughbred 'weeds' still occur – scatty, weak and malconformed – and temperamental differences can be unreliable to say the least. Generally considered 'hot' and fiery, nervous and highly strung by nature, some Thoroughbreds are quite phlegmatic. Many are not as amenable as their Arab ancestors, are unwilling to work and are known for developing 'mental blocks' for no apparent reason.

This lack of uniformity within the breed is said by some to be another of its attractions – how boring it would be if they were all clones – and those in the racing industry seem to accept that true greatness on the

Plate 7 Welton Ambassador, a registered sports horse stallion, by Welton Louis (the advanced event/dressage stallion) out of Minerva (full sister to European Champion eventer Nightcap and by Ben Faerie). He is $\frac{7}{8}$ Thoroughbred with that dash of Irish Draught, a combination which was produced so many successful British and Irish competition horses and hunters. Bred by the Limbury Stud, he combines Welton blood with that of Ben Faerie. (Photograph kindly supplied by Mr Sam Barr of the Limbury Stud, Hartpury, Gloucestershire.)

racecourse often, although certainly not always, accompanies temperamental difficulties that just have to be lived with.

Big, well-conformed Thoroughbreds with substance, quality and that extra special indefinable attribute which can probably best be equated with star quality are still rare, but they do exist and will always be in demand for producing performance horses. Size, however, can come from the mare as well as from the stallion and, in practice, we have long reached the point where we can breed horses as big as we want. Only in the dressage arena has size been seen to increase noticeably recently. It is a definite disadvantage in most disciplines, but for competitive dressage these days it seems that size plus the requisite movement is what impresses judges and therefore this is the type of horse that buyers will seek.

Again, the Thoroughbred is unlikely to be surpassed or even equalled in the forseeable future as the major ingredient in performance horse production.

Plate 8 It's Without Doubt, a $\frac{7}{8}$ Thoroughbred stallion, son of Ben Faerie and out of a full sister to Priceless by Welton Louis, representing an exciting blend of Ben Faerie blood with that of the Limbury Stud, another consistently successful British event horse stud. (Photograph by Exmoor Landscapes; copyright of Mrs Diana Scott.)

Anglo-Arab

The Anglo-Arab horse, except in France, is purely a cross between the Arab and the Thoroughbred (the Anglo or British part of the cross). In theory and very often in practice, the Anglo-Arab possesses the best qualities of both the Arab and the Thoroughbred, giving the size, scope and presence of the Thoroughbred plus the intelligence, extra docility, hardiness, stamina and quality of the Arabian. Anglo-Arabs, too, can be bred big or small, as required; some look very Thoroughbred in appearance, some very Arab-like and others clearly show both ancestries.

Anglo-Arabs have frequently distinguished themselves in competition in many disciplines but the use of Anglo-Arab stallions for some reason never seems to have really caught on in most countries as much as the use of pure Arabs or Thoroughbreds. It is often left to the mares to infuse both breeds into some other breed or to produce more Anglos with more or less of one particular breed's blood.

Fifty-fifty Anglo's (50 per cent Arab and 50 per cent Thoroughbred) can be super horses, well up to size, and those with three quarters Thoroughbred blood and one quarter Arabian can provide a suitable competition horse for the most discerning purchaser, depending on exact requirements.

The increased use of Anglo-Arabs in their own right would, I feel, be to the benefit of competition horse breeding and would save time, at least one generation, by infusing both breeds at one shot into other, probably warmblood, breeds. It would be good to see them used more, both in competition and at stud.

Cleveland Bay

This is another British breed which has been used to add its qualities to other breeds, although much less extensively than the Thoroughbred and the Arab, which it also possesses in its ancestry. Its true origins are obscure, but it is definitely known as a type from mediaeval times. Originally known as the Chapman Horse (from its use as a chapman's or travelling salesman's animal), its breeding came to be concentrated in the Cleveland area of Yorkshire (also the original home of the Thoroughbred), hence its name, taken from its locality and its colour of bay to bay/brown, with only a small white star and a few white hairs on the heels and coronets being permitted.

Like many driving breeds, it went through a crisis earlier this century but is now so popular and in demand – principally for carriage driving and crossing with the Thoroughbred to produce carriage horses, hunters and competition horses, not to mention carrying out royal and state duties – that demand exceeds supply, both at home and abroad.

A medium-weight, clean-legged horse, it was also used in agriculture, mainly in Yorkshire, because of its great strength, yet a good specimen is not at all coarse. Its slightly Roman nose gives it a handsome rather than common look. Its height is from 15.2 to about 16.1 hands. Many competition horses in various disciplines have had significant amounts of Cleveland Bay blood in them and the straight Cleveland Bay/Thoroughbred cross produces excellent middleweight hunters for most hunting countries.

Irish Draught

There aren't many horses that can claim to be farm horses, family driving horses, hunters, Grade A show jumpers, event horses and in

Plate 9 The Irish Draught stallion Finbarr showing his scopey, elastic paces on the lunge. He is a lovely example of his breed, which is ideal for crossing with lighter horses, particularly and traditionally the Thoroughbred and near-Thoroughbred, for producing hunters and in subsequent crosses high-class competition horses, with equable temperaments, courage, speed, stamina and soundness. (Photograph by Susan McBane.)

possession of sufficient sense to bring an incapacitated owner home unassisted from a Saturday night *ceilidh*, but the Irish Draught can lay just claim to all this!

Its legendary reputation as the ideal cross with the Thoroughbred to produce quality, fast hunters with jumping ability, the agility to tackle formidable Irish banks and a sensible temperament too, fits it as a highly suitable breed for producing competition horses with toughness, stamina, commonsense and athleticism, not to mention that essential asset, courage.

Itself made up of Spanish and Arab horses on native Irish mares, it is a clean-legged horse with a straight profile and proud outlook, not coarse but with plenty of strength and substance and a surprisingly light, springy action with enough knee and hock action to produce the type of easily-flexing action required in today's competition, and particularly dressage, horses. There is also a significant amount of select Thoroughbred blood in the breed.

Although no longer regarded as in danger, following a decline some decades ago in common with other farm and driving breeds, numbers are still rather thin on the ground. As with any breed in short supply, this matter could be rectified relatively quickly if the breed authorities made it a temporary regulation that Irish Draught mares could only be put in foal to Irish Draught stallions and not be used for crossing, that job being easily left to the stallions. However, such a step has not been taken.

The breed is following up its earlier fame on a whole new generation of horsemen and women, principally interested in the horse as a competition vehicle. Used with selected Thoroughbreds, Anglo-Arabs and Arabs, it is the ideal breed for producing the type of horse exemplified by the Warmbloods today. The resulting stock could easily compete on equal terms with its continental cousins and it is hoped that this will prove to be the case in years to come.

Welsh Cob Section D

Here is another breed well suited to competition horse breeding when judiciously crossed with the Thoroughbred, Anglo-Arab and Arab in carefully judged amounts.

Welsh Cobs are renowned for their stamina and particularly their spectacular trotting ability, the 'trotting of the cobs' being the main attraction at Wales' premier show, the Royal Welsh. The words 'Flyer' and 'Express' and similar expressions abound in Welsh Cob pedigrees, and not without reason. A top speed trot may not be what is wanted in carriage horses today but the inherent ability is there to use, along with the Welsh Cob's proven stamina, soundness and tractability.

Welsh Cobs, in fact, pure and crossed, compete successfully in top-level driving competitions, and many three-quarter and seven-eights Thoroughbred crosses have Welsh Cob for the rest of their make up.

Again, their action shows plenty of flexion and lift in both knee and hock – just the thing to give more height and extravagance to the long, low stride of the Thoroughbred or Arab. The breed is sturdy, well muscled and compact, with great strength and agility. The earth is *not* supposed to move under them! The hooves are of good size for the build of animal, another point in its favour for competition horse breeding as so many breeds today have too-small hooves with consequent unsoundness problems.

Altogether, the Welsh Cob is a quality, sound, capable animal with much to commend it for competition horse production.

British and Irish native ponies

All the British and Irish native ponies are noted for their hardiness and commonsense and some of the larger ones, such as Connemara, the lighter Highlands and the New Forests, are frequently found a little way back in performance horse pedigrees. Even the smaller ones are found in seven-eighths Thoroughbred horses. Some, such as the Fells, are used in their pure form for national competition carriage driving, but any of them, carefully selected of course, are suitable for breeding up (crossing) for the purposes of producing competition horses.

Types rather than breeds

British and Irish hunters and cobs, riding horses and show working hunters are types, not specific breeds. More of them are geldings than mares, but any good female specimen can be used with compatible stallions, although it is far preferable to use one which has proved itself in performance than one which has merely been shown and done no actual work. There is more on this topic in Chapter 3.

The stud books of specific breeds sometimes allow outcrosses of suitable breeding, type and performance ability – not all of them are closed, not even the General Stud Book for Thoroughbreds – and this is one way the owner of a good mare of uncertain breeding can enter the competition horse breeding field.

Akhal-Teke

In passing on to breeds of other countries, some readers may be surprised to see mention of that magnificent Russian horse, the Akhal-Teke. Russia has many superb competition-type horses which

Plate 10 An example of a type rather than a breed, this is a British show hack of yesteryear, the famous June. Animals of her type and refinement are extremely difficult to find today. Part Arab herself, she was put to the late Mr Henry Wynmalen's Hungarian Shagya Arabian, Basa, and founded a line of superlative show hacks. She was owned by Miss Marguerite de Beaumont of the Shalbourne Stud.

are unfamiliar to those in the western hemisphere. There is not exactly a roaring export/import trade in Russian horses, despite some attempts in the 1960s to import some breeds into Britain, but this is one breed in particular I should like to see much more of. The Soviets do use them, and their other breeds, in competition at home and abroad.

The Akhal-Teke is an extremely hardy horse with phenomenal stamina and is famous for the feat of trekking from Ashkhabad to Moscow in 1935, a distance of 2500 miles (4000 km). Part of the trip involved 900 miles in three days across the Karakum desert, which they completed without water.

Closely related to the ancient Turkmene or Turcoman horses of Iran, to Westerners Akhal-Tekes most closely resemble a rangy Thoroughbred. They are usually 14.2 to 15.2 hands and of good, fine riding horse conformation in general, with long legs, a longish neck with fine, well set-on head, and proud bearing and outlook. The front is good with pronounced withers and a sloping shoulder. Sometimes appearing a little tucked up, the breed is naturally lean and spare, and they are good doers. The pasterns tend to be long and the feet large and sound and well-formed. Probably the Akhal-Teke can best be described as a greyhound among horses. It is particularly noted for its speed, stamina and jumping abilities. Temperamentally it is lively and courageous, but is known to be rebellious and stubborn, needing a most tactful rider.

Possibly one of the most remarkable things about the Akhal-Tekes' appearance is the metallic sheen most of them have to their coats, which are usually of a deep to pale gold colour. Black points are favoured although they are not universal in the breed, and bays and greys are also known.

In any sport where endurance is required, these free-going, independent horses would be sure to distinguish themselves and give the more famous Arab plenty to think about. They have, however, distinguished themselves also in dressage and jumping events and, with the right rider, could compete more internationally with undoubted success.

Standardbred

The Standardbred is known mainly for harness racing, either trotting or, according to individual inclination and ability, pacing. However, the breed has also distinguished itself in endurance riding, in dressage, hunting, jumping and as a private pleasure horse. Many owners find its natural pacing gait most comfortable to sit but others dislike it.

Having much Thoroughbred blood in its veins, it is not surprisingly very like a Thoroughbred to look at, but is longer in the back, with shorter legs, longer ears and longer and more sloping pasterns than is desired in the Thoroughbred and with a more substantial, muscular appearance. It derives from the Thoroughbred stallion, Messenger, who was exported to the United States of America in 1788, but also owes much to other breeds, including Morgan, some Arab and, particularly, to the Norfolk Trotter stallion Bellfounder, who made the trip to America in 1822. (The Norfolk Trotter is a superb trotting/harness breed, or rather was, as only a tiny nucleus of the breed's blood now survives in reasonably pure form, the Shales line still existing in Northamptonshire. It would, however, take many generations of careful breeding to recreate this phenomenal breed which was allowed to die out.)

Standardbreds are popular for harness racing in their homeland, the

United States, in Canada, Europe (other than Britain) and Australasia. Standardbreds are bred and trained in Britain but in relatively small numbers, harness racing never having caught on in a big way.

The horse's great quality is speed which, combined with a willing and apparently competitive temperament, makes it a pleasure to handle and train. The Standardbred is a perfect example of a man-made, homogeneous or uniform and firmly-fixed breed. It is far more homogeneous than the Thoroughbred, despite being a more recently-established breed; it was only in 1879 that the National Association of Trotting Horse Breeders laid down strict standards (hence the name) to which the horses should be bred. Although, like the Thoroughbred from which it is descended, it was bred purely for speed and performance on the racetrack, much tighter selective breeding was practised and there was not the variety of race types and distances or the same extent of tactical racing as in Thoroughbred racing. Therefore, the type of horse produced conformed very closely to one particular type as a result of the requirements laid down. Again, it was bred for performance and speed, not for conformation or 'looks'. The demands on the horses produced the type or 'standard'. Choosing proven top performers to breed from also 'programmed' into the breed pre-potency or the ability to fairly certainly pass on to offspring the breed qualities, and for this reason Standardbreds are used in other countries to improve other trotting breeds.

French Trotter

Containing much Standardbred blood, the French Trotter (also used for mounted trotting races which are quite a feature in France) is nevertheless different in that its early origins are based on the native Norman horse and the Norfolk Trotter. It is slower to mature than the Standardbred, has even greater stamina and is more compact, having a shorter back. While the Standardbred averages fairly closely 15.2 hands in height, the French Trotter ranges from 15.2 to 16.2 hands.

Orlov Trotter

No mention of trotting horses could be complete without referring to the famous Orlov Trotter of the Soviet Union. Developed by Count Alexei Orlov, the breed was based on the Arabian stallion, Smetanka, and a Danish mare who produced a colt, Polkan, to him. Polkan was mated to another Danish mare who produced Bars 1, a trotting legend in his own lifetime and regarded as the real founding father of the Orlov Trotter.

Using the blood of Bars 1 and several English Thoroughbred

stallions on carefully selected Arab, Polish, Danish, Dutch, Russian and English mares, the breed developed. Initially, any animal could also be registered in the stud book who had achieved a speed of under two minutes for the kilometre, but now the stud book (and therefore the gene pool) is closed and only animals whose parents are already in the book may be registered.

It is a strong, substantial animal and is also used for light draught and farm work. As a trotter, it has lost pride of place to today's Standardbred and French Trotters but Orlov races are still held in the USSR.

Metis Trotter

The new Metis Trotter is the result of crossing the Orlov with the Standardbred, the aim being to keep Orlov blood but improve the speed of the old Orlov. This has happened, but the Metis still does not come up to the speeds of the Standardbred and other trotters such as the French.

A peculiarity of the breed is that it tends to be knock-kneed and cow-hocked to some extent and, although this causes dishing, it is thought to enable the horse to lengthen its stride more quickly and with less risk of brushing or over-reaching.

East European breeds

Along with the already-mentioned Akhal-Teke, Russia has other riding breeds of which we see relatively little in the west but which are excellent riding horses: the main ones are the Budyonny, the Don and the Tersky. They are based on indigenous blood with oriental and Thoroughbred blood, and the Don in particular is used to improve and create other breeds. The Soviets go for good temperament and character, intelligence and 'trainability' in their horses, not perform- ance alone, and, like their colleague the Akhal-Teke, it would be good to see more of these super riding horses in the west.

Poland and Hungary have long been respected horse-breeding countries. Poland's two breeds of note from the riding horse/ competition horse outlook are the Malapolski and the Wielkopolski. The Malapolski is based largely on the Furioso (Thoroughbred/Norfolk Roadster) and Gidran (Hungarian Anglo-Arab) plus other oriental blood and straight Thoroughbred infusions. Also known as the Polish Anglo-Arab, it is similar to the Wielkopolski which is rather more uniform in type based on indigenous Polish/Eastern European horses crossed with Arab, Thoroughbred and West European stock. Both breeds are well-suited to general competition work and are particularly noted for their jumping ability, well-balanced temperaments and sturdy builds.

Bulgaria has its own elegant and well-conformed breed, the East Bulgarian, which they are promoting as a sports horse. Mainly of Thoroughbred blood, it also possesses Arab and 'English half-bred' blood. It seems inconceivable that there is no native blood in this breed, but I have been unable to find any evidence to support this.

Plate 11 A four-in-hand team of Hungarian horses owned, and driven here through a water splash in training, by international carriage driving competitor and former stunt man Peter Munt. The Hungarian breed has presence, action, tractability and stamina, essential qualities for this demanding sport. (Photograph by Susan McBane.)

Also well-distributed throughout Eastern Europe is the Furioso-North Star. Originating in Hungary, it is based on the Norfolk Roadster, North Star, and the English Thoroughbred, Furioso, hence the name. The famous Hungarian stud Mezohegyes crossed these two stallions with mares of native Nonius blood and developed this lovely horse mainly as a carriage horse. They concentrated on the lighter specimens of the breed, but it is also now suited to ridden events, while retaining strength and substance.

A slightly heavier Hungarian breed, the Nonius descends from a Norman draught mare and an English half-bred (i.e. half Thoroughbred) stallion who proved most pre-potent, stamping his stock with his type. He was put to mares of different breeds. The Large Nonius (the strain most suited to competition) is a little too heavy in appearance for today's sports horse standards but, being based on Thoroughbred and Norman blood, is a good driving horse, and many of their successful international teams have consisted of the Nonius. As any whip will tell you, the Hungarians are *very* hard to beat.

The Shagya Arabian is a horse of which Hungary can be justifiably proud. It is well distributed throughout Europe, particularly in the east, and is now popular in the USA as well. A few have been brought to Britain, probably the most famous having been the late Henry Wynmalen's Basa, noted for his High School abilities.

The breed was founded at another famous Hungarian stud, Babolna, in the first half of the 19th century, when native mares were crossed with oriental and later entirely Arabian blood. The stallion Shagya proved the most pre-potent and influential, nearly all his descendants being remarkably like him in both type and temperament, and most possessing his grey colour. Shagya Arabians are superb light carriage and riding horses, possessing both stamina and speed and having active, keen temperaments needing a calm, competent driver, rider or groom.

The breed is a homogeneous, well-fixed type thanks to careful line-breeding. It is interesting to note the historical and scientific fact that the Hungarian horse, from examination of skulls dating from around the 10th century, seems to have had wild Tarpan and Mongolian blood in significant amounts. Oriental infusions plus heavier draught type blood resulted in the Hungarian farm horse which is an ancestor of the Shagya Arabian.

West European breeds

Travelling further west, the Swedish, Danish, Dutch and Germans inhabit the area which has come to be regarded as the cradle of warmblood (competition horse) breeding. Say 'western Europe' to a performance horse breeder, trainer, owner or competitor, and they will invariably think of warmblood horses and particularly German horses, and even more especially, the Hanoverian.

However, as already discussed in the Introduction to this book, most of these horses, particularly today with comparatively simple import/export practices, are so inter-related as to be almost indistinguishable. In fact, horses are frequently eligible for registration in various stud books and/or sections or more than one formal breed of warmblood. It mainly hinges on physical appearance and ability. If a horse satisfies the requirements of the breed societies of more than one country, it can have multiple 'nationality', as it were, and seek acceptability in the stiff and painstaking 'grading' inspections of horses which most western European countries insist upon and which have produced the superlative dressage and show jumping horses for which they are famous.

It is a little tricky, therefore, to attempt a description, however potted, of all the individual western European warmbloods as they are so alike. Belgium has its own warmblood, Denmark's is well-established and very highly regarded and Sweden's is a repeatedly-proven competition horse with a real blend of widely differing breeds in its make-up – the ubiquitous Thoroughbred, of course, with (in alphabetical order) Arab, Andalusian, Friesian (from Holland and an excellent driving horse in its pure form), Hanoverian and Trakehner, all amalgamated with native Swedish stock. Swedish warmbloods have won Olympic gold medals in all the equestrian disciplines.

The Swiss warmblood was originally based on the old Einsiedler breed, a strong horse of willing, kind temperament used for riding and driving, itself made up largely of Anglo-Norman and British Hackney in later times, although it is believed that it was bred from mediaeval times from native stock (that expression again!). Today's Swiss warmblood, like the others, has its own foundation stock plus other warmblood breeds and, as ever, the Thoroughbred. Earlier this century, French blood was repeatedly infused. Today's horse is a good, all-round competition horse with generally docile temperament.

Possibly the Germans are more publicity conscious than some other nations, but it is certainly their horses most people think of first when warmbloods are mentioned, even though many think them no better than other countries' horses and not as good as some – depending always on that fickle whim, individual preference. There are several excellent competition breeds in West Germany: the Westphalian, the Wurttemberg, the Oldenburg, the Trakehner, the Hanoverian and the Holstein. It's a case of being spoilt for choice when you go to Germany for a dressage horse or a show jumper.

The Westphalian is certainly one of the world's premier sports horses but of very mixed type, having an open stud book and accepting any foal from registered stock which is born in the area. However, all Westphalians must have substance, being slightly heavier than some other warmblood breeds in general. They are powerful, docile and intelligent.

The Wurttemburg is a steady-tempered, hardy horse used for riding and light draught work and competition on a regional and national level, although not noted for producing international winners.

The Oldenburg is known mainly as a carriage horse although recent infusions of lighter blood, including the obvious choice of Thorough-bred, has produced a breed more suited to saddle work as well. Almost three centuries of careful selection and crossing of the original East Friesan stock with Spanish, Neapolitan, Anglo-Arab, Thoroughbred, and other oriental stock produced a superb carriage horse by the beginning of the 20th century. There were also infusions of Cleveland Bay, Norman, Hanoverian and Yorkshire Coach Horse blood from the stallion Stavee. Today's breed representatives have more Thorough-

Plate 12 An Oldenburger stallion, the late Adel, belonging to Miss Sylvia Stanier, LVO. (Photograph by Peter Sweet.)

bred, Hanoverian and Anglo-Norman blood in their veins, to produce not only international carriage horses but competition horses under saddle.

Probably the three German breeds which need individual mention are the Trakehner, the Hanoverian and the Holstein.

The Trakehner (East Prussian horse)

This is the lightest of the German warmbloods and is often used on a par with the Thoroughbred to add quality and finesse to other breeds.

Plate 13 The Premium Trakehner stallion Illuster, by a Thoroughbred stallion specially selected for the Trakehner breed, Osterglanz. Illuster, performance-tested and graded in Neumunster, Germany, has sired many high-class perform-ance horses and has a graded son, Kalluster, standing in the USA. Illuster is owned by Mr and Mrs David Clark of Liberty Lodge Stables near Darlington, Co. Durham.

Based on the old Schweiken breed of East Prussia, plus Arabs and Thoroughbreds, the Trakehner breed was developed mainly at the Trakehnen Stud, founded by Frederick William I of Prussia in 1732. As with most light horse breeding up till the present century, the aim was to produce a superb cavalry horse and this the Trakehner proved to be. It is now a sought-after competition horse.

The stud itself was destroyed during World War II but over 1000 horses were taken to West Germany where breeding has continued ever since, those horses which remained in southern East Prussia, now part of Poland, being incorporated into the Wielkopolski breed.

With all the usual good points of conformation, the Trakehner is particularly noted for its stamina, style and its basically quiet but go-ahead temperament.

The Holstein

It is likely that the Holstein has been bred as such since mediaeval times or at least the middle ages, in the north-eastern part of West Germany, initially a rather heavy war-horse on a par with the so-called Great Horse. Subsequent refinement, as war requirements changed, using oriental, Spanish and Neapolitan stock increased its international popularity and Holstein horses were steadily exported during the 16th, 17th and 18th centuries.

Its military use, up to World War II, was mainly that of an artillery horse, but, like other breeds worldwide, it has been the subject of refinment while attempting to retain its native characteristics, to produce a competition horse capable of work both in harness and under saddle. A biggish horse, usually over 16 hands or even sometimes over 17 hands, it is slow to mature but worth the wait. Often a little long in the back with a sloping croup, like other warmbloods it is most in demand as a dressage or show jumping mount. It is a strong, sound animal with presence, stamina and free paces.

The Hanoverian

A little lighter than the Holstein but with more substance than the Trakehner, many people consider the Hanoverian as the warmblood sports horse above all others, and it does seem to produce top level horses in abundance. It is normally sensible, courageous and calm.

Again initially a heavy-type war horse of friendly temperament, willing to go all day, the usual refinements took place over the years. In this case, Britain's House of Hanover contributed greatly to the development of the breed, regularly exporting Thoroughbreds and

Cleveland Bays to refine this rather heavy and, it seems, ugly breed.

After the end of World War II, the Hanoverian too was subjected to a flood of infusions of Thoroughbred, Arab and Trakehner blood, ultimately producing today's handsome middleweight horse and retaining the kind temperament. The presence and size of the horse, plus its power and supple, ground-covering gaits, make it particularly sought-after as a dressage horse, but many top show jumpers are Hanoverian and at present it does seem to be at the top of the tree as far as warmbloods are concerned. It is used itself to improve other breeds and to establish other warmblood breeds world-wide.

Dutch Warmblood

Probably the breed most on a par at the time of writing, as far as popularity as a competition horse is concerned, is the Dutch Warmblood. Consisting mainly of native Dutch breeds (the Gelderland and the Groningen) with Thoroughbred blood, it also possesses the blood of other French and German breeds. Lighter than the Hanoverian, its most desirable feature is its particularly free, flowing action and normally comfortable ride, which make it particularly desired as a dressage horse, although it also produces top show jumpers.

Marketed as a riding/sports horse and light carriage horse, its stud book goes back to only 1958 so in only 30 years it has made great strides to reach the top of the tree in today's competition horse market. It is a justifiably popular breed which is freely exported for the establishment and improvement of other warmbloods worldwide.

British Warmblood

The British Warmblood Society was formed in 1977 and is currently going from strength to strength in its efforts to establish a British Warmblood competition horse, although it is far too early for a recognisable type to have emerged from the varied types initially involved. Importations have been made in substantial numbers from other European countries and selected British horses of various breeds and types are also involved, with a view to ultimately producing a general purpose horse for the 'ordinary' rider and also for show jumping and dressage.

The performance and progeny testing carried out in continental Europe has been found impractical in the UK for reasons discussed later, but grading and strict attention to conformation, veterinary and pedigree examinations are carried out with every bit as much thoroughness as in the rest of Europe.

American Warmblood

An even newer organisation, the American Warmblood Society, formed in the early 1980s, is also surely set to make its mark in this field. It was formed 'for the purpose of establishing a superior performance warmblooded equine in the US'. American Warmbloods can consist of any stock except 100 per cent hotblood (Thoroughbred/ Arab) or 100 per cent coldblood, so this gives plenty of leeway and developments should prove interesting, particularly in view of the Americans' hitherto preferences for bold, big, free-going Thorough-breds, particularly in their show jumping teams.

American Performance Horse

This project started in 1981 and consists of crossing champion Thoroughbred racehorses with draught horses, usually Percherons, a breed having Arabian ancestry despite its heavy build. The stock would seem to be most suited to dressage and show jumping but this depends on whether the Thoroughbred infusions will be sufficient to give the necessary speed for eventing.

Quarter Horse

The American Quarter Horse is an extremely popular breed in America and Australia and also has many advocates in the UK and continental Europe. It was originally developed by early American settlers for quarter-mile races and is said to be able to hold its breath for as long as it takes to gallop that distance. In fact, over that distance it is the fastest horse in the world and its standing starts are incredible.

It is a stocky, well-muscled breed, as must be any sprinter. Extremely sharp and handy, it would be ideal for polo if it had more stamina but it is felt unable to stand up to a series of chukkas of seven minutes more or less constant galloping and turning. As it is, Quarter Horses are used extensively for western riding sports such as cutting, roping, barrel racing and so on and also make very good general purpose competition horses at the lower levels of the Olympic discipline sports – show jumping (stadium jumping), dressage and eventing. Most have equable temperaments and are suitable, because of this, for most amateur enthusiasts.

Morgan Horse

This is another tremendously popular breed in the USA and is gradually spreading overseas. Believed to be of mainly Welsh Cob stock originally, all the horses in the breed today are descended from one prepotent stallion, Justin Morgan, who seems to have excelled at just about everything asked of him. Morgan and Welsh Cob young-stock, in fact, are extremely hard to tell apart about the head, only the stockier body of the Welsh Cob giving the game away.

Like the Arab, the Morgan could be said to be a 'Jack of all trades and master of one'. Both breeds are excellent general purpose horses with a particular affinity for long distance and endurance riding, the Morgan having been at one time the official remount breed of the American army and required, like any army horse before mechanisation, to be sound enough, willing enough and with sufficient stamina to undertake long marches day after day, as well as carry soldiers into battle.

There are Pleasure Morgans and Park Morgans, the former having the type of average make and shape to fit them for general riding but the latter with a naturally higher head carriage and action and with the proud, lofty bearing which ideally suits them for parade work, like the old fashioned European and particularly Iberian breeds such as the Andalusian and Lusitano. In the context of today's competition horse, I have always felt they would be ideally suited to dressage at advanced levels and above provided they were conventionally turned out as regards their manes and tails and their feet trimmed normally rather than being kept purposely long to encourage a high action. The Park Morgan naturally inclines to higher action suited to higher levels of dressage calling for such movements as *piaffe* and *passage* and extreme collection, and there is no need to have long feet in this breed for such work.

Unfortunately, in today's competitive dressage arena, larger and larger horses seem to predominate and spectacular extension seems to be called for as well as collection, and on these two points the Morgan would not score. There are exceptions to every rule and I should be very interested to see someone seriously taking Park Morgans into the world of high-level competitive dressage.

Appaloosa

The Appaloosa was originally founded by the Nez Percé Indians who inhabited the Palouse River area of Central Idaho and Eastern Washington. It is based, as are many American breeds of long standing, on Spanish horses abandoned by or captured from the *conquistadores*, although the distinctive and mainly spotted colouring patterns for which the breed is noted are known to have existed on oriental and particularly Chinese horses many thousands of years ago.

Appaloosas today have a good deal of Thoroughbred blood; I

remember some years ago seeing in quarantine in England a superb $\frac{7}{8}$ Thoroughbred 2-year-old Appaloosa colt on his way to Australia to found a racing strain of Appaloosas. Staying at Lovegroves Stud in Berkshire, he was called Ole Man River and I often wonder how he got on.

There is also Arab blood in the breed now and this makes for an extra dash of elegance and panache so desirable in a riding horse. Of compact conformation, less chunky than the Quarter Horse, they are easy-natured yet lively and justifiably popular as general riding horses and, because of their colour, as parade and circus horses.

Saddlebred

A combination of old English, European and oriental blood has gone to make up this very elegant riding horse which was developed by early American settlers to provide a horse with speed and comfort for riding long distances over their vast, new country, and which would adapt to going in harness too. Later, new American breeds such as Standard-bred and Morgan were added and today's Saddlebred is a refined, quality horse which is, however, little known outside its own country. It has strength and stamina with a docile and lively temperament and would make a most useful competition horse if most of the breed were not directed towards the specialised American saddleseat equitation classes.

This seat, it has to be said, is quite contrary to the classical seat and to that used in the type of competition covered by this book. The rider sits back towards the horse's loins with the feet (intentionally or otherwise) forward and is, therefore, out of harmony with the horse's natural centre of balance just behind the withers. The hooves are kept very long and are even often artificially augmented with attachments, all with the aim of encouraging a very high, flashy and strenuous (for the horse) way of going in the three or five gaits which these horses can perform. In addition to walk, trot and canter there are the stepping pace (a four-time pacing gait) and the rack (a fast, four-time running gait). These points, and the fact that show Saddlebreds are still subjected to the unfortunate practice of nicking and setting the tail, do disguise what lovely horses they are and what good general riding and competition horses more of them would make. Some are used in this way but the training and manipulation they undergo and the seat with which they are ridden give them a superficial grotesqueness which horsepeople unused to saddleseat equitation and presentation may have difficulty seeing through; until this can somehow be overcome it seems the Saddlebred will be denied the chance of displaying its talents in other spheres of competition, to any great extent at least.

Plate 14 Jennie Loriston-Clarke MBE, FBHS, with Dutch Courage, a Dutch warmblood and Britain's most successful competitive dressage horse of recent years. (Photograph by courtesy of Horse and Rider magazine.)

Cheval de Selle Français

Back across the Atlantic, the horses of France generally seem *not* to be regarded as conventional warmbloods although that is technically what they are.

The Selle Francais (French Saddle Horse) is based on and directly descended from the Norman horse, which no longer exists in its original form. The Norman's exact origins are somewhat obscure, but it undoubtedly contained oriental blood dating from the Crusades. From the early 19th century considerable crosses of other blood, such as Thoroughbred, Anglo-Arab, Arab, Norfolk Trotter and other French and Dutch breeds, have been introduced, with the result that the Selle Francais today is certainly not a uniform type but is capable of producing a top competition animal for virtually anyone's requirements. It excels in most sports, but it is particularly noted for producing show jumpers of the highest level.

There are five different types of Selle Français: three of medium weight (small up to 15.1 hands, medium 15.1 to 16 hands and large over 16 hands) and two heavyweight (small up to 16 hands and large over 16 hands). This enables the breed to field an individual suitable for just about anyone.

It is a keen, willing but easily-handled animal (although there are exceptions as in any breed); it is justifiably and increasingly popular and has become firmly established since the setting-up of the stud book in 1958.

French Anglo-Arab

Unlike its British counterpart, the French Anglo-Arab does contain some blood other than Thoroughbred and Arab. The breed is founded on oriental broodmares abandoned by the Moors after the Battle of Poitiers in 732 AD. The Tarbes and Limousin breeds resulted from the crossing of these mares with local horses. Thoroughbred and Arab crosses took place, and in more modern times were reinforced by the use of three English Thoroughbred mares, the Arab stallion Massoud and the Turk stallion Aslan.

Today, the authorities insist that the French Anglo-Arab has at least 25 per cent of Arab blood and that for at least the last six generations of a horse's pedigree there must be no other blood than Arab or Thoroughbred. An interesting proviso is that, from 1976, horses with less than 25 per cent Arab blood can be used and known as *Facteur d'Anglo-Arab*, for by mating such a horse back with a pure-bred Arab or an Anglo with a high percentage of Arab blood, it is possible to produce an animal meeting the registration requirements.

The French Anglo-Arab is one of the best riding and competition horses in the world, with its tough constitution, proud bearing, kind nature, intelligence and good conformation and action. The French style of riding, like their style of life, is more *laissez-faire* than that of their neighbours in the competition horse scene. They have, knowingly or otherwise, produced a horse that suits this attitude to life and not surprisingly, having a good deal of Arab blood in both breeds mentioned here, is not suited to the dominating style of rider. The horses are willing co-operative partners in an enterprise; they do not submit to bullying in any form but neither are they wild and disobedient as their successes in international competition regularly show. For those who want a partner and friend rather than a polite servant, the French breeds are perfect.

Breeding schemes and registries

I hope the protagonists of those breeds I have missed out will forgive me; however, I feel I have mentioned the major, and some of the less major, competition breeds currently active in the field.

It may have been noticed that, in the descriptions of the various warmblood breeds, it was stated that they are ideally suited for dressage and show jumping, eventing not having been mentioned. Of course some of them do excel at eventing but warmblood breeds as a whole are better-known and suited to the first two disciplines. In the field of eventing it is usually felt that they do not normally have the speed or the spirit for such a fast, tough, endurance-type sport, despite the high percentage of Thoroughbred blood warmbloods possess. In this sport, it really does seem that British-bred seven-eighths Thoroughbred horses are the best in general. We export them world-wide and not uncommonly find ourselves being beaten by our 'own' horses ridden by foreign teams. Irish horses of the same breeding are similarly in demand.

But production of them is fragmented, hit-and-miss and disorganised. A few years ago the British Horse Project was formed to try to meld together breeders, trainers, riders and sponsors, but it fell through. At the time of writing attempts are being made to try and revive it, especially in view of the steps taken in warmblood breeding in this country, together with the greater interest in them and the acceptance of the need for a cohesive competition horse industry after the fashion of the bloodstock industry. This is not unthinkable but quite feasible. Prices rise for competition horse all the time and it is now possible to get a moderate racehorse far cheaper than an equally moderate competition horse. The fully-trained, proven article frequently fetches prices way above those paid for good racehorses, even flat horses.

The model that many breed societies and similar organisations are generally trying to adapt to their individual requirements and circumstances is that operated by the most successful warmblood-breeding countries. Schemes and regulations do vary from country to country, but generally they involve inspection of stock both for conformation and veterinary aspects, and performance testing.

Basically, before a stallion can stand at stud he must have a pedigree going back at least four generations. He will have been registered at birth with a relevant society. Then, at a minimum of $2\frac{1}{2}$ years old, he attends the society's grading show. He will be shown before a panel loose and in-hand so that his way of going, his suppleness, agility, balance, ability to gallop, conformation, apparent character and willingness, bone, height and girth can all be assessed. Should he pass his grading, the young stallion may then stand at stud for one year and his progeny will be eligible for initial registration.

A year later, the young horse must be shown under saddle for a further grading. If he passes this test, he may continue to stand at stud but only receives full grading status once his progeny have been inspected and passed as up to standard.

Mares are also graded at three years old by being shown in hand; during the inspection they must be trotted out fast to ensure that they have good natural balance and are capable of extending. There are normally three levels of stud book and mares succeeding in entering the top level are further shown against one another, the top three receiving gold, silver and bronze medals. All stud book mares may produce progeny eligible for registration, which will then go through for grading in their own right, the mare's status not affecting her progeny's potential.

Probably the crux of the whole continental system is the 100-day performance testing which the stallions go through (and in Germany performance tests for mares have recently started). The system in Germany produces a uniformly trained 'Bereiter' or 'Master Rider' squad, or team, of trainers able to produce and school horses in all disciplines up to top levels. In Britain the system produces mainly teachers of people, not horse trainers. Although British Horse Society-qualified personnel, and those qualified by the other organisations (The Association of British Riding Schools and the National Pony Society) are, at least at the higher levels, capable of training horses, obviously, the *emphasis* is on teaching them to teach people, not to train horses. Ireland's system is more horse-trainer orientated and in America, there being no national qualifications after our style, it depends very much on which private (i.e. non-government) establishment you go to as to where the emphasis lies. They have imported many more continental trainers than we have, but there is still no national system which, like it or not, is so successful on the continent.

Basically, the 100-day performance testing will run something like this, with differences for the various countries:

The horses are sent to a central training centre and trained under a head trainer by the team of Bereiters. They are, during their training, continually assessed on trainability, temperament, manageability, ride quality and talent in both flat work and jumping. At the end of the period, approved experts in the disciplines (from outside the training team) test the horses under saddle (both on the flat and over obstacles), loose jumping and for general character. They must complete a walk of 300 metres, a trot of 750 metres and a gallop of 1500 metres each in $2\frac{1}{2}$ minutes. There is also a 6000 metre cross-country course followed immediately by a gallop of 2000 metres.

If the horses are felt to have performed satisfactorily they are graded – a highly desirable state because if they fail they are of little or no value and the potential in the eyes of a purchaser of their progeny is also adversely affected.

Because of the somewhat erratic nature of our British training system and, as mentioned, the emphasis on teaching people rather than training horses, it is felt that it would not be possible to give each animal an equal chance in the testing and training period. It is also felt that British owners, with their independent spirits and ethos of free enterprise, would object most strongly to being 'forced' to send their horses to a central venue with the possibility of their being rejected at the end of it.

As the whole purpose of a stallion standing at stud is for him to produce competition horses (and they say that there is no greater compliment to a stallion than for him to produce something better than himself), progeny testing or a system based on the successes of his offspring, similar to the French system, would seem to be best for Britain and, if I may suggest it, for America, Australia and similar countries.

In France, competition horse classes for three- to six-year-olds are run and the stallions that sired the entrants are rated according to their progeny's performances. In Britain we now have similar classes which it is hoped will become more widespread and firmly established.

British schemes

As for the warmbloods in Britain, many of the stallions are imported from their homelands already graded. The British Warmblood Society has adopted a system without the performance tests but involving the strict examination of horses (male and female) for conformation, pedigree, temperament etc. as described earlier, and giving points to subsequently graded stallions according to not only their progeny's performance in competitions of all kinds, but also their own. The increasing number of stallions to be seen (of all breeds, not only warmbloods) in our competitions is very heartening and quite fascinating, especially in view of the old-time view that stallions could not be expected to work successfully like other horses and were, indeed, dangerous in public! True, they do need expert handling, but if they are not handled in competition by experts they are unlikely to acquit themselves well anyway.

Many other breed societies are now setting up similar schemes based on performance in competitions, not merely in the ordinary showring, and those requiring a performance horse of any breed or cross are advised to contact the relevant societies to obtain precise details of the schemes operated and their implications on the abilities and possible values of stallions and progeny, and mares where suitable schemes for them exist.

Britain's National Light Horse Breeding Society (HIS) has run its famous Premium Stallion Scheme for many years. Initially called the Hunters Improvement Society, it was first intended to improve the quality of hunters by offering the services of approved (conformation-inspected), sound stallions, free from hereditary disease, at subsidised fees to mare owners. The horses could serve Thoroughbred mares at their normal fees. It was not intended to be a cheap way of producing bloodstock!

The stallions are still used for that purpose, but increasingly for producing competition horses. The big flaw in the system is that they are not performance tested in any way relevant to producing competition horses and not all of them have even raced or done well on the racecourse. The proven ability to race is fine if you want to produce racehorses but no good at all if you are looking for eventers, show jumpers or dressage horses as the qualities required are so different.

Possibly more by good luck than good management, the HIS stallions *have* been responsible for producing many top competition horses. Maybe because of the increasing publicity given to warmbloods and their continental marketing and organisation systems, the HIS are becoming increasingly aware of the competition horse maket. Being a privately funded society with no government assistance either financially or otherwise, it could not afford to set up performance training and testing facilities like those on the continent of Europe, but it has opened its doors to some warmblood, Irish Draught and Welsh Cob stallions, most of whom have proven jumping ability.

HIS also has three grades for mares, and grants premiums to the owners of the best ones. Grade 1 is simply an identity record for mares approved by inspection as to conformation, action, type, performance ability and quality of progeny produced to date. Grade 2 is for mares bred according to approved HIS breeding lines or who have proven performance ability under British Horse Society, British Show Jumping Association or Jockey Club (racing) rules or who have won at least at County level in the showring.

Because owners of horses seem reluctant to provide precise breeding details of their stock, or sometimes do not even seem to care about it even if they know it, the HIS is trying to ensure that in the forseeable future all types of competition will be restricted to registered horses, with a view to collating details of successful performance bloodlines and individual mares and stallions, which will obviously enable purposeful breeding policies to be developed.

Commencing from the 1990 showing season, the HIS requires all horses entering in hunter breeding classes at affiliated shows to be registered on the society's Basic Identity Record. Foals up to three months old may be entered at shows but must be subsequently registered. Foals un-named will be recorded under their dam and a naming fee charged at yearling stage. All horses applying for inclusion on the ridden show register must also be identified.

The identification record is for life, open to all horses exceeding 14.2 hands (except stallions over three years of age). The society's aim is to encourage the adequate identification of horses at an early age, particularly as this is likely to become compulsory with the advent of the free market between EEC countries in 1992.

One of the advantages with the warmbloods is that they do tend to breed true to type as regards performance abilities and 'duffers' are much rarer than with other breeds and types. Purchasers can be told with some certainty what abilities their horse will have, what quirks and so on, and although it will take us some time to catch up, better stock records, whatever the breed, cannot but assist this aim.

Some years ago, as mentioned earlier, a project called The British Horse Project was founded with a view to producing a British competition horse, comprising various breeds (not all warmblood – indeed, many wanted there to be no warmbloods in the scheme at all), with the ultimate aim of producing our own competition breed. It floundered due to lack of real commitment and finance, and fragmented interests, general apathy and lack of agreement. Attempts are being made to resurrect it and it is hoped that, in view of the increasing support for the competition horse market and its obviously burgeoning importance, it will succeed this time.

British Warmblood Society

The already-mentioned BWBS grades its mares and stallions and registers foreign bred warmbloods and British-bred ones by or out of BWBS-graded parents. It will also register some Thoroughbred, non-Thoroughbred (i.e. part Thoroughbred!) and Anglo-Arab mares in foal to BWBS-graded stallions. Even if a stallion was graded abroad it must still be approved by the BWBS before being accepted into the British stud book and must still pass British grading. Foreign-bred stallions who have failed grading in their own country will not be considered for grading or even registration here.

Unproven stallions are graded into Class III. When a horse is competing at intermediate level show jumping or eventing or medium level in dressage, he is 'promoted' to Class II, and when his progeny are awarded 21 points out of 25 in a BWBS progeny class he achieves star status – Class I.

British Sports Horse Registry (*run in conjunction with the BWBS*)

This most useful registry is suitable for animals whose pedigrees are not fully documented a few generations back but whose performance and/or appearance indicate high quality competition ability. Mainly intended for horses of warmblood breeding (even a small percentage), it is also suitable for non-warmblood British-bred stallions from proven competition families, and for mares not graded by the BWBS but covered by BWBS or BSHR graded stallions, including non-warmblood ones. To be registered in the BSHR the animal must be approved at a BSHR grading show.

This is not a second-class register, it must be stressed, because the animals must be of the same standard as BWBS graded stock regarding

Plate 15 A grand stamp of horse, this 5-year-old stallion is Haddon Conquest. By the popular and successful Irish Draught stallion Skippy out of Quiffy of Catherston, who is in the British Warmblood Society main stud book and by the Thoroughbred Xenocles, Haddon Conquest is himself graded in the British Sports Horse Registry. A prolific winner in hand, he is now competing lightly under saddle and showing great talent. (Photograph Kit Houghton, kindly supplied by Chris Hewlett of Haddon Farm Stud near Sturminster Newton, Dorset.)

action, conformation, character etc. and may subsequently be performance tested. Indeed, performance ability in the pedigree is desired. This register is ideal for British mares whose breeding is not known a few generations back, as is so often the case here.

Great strides are being taken to enable owners and breeders of any good competition-type animal to register their stock, no matter (within reason!) how it is bred. There is a suitable stud book or register for just about any good animal and even if the highest sections of a stud book or registry cannot be attained with a particular animal, its initial registration enables its progeny to 'rise up through the ranks' in their own right if the right stallions are used.

'Papers' are going to be essential in future if a horse is to be worth anything in the market, so it is not before time that we have finally begun to get out act together in Britain. We are evolving systems which suit our horses, our human characteristics, our society and the world-wide sports horse industry. Other countries that feel unable to operate the continental system of warmblood grading and performance-testing in its entirety, may feel our schemes have something to offer them too.

2
Conformation, Action and Temperament

As far as performance/competition horses are concerned, it is very much a case of handsome is as handsome does. They seem to come in widely differing shapes and sizes, and relative novices to the game are often understandably at a loss as to exactly what to look for. There are many facets which make up the competition horse: conformation, action and temperament are three of the most important, but there is also the way you do or do not gel together, there is the horse's quota of guts to battle on when the going gets rough, whether his constitution (which belies all external appearances) will withstand the training let alone the competition, and whether or not his human connections have the sympathy and vision to amend their management regime to suit the horse rather than forcing him to conform to their usual system.

One thing is for sure, however, and that is that a badly-built horse who cannot use himself effectively will never be even moderately successful and will probably bring his owner or rider nothing but disappointment, disillusionment and wasted time, effort and money, no matter how lovable a character he is or how hard he tries. There are always exceptions, but basically if you want to be reasonably sure of some success you should start off with the best conformation and action you can find and afford.

Conformation

The nuances of conformational requirements in relation to the different disciplines were discussed in Chapter 1. Here we will look at the basic conformation of a horse meant for athletic work, a conformation blueprint from which to work in the search for a horse really able to perform. You can develop an eye for the sort of horse which should meet your requirements by frequenting the type of competition in which you are interested (you will probably be doing this anyway) and really studying the winners' conformation and way of going. If you can get them, collect posed conformation photographs of such horses and use them for analysis at home, and apply to them the criteria outlined in this chapter to see just how many of them 'fit the mould' despite differing looks on the surface.

Looking at the placed horses in conventional (non-performance horse) show classes, however, is not the most effective way to learn to recognise the type of horse you want. There are exceptions, but generally their conformation is not as workmanlike as a true performance horse and, because most of them are shown too fat, it is difficult for all but an expert to see through the blubber to the framework underneath.

A basic pattern

There are various systems for assessing conformation but the one given below has stood the test of time and, after repeated analysis, you will find that most successful competition and performance horses come very near to the proportions outlined, whatever their discipline. Plate 16 may help to clarify the points made.

The horizontal length from the poll to the point of the withers should

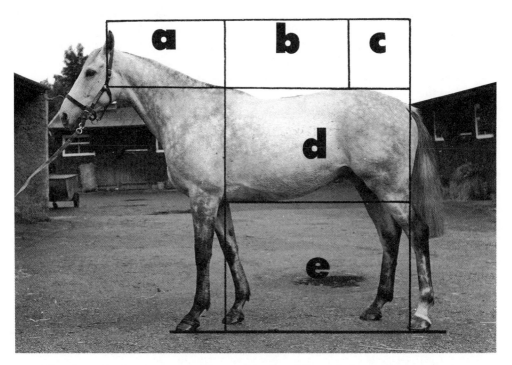

Plate 16 A basic pattern. A Thoroughbred gelding of the perfect proportions described in this chapter. This horse is an ideal type for steeplechasing, point-to-pointing and three-day eventing. Draw the lines on a photograph of your horse as a means of assessing his conformation.

be about the same as that from the withers to the croup. The distance from the croup to the root of the tail should be about half one of the first two distances. The vertical measurement from the withers to the breastbone should be at least half that from the withers to the ground, and the croup-to-ground measurement should be the same as the withers-to-ground.

Within these fairly precise guidelines, the horse must look symmetrical within himself, as though he is all of a piece, not as though he has one animal's quarters and another's forehand, or whatever, despite the measurements.

The head and neck are vital to the horse for balance. If measurement A (see Plate 16) is too long, especially if the head seems too large and therefore heavy, it may not mean that the horse has a super front with plenty in front of the rider, length of rein and so on, but simply that the neck itself is too long and the horse will have a natural tendency to go on the forehand, especially if it naturally carries the head and neck forward and low. An over-short neck, particularly a ewe neck as opposed to one with a gentle crest to it, does not compensate but usually makes for a hollow back with lack of engagement of the hind legs, particularly if the head and neck are carried rather high.

The withers should be moderately well-defined, not so low as to cause the saddle to slide around nor so high as to cause it to slip back or present fitting problems. The well-known 'well-laid-back, sloping shoulder' is a classic feature to look for and generally an angle of 45° from the point of the shoulder up towards the withers along the spine of the shoulder blade is what is wanted, although a more upright shoulder seems to help *puissance* horses. Incidentally, this imaginary line does not necessarily end at the point of the withers; you have to feel for the spine on the shoulder blade to be sure you are following the right angle.

With the horse standing naturally but to attention, look to see if the point of the elbow comes in front of a vertical line dropped from the point of the withers, in other words see that the forelegs are not set too far back under the shoulders, to ensure that, combined with an open elbow (not tied in to the trunk), the horse will have free movement with plenty of scope in front to make for a ground covering stride and good forearm lift over fences.

The breastbone should run parallel to the ground for its length, not slope upwards giving a herring-gutted appearance, and the belly should then slope gently up towards the stifles. Ideally, there should be a noticeable girth groove behind the elbows. The saying 'well ribbed up' means that you should just be able to fit the width of your hand between the last rib and the point of the hip (or rather pelvis) which should mean that the horse's back is neither too short nor too long. The back itself should neither be roached (seeming to arch upwards –

extremely uncomfortable, if strong) nor swayed (sunken downwards – fairly comfortable if not extreme, but weak). The measurement C is particularly important in competition horses as the horse's forward thrust and power come from his quarters. If the horse is wanting in this measurement and it is too short, it could mean that the quarters are not strong enough to provide that forward motion. The engine is vital in a performance horse; all too often people's eyes are riveted on the shoulder without paying enough attention to the hindquarters.

Apart from having a good, deep girth (withers to breastbone) measurement from the side, the ribcage from in front should appear neither too flat (slab-sided) nor too rounded (barrel-chested) with, respectively, too narrow or too wide a chest. This may be difficult to assess in moderate cases but much will also be decided by the ride the horse gives. A slab-sided horse may make you feel insecure with not enough between your legs and, despite a good girth measurement, may not have the lung room for really efficient breathing. A too-rounded shape could produce an unpleasant rolling gait and be uncomfortable to sit, also presenting problems with the stability of the saddle.

Seen from behind, the quarters should give the impression of a muscular square shape, with the thighs as wide as the hip bones above them and muscles which meet between the hind legs. The stifles should be smooth and open so the hind legs have plenty of scope to produce that ground-covering thrust so important especially in galloping, jumping and driving horses.

Much is heard about a horse having 'straight' legs. Of course, the legs are not rod-straight, but the expression does give an indication of what to look for. The forelegs carry two thirds of the horse's weight, plus whatever he may be carrying in the way of a rider and weights. It is they which give most concern to horsemasters and which are most prone to sprain and concussion. From the front, you should be able to see an imaginary vertical line dropping from the point of the shoulder, bisecting the knee, cannon, fetlock and foot, reaching the ground right in the middle of the toe. From the side, a line should fall from the point of the elbow, down the back of the forearm to the back of the fetlock. The horse should not 'lean' either forward or back.

The reason for this desirable conformation is so that the forces run up and down the leg distributing themselves equally along its structure. Any deviation from this 'straight' leg conformation results in uneven force being applied to some part of the leg, which likewise results in that part bearing too much weight/force, with the constant risk of injury.

The pasterns are normally required to be at the same 45° slope as the shoulders to give a comfortable ride and to absorb the forces and dissipate concussion. If they are too upright the legs could be subject to too much jar and vibration, and if too sloping the soft tissue support system (tendons, ligaments etc.) could be overstressed and injured. However, if the pasterns are, in the first case, longish, and in the second shortish, this compensates and reduces the ill effects. Extremes (short, upright or long, sloping) are the worst combination. The 45° slope of the pasterns and shoulders should be echoed down the front wall of the hoof and in the heel wall at the back to aid even distribution of forces.

The hind legs are obviously not the same shape as the front and different criteria apply. From the back, you should be able to imagine a straight, vertical line dropping from the point of the buttock bisecting the hock, cannon and fetlock. It is often extended to the heels but in practice most horses have very slightly turned out hind feet and equally slightly turned in hocks, although not to the extent that you could call them cow-hocked. You have to look carefully to spot this natural equine conformation. Animals which have 'dead straight' hind legs have been selectively bred by man to be so conformed as that is our idea of how they should be. In work, this variation in natural and imposed conformation seems to have no noticeable effect on performance or soundness one way or the other.

The hind legs from the side are best judged with the horse standing square rather than in the traditional posed conformation stance as for a photograph, with one hind leg slightly in front of the other. Taking your vertical line again, it should drop from the point of the buttock to the point of the hock, straight down the back of the cannon to the fetlock. If the cannon comes equally in front of this line the leg is termed too straight and could be subject to concussion and lack of thrust. If the cannon falls behind the line with 'hocks in the last county' it is termed too bent and weak. Should the cannon slope forward from the hock the leg is 'sickle-hocked' and too much soft tissue stress could result, plus again reduced thrust.

The hind pastern/toe angle is generally regarded best at about 50°, slightly more upright, and with slightly shorter pasterns, than in the forelegs. The term 'good bone' is often applied to the forelegs, indicating the measurement round the leg just below the knee. Of course the measurement obtained is not that of the bone as it includes space taken up by tendons and ligaments. The measurement also gives no indication of the strength of the structures concerned, either, so is best disregarded. What really matters is that the legs are neither big, clumsy and fleshy nor too 'fine' (spindly) for the body of the horse. This can only be assessed by eye and experience; even so, it is the strength of the bone and its associated structures which really matters, and you cannot measure that.

The question of individual symmetry in the horse's conformation has already been mentioned. One other aspect related to conformation and the way the horse goes is natural balance. This, again, can really best be learned by constantly watching as many horses as possible and developing an 'eye' for balance, nimble-footedness, agility and self-confidence in the horse's own attitude when he is moving. The horse with good natural balance will be so much easier to school, so much more reliable in action (and likely to stay on his feet!) and so much more economical in his movements than a clumsy, non-athletic type, that this aspect of the performance horse is well worth seeking out. Poor natural balance *can* be improved with schooling and maturity, plus experience in the field, but you are starting out with a disadvantage in a highly competitive field, so why make things difficult for both yourself and the horse?

Action

It seems to be generally agreed that if a horse has a good walk his other paces will be good too. Fortunately the walk is a sufficiently leisurely pace for us to be able to judge it without too much difficulty.

Again, the horse's natural balance should be noted, whether he seems able to relax into his walk and swing his back and tail – although inability to do this can indicate unsoundness even if the horse is going sound and level, say in the back or neck, and a handler who insists on hanging on to the horse's head can significantly interfere with his action.

Looked at from the side, check that the horse overtracks well, that is that he puts his hind feet down well in front of the fore prints, preferably by several inches. The forelegs, for their part, should reach well forward so that the forefeet come down well towards the head when the head is held naturally. This can only happen when the horse moves from a well-sloped shoulder, not simply appearing to do so from his elbow joint, and the elbow as previously mentioned needs to be nice and open, able to take a lady's fist preferably. In trot, the hind feet should come down on the fore prints, but this can be improved with training, encouraging the horse to go from his hind end.

Many competition horses are Thoroughbred, nearly so or stem from breeds based on the Thoroughbred. Unfortunately this can often mean an action which is too long and low with little knee and hock action – too much daisy-cutting. Competition horses need an element of this for speed but also require moderate joint action for the ability to negotiate fences, as obviously do steeplechasers and point-to-pointers. If they do not have this, they will never be able to 'snap' up their legs in front over a fence, a movement also facilitated by an open elbow.

When watched from in front and behind, the fore and hind legs should seem to follow the same plane or track, swinging straight back and forward. Although some slight deviations from this can be tolerated, it should be remembered that *any* excess/crooked movement takes up energy and time and causes uneven stress on the leg, particularly if it is also put down crookedly. You do not want that in a performance horse if you can possibly avoid it. Horses whose action may cause them to interfere, such as splay-footed horses, those who go too close or who carry their legs too far in rather than out (as in, for example, slight dishing) are particularly inappropriate. Not only can they injure themselves but they are prone to bringing themselves (and their riders) down.

The terms 'short cannons' and 'well let-down hocks' abound in descriptions of horses' conformation. Everyone knows they are desirable points, the reasons being that the horse's lower legs are not muscular but, from a locomotion point of view, contain only the vital tendons and ligaments which run from the muscles to various points of attachment in the lower legs so creating movement when the muscles contract (shorten), and, in the case of ligaments, help 'bind' together and support the bony skeleton.

Short cannons (the hind are always a little longer than the fore) mean shorter tendons and ligaments below the knee/hock. A short structure is always stronger than a longer one of the same circumference; in the case of a living organism like a horse, therefore, short(ish) cannons make for strength under stress and maximum thrust or 'leverage' with the minimum strain.

When looked at from behind (see Figure 4), the rectangle enclosing the hind quarters from the croup to the bottom of the thigh muscles should be the same height as that enclosing the hind legs from the points of the hocks to the ground, more or less. From the side, to give a judgement for the length of the front cannons, the point of the hock should be level on a horizontal line with the chestnut inside the foreleg above the knee.

Jumping conformation

Equine research is constantly improving our knowledge of various aspects of horsemastership. Most of the work done is of a veterinary nature, but in 1981 and 1982 EQUI magazine published a series of articles by Christopher Biddle, BSc, MSc (Equine Studies) on the ability to jump in horses. It was based on original work carried out using approved, scientific methods in a practical, 'in-the-field' situation studying show jumpers at shows and at home.

Biddle showed, using control groups of horses, (unsuccessful,

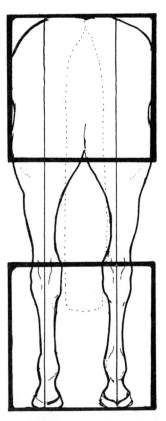

Fig. 4 Well-muscled quarters from the rear. The top and bottom squares should be the same size for good, strong proportion.

unproven and international), that the following aspects of conformation are relevant to successful jumping ability:

- The international class horses were about 3 cm ($1\frac{1}{4}$ in) taller than the other horses and it was concluded that height is necessary for a show jumper.
- The length of the back is *not* significant, which is contrary to the traditional opinion that a good show jumper needs a short back.
- The length of the neck *is* significant, a factor usually overlooked; a longish neck is an advantage.
- The length of the head and the measurements for knee-to-ergot (fore cannon), fetlock-to-ground and the measurements of the pelvis were *not* found to be significant, but a long forearm *was* found to be desirable.
- The measurements of the femur (thigh bone), tuber calcis (the bone forming the point of the hock), hind cannon, pastern and

the circumference of the girth, hocks and fetlocks were found to be of no special significance in relation to jumping ability, but the circumference of the knee was found to be significantly larger in the internationals, so a large, strong knee joint is important.

- The traditional terminology of 'bone', as mentioned in the previous section, was found *not* to be significant, which is again contrary to expert opinion which lays great emphasis on this measurement.

- The most significant difference between the control groups was found in the length of the tibia (second thigh bone) which was found to be some 16 per cent larger in the internationals and was actually 48 per cent larger in the British High Jump Champion, Lastic. Therefore, it is essential to have a good, long second thigh (length from stifle to hock) for above-average jumping ability, a more precise criterion than the usual hip-to-hock length.

Unfortunately, I know of no similar studies which have been done on the conformation required for dressage or driving horses.

In any discipline, actually competing is a very small part of the horse's work. The training needed to get the horse fit enough to

Plate 17 Everest Lastic ridden by Nick Skelton achieving his British High Jump Record of 7 ft $7\frac{5}{16}$ ins (2.32 m) at Olympia, London, in 1978. (Photograph by Kit Houghton, kindly supplied by Caradon Everest Limited.)

compete takes a considerable toll on the horse's natural resources. No matter how good the horse's conformation or how brilliant his action, it is all for nought if he does not have the constitution to withstand the training, and this is something you cannot tell until you get him in work.

Sometimes you come across a horse with the most superb action, a *real* jump, terrific extension or whatever but his actual conformation, despite producing that action or making it possible, cannot stand up to the pressures the horse puts on himself – his conformation cannot stand up to his action. Again, unless you have been following the horse and know something of his history – the 'inside story' – you cannot be sure of his inherent soundness until you work him. The best you can do is assess his conformation, with other expert help possibly, and be guided by that and his overall balance and symmetry, mentioned earlier, plus the appearance of 'substance' he gives you.

It often seems to be the case that given two very similar horses, one a good height for his discipline and one rather bigger, the bigger horse is the least sound, the most likely to break down or generally disappoint. Conversely, there have been several outstanding small individuals in equestrian sport. If often seems to be better to err on the side of caution when a big horse is in the offing, all else being equal.

The feet

There is an unfortunate trend in some disciplines today, notably dressage and showing, for horses to be purposely bred with feet too small for their bodies. No hard and fast rules can be given, but every effort should be made to train the eye to recognise when a horse appears to have over-small feet. By studying many different horses who perform and regularly win in disciplines where the horse is placed on his deeds and not on a judge's opinion, you will fairly soon get a good idea of symmetry and balance in this respect. Large, clodhopping feet have often been seen on winners of yesteryear, although not so often today.

The horse's weight is obviously borne on those feet and most lameness seen by veterinary surgeons in general practice apparently originates in the feet. The higher up the leg you go, the rarer becomes the likelihood of disorder. This may sound surprising to those who may be a bit obsessed with tendon and ligament soundness.

Another problem fairly common in Britain at the present time is the apparently widespread practice of farriers shoeing horses short with insufficient heel support. Over months and years, this can lead to low, weak heels and long toes, a conformation fault most likely to lead to the development of laminitis and to excessive tendon strain and other foot disorders.

The first thing to look for when assessing the conformation of a horse's feet is, again, their symmetry. The front and hind feet should respectively look as though they are a pair. If one is smaller than the other or one seems mis-shapen it could well indicate a longstanding lameness or some sort or faulty weight distribution which has meant uneven stress on the mis-shapen foot or extra weight having been placed on the larger of the two feet; look elsewhere in the body for the cause, and pay particular attention to the straightness and evenness of the horse's gaits.

The forefeet are nearly circular in shape whereas the hind are more oval and a little smaller. Figure 5 will help make desirable foot conformation clear, but basically when the foot is viewed from the side you should be able to imagine a straight line running up the toe and long pastern bone. If the line is 'bent' up or down just above the coronet, there is something wrong somewhere. In the first case the toe will probably be too short and the heels too high; the foot may be contracted the boxy. In the second case, the previously mentioned low heels and long toe will probably be present.

The hoof/pastern axis, as it is called, should form a straight line so that the toe and long pastern bone form the same angle with the ground. The wall at the heels should match that angle. From in front, the coronet should be the same height from the ground on both sides of the feet with the wall sloping out at the same angle each side, although it is in order for the inner wall to be *slightly* more upright than the outer.

If there is any significant deviation from these guidelines the result

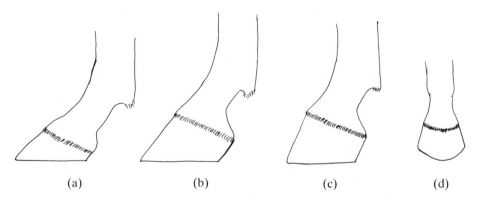

(a)   (b)   (c)   (d)

Fig. 5 Hoof conformation: (a) An over-sloping hoof and pastern with low, weak heels; (b) Good hoof/pastern conformation with strong heels having the same angle of slope as the front of the hoof wall and pastern; (c) An upright, boxy foot prone to concussion which is exacerbated by the short pastern. The hoof/pastern axis is 'broken' upwards at the coronet; (d) The ends of the coronet seen from the front should be the same height from the ground at each side.

will be uneven stresses on the feet, with some parts not receiving their share and others being overburdened, with the risk of injury and further compounded foot deformities.

Corrective trimming to put right naturally mis-shapen feet can only be applied up to the age of about six months with any success. The weight falling on the feet is transferred to the bones, so uneven stress on the hooves means unevenly stressed bones and joints higher up the leg with the result of possible unsoundness, although the bones and surrounding soft tissues will compensate somewhat by producing more and stronger material. This can, however, lead to permanently deformed feet and limbs, so the best course of action is to catch any problems early, while bones are malleable.

However, should the feet and action be incorrect due to faulty trimming or neglect after the age of six months or even after maturity, whether recent or of long standing, gradually correcting them by careful dressing to restore correct hoof balance and action is usually feasible. Every attempt should be made to do so as unbalanced feet not only unevenly stress the limbs but can cause faulty action which can result in the horse interfering or bringing down itself and its rider, or team mates if in harness.

The type of shoe most generally used in Britain and many other competitive countries is the standard fullered concaved shoe with pencilled heels, stemming from the English hunter shoe. Some farriers, however, feel that a thinner, wider-webbed shoe would be more appropriate for performance horses as this would allow more frog pressure and give a little more protection to the underside of the foot.

In trotting and sometimes in mounted racing, grips or grabs are often used to give grip and increased stability during fast work or in less-than-perfect conditions, particularly on dirt tracks as opposed to the more stable turf courses. They consist of wedges or strips of metal or alloys rivetted, moulded or forged to the shoe itself or set into the fullering, according to the ideas of the farrier or manufacturer concerned. Although they may very well achieve their purpose of keeping the horse on his feet on a slippery track or tight turn, they are not without their cost in terms of soundness and overstress on the horse's feet and legs. The main disadvantage they create is the risk of torsion or 'twist' injuries as the foot and leg are denied any 'give'. Not only severely torn soft tissues have been caused by grabs but actual fractures, usually low down in the leg or feet, and also badly torn hoof horn.

Grabs may be regarded as necessary in some disciplines, but many people feel that better conditions, and not racing/working animals in poor conditions, would make them unnecessary and make for sounder horses able to work longer.

Studs, of course, are not without their disadvantages either. Commonly used in sports such as eventing and show jumping, their use should be most selective according to the conditions prevailing; they should not be used as a matter of course. It should be remembered that as soon as they are fitted they unbalance the foot, particularly if fitted in one heel only, usually the outside heel, to lessen the risk of injury should the horse tread on himself. Usually, large blunt studs are used in the mud and shorter, sharpish ones on hard going. The horse's feet and legs are under particular stress during work, and working with deliberately unbalanced feet seems rather foolish even though it is a widespread practice. Some experts advise the use of a blunt stud on the inside heel to alleviate this unbalancing effect at least from side to side, but the foot will still be 'tipped' forward even then.

The whole matter should be discussed with your vet and farrier to reach a solution appropriate for your horse, his job and action. In any case, put the studs in as late as possible (certainly do not let your horse travel to the venue wearing them) and take them out as soon as you have finished. Studplugs are now available to make the job of packing the studholes easier and quicker, although it does not take long to do with oiled cotton wool anyway.

Psychology and temperament

That intangible quality, courage, has already been mentioned in Chapter 1 as a prerequisite for competition horses. People always attribute all sorts of qualities to horses which they probably do not have due to their nature of being a live-and-let-live type of animal, a grazing animal with no hunting instincts that basically wants to be left alone to get on with its life – not unlike many humans! A top event rider was heard to say that she sold one particular horse because 'he didn't have enough ambition'. Her meaning is clear enough to those involved, even though horses obviously do not have any ambition at all in the accepted sense. What they must have is determination and bravery to tackle the fences without considering the possible outcome too much. Another top rider described a horse she had acquired as being 'probably too much of a thinker' to make a successful three-day eventer. Yet another rider, a gentleman this time, said he liked his horses to cultivate 'blind obedience, rather like a soldier as opposed to a policeman' so that they would jump anything asked without asking why or wondering what might happen on the other side.

Unlike hunting predators, horses only seem to become crafty with experience, not by instinct, but the more intelligent ones certainly do learn quite quickly what their particular game is about and if they don't like it can devise all sorts of ways of evading the issue if they are clever enough.

Over many generations, Thoroughbred horses have been bred for more or less one quality only – speed. Other matters, even soundness, and certainly temperament have received little or no consideration which is why the breed in general has such widely varying qualities of temperament. This seems to be tolerated in the racing world where the horses are handled by professionals, but in other fields of competition temperament becomes much more important because so many of the horses are handled by their amateur, if highly competent, owners, as well as, possibly, professional grooms. The differing skills demanded of a competition horse today require a more equable temperament than does racing and, like other qualities, temperament can be selected for or against in a breeding programme, as is so plainly shown by the warmbloods whose breeders have produced a predictable, reliable stamp of horse in many cases, both physically and mentally.

Competition horses must have 'trainable' temperaments; they must be willing and preferably must not 'hot up'. They must have the courage (that word again) and mental endurance to stick with whatever is happening until the rider/whip says 'stop', and although they cannot be credited with a will to win as they cannot understand competitive conditions, no matter what people may say they must display an eagerness for their work and a tendency to rise to the occasion, for they certainly do understand special occasions. They also understand when their human connections are pleased with them or *vice versa*. Many competitiors also feel that horses understand adulation and applause and the electric atmosphere pervading important events. There are any number of horses who will not work well at home but self-ignite at a competitive event.

All in all, a malleable temperament with that vital spark when you need it is what to look for. Unfortunately this is the sort of thing you can only be certain of in practice, although the horse's facial expression and particularly the eyes and ears can be a good guide.

3
Heredity and Selective Breeding

There is an old and well-known saying concerning breeding, whether it be horses or any other animal: 'Mate the best with the best and hope for the best'. While that is good advice as far as it goes it is an over-simplification, and to do it could, in practice, lead to disaster or at least dismal failure.

The traits or characteristics possessed by a horse are inherited from its parents by means of genes, groups of chemicals which act as hereditary 'instruction leaflets' present on protein, threadlike structures called chromosomes. There are chromosomes present in pairs in the nuclei ('control centres') of each cell in the body. The horse has 32 pairs of chromosomes.

Each gene is present in its own locus (position, location) on a chromosome. As the chromosomes are in pairs, there are obviously two genes for each characteristic. The chromosomes, however, are passed on singly during mating. The stallion's sperm and the mare's ovum (egg) each contain 32 single chromosomes; then, when the sperm pierces the ovum at the moment of conception they link up, so the fertilised egg contains the necessary 32 pairs, half of each pair coming from each parent along with the genes for all the various characteristics. Therefore, the resulting foal is in practice 50 per cent its dam and 50 per cent its sire.

However, this does not mean the foal is an equal blend of its parents' characteristics, for some genes may be dominant (overpowering) and others recessive (submissive), while yet others may be additive (equal in their ability to pass on traits). Characteristics themselves may, of course, be both good and bad and if a horse passes on dominant genes for a bad characteristic, say weak constitution or sickle hocks, his or her offspring will inherit that characteristic. The same obviously goes for good characteristics such as strong, well-conformed forelegs or a good temperament.

There are thousands of genes controlling as many traits and although genetics, as the science of heredity is known, has been refined into mathematical formulae and well-defined rules, the highly complicated interaction of genes still makes for a degree of uncertainty in breeding and you can never be absolutely certain what your resulting foal will be like mentally or physically. We do know enough, however, to be able to make practical use of our present state of knowledge and reduce the gambles to an acceptable level if we apply it in a fairly intelligent and commonsense way.

Although a foal is 50/50 its parent's genes, the number of dominant genes it inherits from the parents will determine its mentality and physique. Because stallions can produce more offspring in a single breeding season than can a mare in a whole lifetime, stallions have far more effect on a breed or population of horses than do mares. Mares *can* be dominant but their opportunities for producing offspring are limited to, on average, two every three years (setting aside the techniques of embryo transplants (Chapter 4), although even then the numbers possible are limited); a stallion, on the other hand, serving 40 mares a season can expect 20 to 30 (or maybe more) of those mares to produce offspring.

However, when it comes to raising the individual foal, even if the mare is not particularly dominant (prepotent is the term more often used for practical purposes), she has a great effect on how well the foal matures. Her milk supply is one critical factor in supplying the foal with its essential nutrients and whether or not she will allow the foal to suckle when it needs to. How well she protects the foal from other field-mates is also important, and whether or not she protects it from the weather and gives it the mental security and confidence of maternal tender loving care are other important factors affecting the finished product. Although human intervention and care can make or mar a foal as well, and can make up for a poor mother, there is really no substitute for a good equine mother in raising a healthy youngster. So it is generally accepted that the mare is responsible for 60 per cent or more of the foal, and the stallion only 40 per cent, no matter how dominant or prepotent he may be.

Old ideas

Before the monk Gregor Mendel founded what is now known as the science of genetics, breeders had their own ideas of how to produce a good horse. They could see that animals and humans 'took after' one or both parents as regards inheriting certain traits, of course, and they had the sense to mate horses with complimentary characteristics. However, they were at a loss to explain why traits sometimes seemed to skip a generation or more, only to appear further down the line. It occasionally happened, for instance, in the earliest days of Thorough-bred breeding that a very fast horse resulted from the mating of two only moderately fast. The parents had carried, unknown to the early breeders, recessive genes for speed which had been overpowered by their own parents' dominant genes for 'slowness', but the recessive genes for speed had resurfaced in their foal as Mendel later discovered and demonstrated.

Unfortunately, it also happens that two fast parents can be mated together but their foals may be frustratingly slow. The great American racehorse Secretariat is an example of apparently being recessive for speed because, despite having had the cream of racing mares sent to him, he was a disappointment at stud, producing nothing approaching his own greatness. When bred to sprinters rather than distance runners, however, his stock performed better and the American trainer D. Wayne Lukas, who has been described as the most successful racehorse trainer in the world, told me that he has trained several successful offspring of Secretariat and he has certainly not been disappointed in the horse. In Britain, many people consider Brigadier Gerard a similar case but, on studying his pedigree and ancestors' achievements, he did not come from particularly fast families and has not produced reliably fast offspring. Some people have even described him as a freak in his family. His conformation is actually superb, as near perfection as you can get, and this has no doubt had a considerable effect on his own achievements on the racecourse.

Old-time breeders also believed that acquired characteristics were passed on too, such as physical fitness and condition and the results of injuries. One belief that persisted to within living memory, in the breeding of other animals as well as horses, was that if a pure bred mare was mated with a mongrel type of animal she would be tainted and unable to produce pure bred offspring again, and that if she were subsequently put to a pure bred stallion he too would be tainted irretrievably! Old books are full of, to our thinking, weird and wonderful theories of this sort. The science of genetics has shown most of them to be untrue, of course, but the breeder of olden times did not have the benefit of such knowledge and must have been quite perturbed when his theories (at least the sort mentioned above) did not work out in practice. Disease could be and is passed on, but acquired traits certainly are not. However, the propensity for developing good and bad qualities if environmental conditions are right *is* passed on. There is probably a genetic predisposition towards such things as respiratory problems, limb weaknesses, behavioural quirks and so on.

In her book *A Breed of Horses* (now out of print) Moyra Williams, a clinical psychologist by profession and a breeder and rider of competition horses, tells many fascinating tales of how characteristics appeared again and again in a related group of horses she owned and in their relations by her stallion, Gamesman, to the point where she could fairly reliably predict how different foals were going to perform and behave as they grew up. Aspiring competition horse breeders would be well advised to try and get hold of a copy of this book not only for sheer entertainment but also for instructive 'lateral thinking' as regards the inheritance of mental and physical characteristics.

Pedigrees

A horse's pedigree is a godsend to prospective purchasers or breeders as it permits them to trace such characteristics in a whole family and acquire some idea of how likely they are to be passed on. Pedigrees and related homework in following them up, contacting owners, breeders and riders with pertinent questions, can give an excellent idea of the characteristics likely to be possessed by a horse one is considering buying or breeding, particularly if the research shows certain traits to be reliably passed down in that family. Acquiring as many photographs as possible of the animals mentioned in the pedigree is also most helpful in judging conformation.

The animal on the top line or extreme left-hand side of a pedigree is known as the 'first generation', its parents the second generation and so on. Most breeders feel that from the fifth generation back the pedigree has little significance, only the latest four counting as regards predicting the characteristics of the animal under consideration. However, genes don't discriminate. They have been passed down since the beginning of time along with the various traits they bring. Each animal's make-up is individual, however, and no horse will be exactly replicated – even brothers and sisters can look and behave quite differently according to just what genes have been expressed as dominant or recessive.

I was watching a private display of lungeing and long-reining some years ago when a horse was brought into the school who was the image of the legendary racehorse St Simon – not that I remember St Simon but I have seen many photographs of him. The likeness was so uncanny that it was like going back in time a hundred years or so. St Simon was very prepotent. He had the proverbial scorching speed of a true champion and headed the winning sires list a record nine times, his offspring winning 571 races in Britain alone. It turned out that St Simon appeared several generations back in the pedigree of the horse in the display, many more than four.

Although that particular horse had inherited St Simon's appearance and apparently his temperament, he did not have his speed, but that speed has been passed down to other families, the great Ribot being one of St Simon's descendants. It is true that Ribot's speed could well have come from elsewhere, but the fact is that the appearance of St

Simon in a pedigree today is still indicative of the good possibility of higher than average speed.

When reading up pedigree details, it should be remembered that it makes no difference whether traits come from the female line (side of the family) or the male. However, for present-day, practical purposes the four-generation watershed is as good as any to adhere to as it makes research that much easier. If genes from prior ancestors have not been expressed within that time their likely future influence is minimal.

Inbreeding and line breeding

Having a properly laid-out pedigree is obviously very helpful not only for researching what traits a horse is likely to have but also in planning future matings, particularly when considering inbreeding and line breeding. The two are pretty much the same thing, i.e. breeding between related individuals. In inbreeding the relationship is much closer than in line breeding, for example mating father with daughter, mother with son or brother with sister. Line breeding involves mating two more distantly related individuals who have a common ancestor, with a view to fixing that ancestor's genes in the line.

Both inbreeding and line breeding fix the genes (both good and bad) in a family, making prepotency more firmly established and likely. In nature, colts are normally banished from a herd when they reach puberty but fillies tend to stay unless stolen by rival males. This does not prevent inbreeding, however; stallions frequently serve their daughters and may be ousted by one of their own sons when the time comes. The value of inbreeding and line breeding occurs when desirable genes (those enabling a family to survive best in its present environment) are expressed and fixed. When the combination is not so desirable the resulting individual can suffer all sorts of mental and physical disadvantages and, in nature, would not usually survive to breed again.

In domestication, breeders must be very careful when inbreeding to ensure as far as possible that they are inbreeding for desirable, dominant genes. Should the individuals involved possess dominant genes for *un*desirable characteristics (say sickle hocks or nasty temper) these will become fixed in the line or family. Inbreeding or line breeding should not, therefore, be practised between individuals who possess the same fault, as the offspring will almost certainly possess it in dominant form. As no horse is perfect, breeders have to weigh up matings by studying not only the individuals concerned but also their ancestors, carefully noting the good and bad points of each and finally mating for as many good qualities as they can while avoiding as many bad ones as possible, and certainly not putting together two horses with the same fault. If a bad point is obviously dominant and continually passed on, a mate should be found who is obviously dominant in an opposing good point with a view to eventually cancelling out the fault in a family.

Outcrossing means mating between individuals who are not related. Some people modify this by taking it to mean mating between individuals who are not related within the first four generations, although this is not, of course, strictly an outcross.

Inbreeding and line breeding are used within families of individuals: to mate two Arabs together is not inbreeding or line breeding unless they are personally related. However, the word 'outcross' is frequently used when mating an animal of a specific breed with one of another breed or type when the individuals are not personally related, for instance mating a Welsh Cob with a Thoroughbred.

It should be borne in mind that inbred and line-bred animals can develop various weaknesses such as poorer constitutions and lack of strength and stamina. Where this is seen to be happening the process should obviously be stopped. In families where inbreeding and line breeding over some generations have already taken place, breeders often outcross outside the family and sometimes outside the breed depending on their policies, to obtain what is called 'hybrid (mongrel) vigour'. This can be very successful if the individuals concerned are carefully selected to be complimentary to each other in their mental and physical qualities. Strictly speaking, however, a hybrid is an animal produced by mating together two different species (such as a horse and a donkey which produce a mule) rather than simply two genetically different horses, although the term is commonly accepted to denote unrelated matings is everyday parlance.

Within a specific breed it usually happens that all its members are related, however distantly, somewhere along the line. For instance, all Thoroughbreds are related as they all stem from three oriental founding fathers and some 40 or so foundation or 'tap root' mares, the exact number being uncertain because of various gaps in the earliest pedigrees which could have been filled by one or more unknown mares. All these genes have been thoroughly mixed over the centuries producing a vast family of closely and distantly related individuals.

When the stock of two individuals seem to be consistently good a 'nick' is said to have occurred – the two animals appear to 'nick' together. This can happen without warning and is a happy occurrence regarded by breeders rather like manna from Heaven. You cannot plan for it, but when it happens accept it with open arms! A nick does not have to be between a mare and a stallion. It can happen between, say, a stallion and mares by another stallion as in the well-known Nasrullah-Princequillo nick in the Thoroughbred world. Stock by Nasrullah out of mares by Princequillo were invariably outstanding. It could also happen, of course, between, say, a mare and various stallions out of another mare. There are any number of possibilities and the individuals may or may not be inbred or line bred.

The whole question of heredity and pedigrees is fascinating if you look at it in an organised manner and are prepared to do your homework. The steady slog of studying as many animals as possible, noting their good and bad points (and considering whether they would be any better with a different rider), keeping records of the ancestry of winners and getting to know as many individuals as possible, cannot be beaten in your search for the ultimate competition horse.

In Britain, we are becoming much better organised as regards keeping records and pedigrees for our competition horses. There seems to be a kind of perverse satisfaction in producing a winner out of nowhere (usually Ireland or a bog in Devon!) with no known antecedents and bought covered in mud only to knock the spots off everything else at Badminton a few short years later. However, this sort of thing does competition horse breeding no good at all, particularly since the animal concerned is almost certain to be a gelding and almost as certainly of unknown parentage. It may be very nice for the horse's owners, but if it happens to you at least try to find out how the horse was bred if you possibly can – the names and, if applicable, breeds of the sire and dam – and keep records so that some effort can be made to trace these parents or their near relatives with a view to recreating your luck in future and, who knows, actually getting the progeny registered somewhere or other.

It is true that 'papers' won't make the horse any better a performer but if we are to take more of the chance, the gamble, out of competition horse breeding, much more attention is going to have to be paid to pedigrees, parentage and heredity in general to continue the good start made in recent years by various private and commercial breeders and breed societies.

4
Breeding Practices

By far the most common method of mating together a stallion and a mare is to mate them in hand, with each held by a human handler. The mating is controlled by the humans and the procedure is fairly familiar, with minor practical differences according to the policy of the individual stud.

Usually there is a prepared, or at least predetermined, area ranging from a paddock to a specially surfaced and sometimes completely enclosed and covered covering yard. The mare may or may not wear hobbles and boots (to prevent her injuring the stallion), be twitched (to quieten her down), have a foreleg held or strapped up (to keep her fairly still) and wear a leather bib or cover over her neck (to protect her from the stallion's teeth).

The stallion is led into the covering area, with little or no prior contact allowed between the two animals in some establishments, and the stallion mounts in the usual way, serves the mare sometimes with some guidance from his handler, and finally dismounts, has an antiseptic wash or plain water thrown over his penis and is led away. The mare is released from her various contraptions, if any, and led around to prevent her straining and possibly ejecting the stallion's semen, then returned to her box or paddock.

This method has been used in various forms for as long as man has attempted to control the mating process. In its extreme forms, with the mare severely restricted and not even allowed to meet the stallion beforehand, and with unsympathetic, maybe even blasé and bored handlers, it can be a traumatic process for her. The stallion, too, can be less than happy in his work under similar conditions, particularly with the type of handler who constantly jabs him in the mouth (a very common fault) and who drags him off the mare too quickly instead of letting him dismount in his own time.

From a practical point of view, this method has as its advantages the fact that the mating is closely controlled and is known to have definitely taken place, the identity of the parents should be clear and it requires a minimum of special equipment. The disadvantages include the possible trauma to the animals if inappropriately handled, the possible spread of disease, the possibility of injury to mare and stallion, the necessity to send the mare away to stud and the inherent expense to her owner, not to mention the unsettling effect of a change in surroundings and handlers. Older stallions may have difficulty in serving naturally and may have to retire from stud due to a simply inability, say, to stand on their hind legs (due to arthritis) to mount a mare. Similarly, some mares may be unable to bear the weight of a stallion during service for various reasons and cannot, therefore, be used for breeding.

Despite the many disadvantages and few advantages, the method is almost exclusively used in the Thoroughbred industry, with a very few stallions being used at liberty, running with their mares.

Natural mating

To have a stallion run with his mares, either singly or in a group or herd, is considered too dangerous for extremely valuable animals like some Thoroughbreds. Running with mares is, however, quite common in some other breeds, particularly on pony and cob studs. The stallion can either live permanently with his mares who are put into and taken out of the herd as they arrive at stud and come into and out of season, or he can simply be put into a paddock with one mare at a time for as long as it takes for the mating to occur.

This is obviously a method much closer to nature and conception rates are known to be higher than with the more usual in-hand method. During the 1970s, the Thoroughbred stallion Tepukei was allowed as an experiment to run with his mares at the Irish National Stud. He was not regarded as a highly valuable stallion despite being nicely bred, and the then manager, Michael Osborne, MRCVS, wanted to see if, as he believed, conception rates would increase, particularly with mares known to be difficult or impossible to get in foal. The mares sent to Tepukei were often 'last chancers' or even 'no hopers' due to be sent to the knacker's yard if they did not conceive – but conceive they did, as far as I can recall without exception.

This method is certainly not without risk. Tepukei bore the scars on his forelegs where his mares had been teaching him his manners, but he soon learned when his mares were truly receptive to him, and then to approach only from the side to enquire first, and became very proficient at doing his job while keeping out of harm's way.

Obviously this method takes up less time and labour from the human point of view and does have better conception rates. One person can supervise, or rather simply watch, the proceedings and note which mares have been served, the animals may be much more relaxed (which is probably why the mares conceive more reliably), the mares will be fully in season and right for serving as determined by the those best qualified for the job (the mare and stallion) and the horses are allowed important and natural social contact and courtship.

On the debit side, it is more energy-expensive for the stallion, especially while he is learning his job, as he may spend all day following a particular mare around to no avail. On the other hand, it is found with some stallions that they repeatedly serve the same mare when she is full in season, ignoring some others who are just as ready. (With Tepukei, it was found advantageous to remove a mare once he had served her so that he would turn his attention elsewhere.) There is the previously mentioned risk of injury, particularly to the stallion, and there is also the need to ensure that mares are compatible to prevent skirmishes breaking out between them.

On the whole, though, the method has more going for it than against it, particularly with an experienced stallion and where conception rates are considered highly important. The method does not have to conform entirely to nature, of course. The stallion and mares could be brought in separately at night if desired (although it has been found preferable to stable the horse in the same yard as his mares as they all settle better in this way), and a point could be made of accepting only experienced, easy mares for a young stallion who could initially be taught his job in hand. Maiden, younger and difficult mares such as those who do not show in hand or have a 'silent' cycle would be best put with a gentlemanly, experienced stallion, as would those who have had a bad time during past services at the hands of a rough or even vicious stallion or unsympathetic humans.

For the purposes of this book, I telephoned six breeders taken at random from advertisements in the equestrian press which specifically stated that their stallions could run with their mares, to ask them if they had ever had a serious or even worrying injury to their stallion. All of them said they had not, and also confirmed higher conception figures than for in-hand mating. I feel there is much to be said for giving this method of breeding more serious consideration than it receives at present.

Scientific advances

Many people in the competition horse industry feel that the two developments which are really going to show the way ahead in this field are artificial insemination and the more recently developed embryo transfer. The former has been used for many decades in agriculture, and most dairy and beef cattle are now produced in this way. Many competition horse registries accept it but no Thoroughbred registry will do so; however, there is nothing to prevent a competition horse breeder using a Thoroughbred stallion in this way bearing in mind that if the semen were used for a Thoroughbred mare the resulting foal would not be eligible for a Thoroughbred registry.

Artificial insemination

The advantages of artificial insemination include the obvious one of the decrease in the spread of sexually transmitted diseases, not simply because the mare and stallion never meet but because the semen is mixed with fluids called 'extenders' which prolong the survival time of the live sperm and contain anti-bacterial substances.

The method obviates the expensive and often inconvenient process of transporting the mare and sending her away to board at the stud, plus the return journey probably with a young foal at foot. Travelling is always stressful and risky.

Mares and stallions which cannot mate in the normal way could still be used for breeding using this method, for instance those with the lasting effects of injuries or degenerative disease, or those with behavioural problems which make them difficult. Even mating in hand can be risky. This risk is removed with AI.

One ejaculate can be split and used for several mares, increasing the number of mares to be 'served' in a season. Semen can be frozen/chilled and transported and used in other countries and even after the stallion's death. It can also help increase conception rates by avoiding possible over-use of the stallion (such as when several mares come 'right' at about the same time).

Should problems occur with the stallion such as his developing a disease or lack of sperm motility (which affects vigour and conception), this can be spotted before the sperm is used as most samples, in a properly administered system, are examined under a microscope before use. This prevents the diseased sperm being given to a mare and, in the case of poor motility, is spotted before suspicions are raised by mares failing to hold to service.

Disadvantages include, as far as the Thoroughbred world is concerned, cheaper 'service' fees for highly-priced stallions as the sperm is more readily available, and difficulty of identity. In practice, the arguments are almost entirely economic, stallion owners understandably jealously guarding their stallions' services. Identity, however, can be checked by blood typing and the up-and-coming techniques of genetic fingerprinting now used in forensic science.

Another disadvantage could be that if close checks are not kept by registries, too much inbreeding could eventually occur as the numbers of horses by a particular stallion or stallions proliferated. Those mare owners who prefer AI to conventional mating may concentrate only on those stallions whose sperm is available, whether or not they are the most suitable for their mares. This could also lead to restricted genetic variation in time and increase in faults of conformation and temperament.

The technique requires a good deal of expertise and attention to detail so personnel must be properly trained in its use and specialist equipment and laboratory facilities must be available. This can be expensive. Veterinary supervision of the system, blood typing and correct record keeping are needed.

A full description of exact techniques is given in *Practical Stud Management* by John Rose and Sarah Pilliner, but basically the stallion is induced to ejaculate into a temperature-controlled artificial vagina, usually by being allowed to mount a mare in season and having his penis gently deflected into the instrument rather than the mare. There is a semen collection bottle attached to the artificial vagina, which is subsequently either placed in an incubator for early use or placed in a vacuum container and gradually cooled for storage for up to 48 hours. For longer term storage, the semen is placed in a container which is packed in liquid nitrogen to freeze it. Not all stallions' semen will freeze satisfactorily and this technique is not nearly so well perfected as that used in cattle. However, obstacles will doubtless be overcome in time.

To inseminate the mare, a catheter, a syringe, an insemination pipette and plastic tubing are needed. The catheter is inserted via the mare's vagina and cervix into the uterus, and the semen injected via the syringe into the mare.

It is important that sterile conditions and equipment are maintained as far as possible during the process of collecting and administering semen, otherwise disease can easily spread. Small studs, because of the laboratory conditions, equipment and trained personnel needed, may feel the accompanying expense not worthwhile, although future trends may change techniques and ultimately bring down costs to a more bearable level. There is no doubt that AI, as it is known, is likely to spread in the competition horse industry and, who knows, eventually into the Thoroughbred industry too, even if it does not take over entirely.

Embryo transfer

Embryo transfer is another, much newer, technique but already well established due, in Britain, to work done by Professor W.R. ('Twink') Allen and his team at the Thoroughbred Breeders Association Equine Fertility Unit in Newmarket. Yet it is the Thoroughbred world which ironically refuses to accept ET and AI. Basically, ET enables a mare to 'give birth' to several foals a year instead of the normal one as her fertilised embryos are developed to full term inside other mares, known as recipient mares.

The real mother, known as the donor mare, is covered by the stallion or conceives by means of artificial insemination, and the embryo is flushed out of her uterus six to eight days after ovulation, before it becomes attached. It is placed into the recipient mare by either surgical or non-surgical techniques. The recipient mare's breeding cycle and that of the donor mare will previously have been synchronised by means of drug therapy to ensure that the embryo is going into a reproductive environment at the same stage and chemical state as that of the donor mare.

The embryo is sucked up into a pipette from the container into which it has been flushed, and transferred into an insemination instrument which is passed into the uterus. This non-surgical method is obviously less stressful for the mare and cheaper for the owner but has some risk of infection and a lower conception rate.

In the surgical method, less often used, the recipient mare can be given a local or general anaesthetic and the horn of the uterus brought out so that a small hole can be made in it to take the pipette from which the embryo is injected.

Although, as mentioned, it is possible for several embryos a year to be produced from one mare by ET, it should be made clear that some sports horse registries and breed stud books will only accept one foal per year from any particular mare, presumably in an effort to keep down the number (and therefore keep up the cost) of good horses coming on to the market. Vested economic interests again.

It must surely be only a matter of time before such prohibitive restrictions fall by the wayside if Britain is to keep up with more forward-looking nations in the competition horse production race. As for availability decreasing value, anything is only worth what someone is willing to pay for it. Competition horses with truly top class potential are so thin on the ground that I feel that the numbers likely to be produced should ET become readily accepted here will still not greatly decrease the purchase price of the final product, a three or four-year-old horse ready to school on. Whenever any advance is made, scientific or otherwise, there are bleatings of protest from those who believe they stand to lose economically. In practice, as far as the horse world is concerned, there have been many advances, from the invention of horseboxes to the facility of vaccination, from the syndication of valuable stallions to air travel, from the now common-place practice of palpating mares to improved management knowledge, and all the price of good horses has ever done is go up. Instead of trying to operate a restrictive practices policy and cartel as regards AI and ET and whatever else of benefit the world of equine science is about to throw at us, we should be taking full advantage of them if we wish not only to keep up with the rest of the world but avoid being laughed at into the bargain!

On the 28 November 1986, Britain's equestrian weekly newspaper, *Horse and Hound*, published a short report on a breeding seminar covering these and other techniques and practices at which Twink Allen was one of the speakers. The following is one paragraph, and a highly relevant one, from that report:

'In the USA one breeder, enlisting the help of veterinarians from Colorado University, acquired 13 top-class and still-competing event mares, selecting for them four of the best stallions and an "army" of recipient mares. From 116 embryos obtained from artificially inseminating the 13 mares and transferring these to the other mares, he now has 104 foals.'

If Britain's registering authorities and breeders do not keep pace with developments like that buyers will simply continue to go abroad and buy there from both conventionally and AI/ET-produced selections of top class stock.

The main advantage of ET appears to be that the true dam has a minimal interruption of her work/competition schedule and can continue to prove her name and bloodlines while 'having' her foal, thereby increasing, rather than decreasing, its value. Traditionalists should remember that no matter how many foals a mare can reasonably be expected to produce by ET they will not be clones. Full brothers and sisters can be as different as chalk and cheese and there is no cast-iron guarantee that any particular one will be a winner. That will have to wait for further advances in genetic engineering, about which there will doubtless be just as much furore, and by which time no one will be able to remember what it was like for a stallion to serve a mare in the 'normal' way or for a high-class competition mare to carry and give birth to her own foal!

The wastage, particularly in the racing world but also in the competition horse world, is so phenomenal that I cannot envisage there being too many high class animals available. Surely no one *wants* wastage – animals who do not fulfil their early promise often because they are simply not good enough (that is, talented or sound enough) to do the job they were bred for. They will always be made of flesh and blood and subject not only to the usual ailments but to the stresses and stains of their jobs and of the environment in which we place them. Inherent ability is only one piece in the jigsaw of producing a competition horse and even that is hard enough to secure. There will still be wastage in the form of injury, travel stress and poor management even at the highest levels, usually due to managers failing to take on board truly effective horsemastership principles but staying bogged down in past methods and misguided beliefs.

And, of course, there is always the skill of the rider or whip. Humans will never (or not in the imaginable future) be produced in large numbers purely for their genetic traits as we now try to produce competition horses. There will always be a high level of fallibility for umpteen reasons so we shall continue to make mistakes for which some may blame our horses, and we shall continue to allow excitement or nerves to affect, often detrimentally, our performance and our handling of our horses. No one will ever win all the time, no matter how many or how good are their horses.

No, you can never have too many *good* competition horses. Those which are not up to the highest grades of competition will find their niches further down the scale with appropriate riders. And not everyone wants to compete at top level anyway, or has the ability to do so. Keeping the supply of good horses small does not help the market in general or the milieu of the competitive world, whatever the discipline. More horses 'disappoint' than come up to expectations. To make for a healthy competitive scene and fulfil the market demands at all levels, surely it is best to breed as many (according to demand) of the best competition horses as we can and allow them to filter through to their own levels.

The best start

Breeders are always faced with the problem of what stock to cull from their studs and when to do it. Keeping horses is expensive and a bad one costs as much to keep as a good one, probably more if it is more prone to needing veterinary or other specialist attention. At the time of writing, if a breeder cannot (in Britain) obtain at least £6000 for a young horse the whole process of its conception, foaling, rearing and marketing is simply not financially viable unless the breeder is producing the horse for his or her own benefit or as a not-too-expensive hobby. Costs are normally required to be cut by culling from the stud those animals not felt likely to make the grade, as soon as this fact is recognised. Unfortunately, judging youngstock is notoriously difficult. A goose can change into a swan within a year and those showing no early promise can suddenly spread wings. Similarly horses can fail to come good.

All the breeder can really do is give each horse the best start possible, taking advantage of whatever specialist help is available such as veterinary, nutritional and so on, and keep a close watch on his or her developing youngsters, selling on those felt to be surplus to requirements and not likely to make the grade. When breeding warmbloods, however, stock will need to be kept to the various prescribed ages to go through the performance/grading processes, but even here, some breeders carry out their own 'tests' and assessments and cull those not up to the required standard of the stud so that they are not presented for grading. It is often felt that to present a sub-standard animal for testing, auction or in the showring, whatever its breeding, does the reputation of the stud no good. Resources can then be concentrated on the superior stock, profits increased and reputation enhanced. As soon as an animal shows definite signs of not coming up to standard, it should be culled and not kept on in the hope that it might undergo a transformation. It might, but the chances are not high – and if it does the stud's reputation will not suffer. It is simply one of those occurrences which makes buying horses a process of eternal hope for the purchaser and maintains the interest of the whole uncertain field of competition.

Because different breeds and types, and different individuals within a breed or type, mature and develop at different rates, care should be taken not to over-work youngstock too early because of impatience to test them. More good horses are ruined because of overwork at the start of their lives and, particularly, the start of their competitive careers, than from any other cause, notably in the Thoroughbred industry where these beautiful and expensive animals are so often regarded as expendable. Unfortunately, practices such as lungeing and even 'popping' yearlings over poles are creeping in more and more with other breeds in an effort to get an early idea of a youngster's potential.

A foal and yearling should have no more imposed on it than the instilling of good manners: it should be taught stable manners, to lead in hand and to obey simple commands such as 'walk on', 'whoa', 'over' and 'back'. It should be accustomed to wearing a foal slip and later headcollar from a very early age, and maybe a foal rug depending on local climate. The yearling can certainly be 'taken for walks' either in hand or on long reins but no attempt should be made to start encouraging an 'outline' or to introduce a 'work' atmosphere at this stage.

Generally, with variations according to breed, a youngster's legs will not really mature and harden till the age of three or later, the shoulders (not the withers) mature at about four and the femur and hip area may not mature till the age of five; also the spine can, in fact, continue to develop till six or even later in certain individuals. Although the growth plates, the cartilaginous areas at the ends of the long leg bones, may be X-rayed to see if they have 'closed' (hardened and changed into mainly bone) at the age of two or a little later, the maturity rate of the rest of the horse's skeleton is often overlooked. Stress on the spine at too early an age is a common cause of later back problems, particularly in jumping horses.

I hope the current attitude of working horses too much too young can be stopped rather than encouraged by formal testing as it seems to me to be at present. Surely, with an animal as strong and long-lived as a horse, it would be better for all concerned to have a little more patience at the start of a horse's life with a view to getting more productive years out of him later on and, indeed, allowing him to live out his full lifespan. Horses are capable of competing internationally well into their teens, in show jumping and dressage in particular, and into their early teens in horse trials and driving. At a less demanding level, horses in their late teens can be seen regularly competing in all disciplines.

The most common life-shortening practices, both actually and from a work/competition point of view, carried on by the less knowledgeable breeders and producers of horses are:

(1) Working too young.
(2) Over-feeding protein to 'force' growth (which in practice results in physical damage).
(3) Feeding an imbalanced calcium: phosphorus ratio which results in bone disorders (there should always be slightly more calcium in the diet than phosphorus, say 1.5:1 as a general rule).
(4) Getting youngsters too fat, maybe to please or impress showring judges or potential buyers. This overtopping, as it is known, because the skeleton is carrying too much weight for its stage of maturity, again causes physical, usually bone, damage, but also soft tissue strain and subsequent possible lifelong weakness, exactly what we do not want in competition animals.

It should be remembered that once a competition horse is retired from a particular discipline it can often go into another – eventers can become show jumpers, for instance, and almost any suitable equine competitor can become a dressage competitor and still compete in its twenties, depending on the individual. Horses who *are* overdone as youngsters are often only fit for the meat trade by the time they reach middle age at 15 or earlier.

What we should be aiming at is producing by whatever means are available to us, *while still putting first and foremost the ultimate well-being of the horses concerned*, as many of the best competition horses we can, commensurate with demand, raising them and working them in such a way as to give them the best possible start to a long, productive and maybe varied competitive life; instead of taking chances and producing almost anything which just might possibly have some sort of future in competition at whatever level, and being prepared to weed out others at an early age by means of over-demanding formal or informal testing and regarding the resultant wastage as just part of the scene.

The horse is an adaptable, strong, not entirely stupid animal normally willing to please who could give us much better, and longer, service with more appropriate breeding, working and management practices.

5
Environmental Considerations

Whether you are keeping breeding stock or mature, working horses, the basic requirements concerning accommodation and surroundings are the same, with some refinements for stud animals.

Although it is marvellous to have access to many acres of parkland or properly laid-out paddocks, it is not essential. Horses can be bred and kept very well on smallish areas, provided that, where pasture is concerned, they are not actually overcrowded. From a grazing land point of view, it is normally recommended that there should be a minimum of 2 acres for the first horse and one more for every further animal, and this should be regarded as minimal. For stud purposes, it is highly desirable that larger acreages are available; such animals are normally kept out a good deal more than working, mature animals and not only consume more grass but batter the ground with their hooves, actually poaching it quite badly in wet weather.

Many people regard actual grazing as unnecessary for working horses although there is no doubt that all horses benefit greatly from freedom, space and the ability to graze their natural food, grass. There is some measure of belief that the grazing motion is programmed into the horse's pysche and that eating cut grass brought to them does not fulfil the same need in the animal.

Paddocks for horses have traditionally, in the western hemisphere, been sited on chalk or limestone land wherever possible and even today the traditional horse-breeding areas of Britain, the Republic of Ireland and the USA, for example, are concentrated in such areas. This is largely because of the calcium content of the soil over such geological features and, therefore, of the grass eaten by the horses, which is believed to make for strong bones and teeth. It is felt by many that supplementing the diets of horses in other areas with calcium supplements, ground limestone and the like is not as good. However, that said, there are many good studs producing superb, winning competition and racehorses in non-limestone areas. Modern dietetics can produce everything the horse breeder/manager needs for the raising and maintenance of athletic horses, so there is no need for a mass exodus to the most traditionally favoured areas of the country!

It could be said that the smaller your stud the higher quality should be the horses you keep and breed. It is far better to keep a few, or even just one, really good broodmares and aim for the top end of your market. This, good management and a bit of luck combined, will bring the best financial returns in relation to the size of your premises and the running costs and labour involved in running your enterprise. Over-stocking paddocks and other accomodation such as covered yards, surfaced exercise areas and stable buildings overstresses horses mentally, provides a ready hotbed of infection should any be on the rounds, intensifies parasite problems if the worming policy is less than scrupulous (false economy with high class animals, anyway) and is generally to be avoided.

Horses do best in areas of mild climate and fairly high rainfall, which helps ensure a good growth of grass maybe all year round in certain regions. Very wet areas, however, are not recommended, even with exceptionally well-drained land, as constant rain depresses animals and humans alike and makes turning out a regularly offputting experience. Very wet land quickly poaches into a morass of mud in wet weather, ruining the land and grass. Very dry districts are subject to drought in summer which, again, adversely affects the growth of grass and bakes the land hard to the detriment of legs and feet, particularly in playful youngstock.

Paddocks should undulate or slope gently to some outlet (which is fenced off from the horses), so that they drain naturally and provide varied gradients for the horses, helping develop balance, agility and young muscles. Very flat, and particularly low lying land, is not the best because of drainage problems and, obviously, has none of the athletic advantages of land with varied contours. Steep fields, however, must be avoided or horses are constantly bracing themselves against the gradient and if they are galloping about they may be unable to stop in time to avoid a collision with the fence, a tree, building or other horses. Negotiating very steep slopes and rough ground is also a cause of strain, sprains and back trouble.

Pasture management *by Gillian McCarthy*

Pasture is an important environmental resources for the competition horse, supplying a 'habitat', exercise area and some or all of the nutritional input at various stages of the animal's life.

It is important that at all times this is a safe, healthy environment, or lasting damage and effects on performance may occur – whether it be injury due to poor fencing; jarring of young limbs due to compacted soil; clinical or sub-clinical poisoning due to toxic plants, paints, chemicals or water supply; nutritional deficiencies due to soil imbalances; or parasite damage which may have a lifelong effect on health and performance.

It therefore makes sense to have a pre-planned but flexible management programme which eliminates or minimises these disadvantages while enhancing the benefits of time spent at pasture. These benefits include healthy exercise for all stock and development of greater bone density, on a good surface, especially in youngstock; development of a healthy 'outdoor' physique; the mental benefits of time spent outside, however short; and of course the nutritional contribution of pasture, whether this be for growth and development in the young horse (including the unborn or nursing foal), maintenance only of the resting competition horse, or a significant contribution to performance for perhaps the endurance horse, gymkhana pony or any competition horse with respiratory problems when stabled.

Take the time to stand back and think about your pasture and what you want it to provide – whether you could be getting more from it by adjusting your management, and how much time, money and effort you are prepared to put into it, set against the time, money (including veterinary bills, loss of training and feed bills) and effort saved over the lifetime performance of your horse(s) as a result of it. This may be difficult to quantify, but as a form of insurance, if nothing else, good pasture management plays a vital role in the lifetime management of the competition horse.

General considerations

If you already own your land you may well be stuck with the six factors listed below, though some modification of the last four is usually possible. If you are about to buy or rent some new land, these points will help to concentrate your thoughts and point out the merits and de-merits of a given location.

(1) *Aspect and position* The slope of a piece of land and the direction it faces, whether it is on top of a hill, down in a sheltered valley or out on a plain, will affect its use and management for horses. For example, a sheltered field might be useful in winter but a more open site would be chosen for early grazing in spring, where grass growth will get away more quickly, so you may enhance this by choosing earlier grass varieties for the spring paddock, and adjusting your fertiliser policy accordingly.

(2) *Climate and weather* Not much you can do about these, but you can benefit from or compensate for them by adjusting drainage/

irrigation, herbage species selected, shelter provided and so forth.
(3) *Size and arrangement of area available* This, when set against the
number of stock you wish the land to carry, and whether you hope to
grow your own cereals or forages, will obviously affect the intensity of
your management.
(4) *Soil profile and depth of water table, drainage* The nature and
depth of your soil (topsoil), its subsoil and the underlying bed-rock will
have a fundamental effect on the nutritional value of the herbage
grown on it, the period of the year when the paddock can be used (i.e.
degree of poaching and flooding in winter, drought and compaction in
summer) and the possibilities for improving the 'going' on that land to
provide a safe but stimulating surface for valuable limbs. The degree of
stoneyness and proneness to rabbit warrens and other potentially
dangerous (to horses) wildlife activities will also be affected by the soil
profile.

The depth of the water table will also obviously affect drainage and
proneness to drought, as well as access to natural water sources, and
combined with the soil profile combines to affect the natural drainage
characteristics of the land.

There is much the horse owner can do to improve drainage, and this
is really the first aspect to examine when looking to pasture
management, whether it be to set-up or renew a whole drainage system
with ditches and tile drains, or supplement existing drainage. These are
rather beyond the scope of this book, but if you have a serious drainage
problem leading to areas of flooding or pockets of standing water,
serious mud and poaching problems – both of which will stunt grass
growth – this is obviously not a good environment for the performance
horse and specialist advice should be sought. Major drainage work will
involve considerable upheaval and expense, but undoubtedly pays off
in the longer term.

However, once you have an existing drainage network there is much
you can do over the year to keep that system functioning effectively.
Damp, soggy ground means mud and the associated inconvenience and
possible health problems (mud fever, etc.), and herbage which is late to
grow in spring and inaccessible in autumn resulting in the loss of
over-all pasture production and a possible 2–3 month annual reduction
in convenient use of that pasture area.

The main points are:

(a) Check that drain-pipe outfalls into ditches are clear.
(b) Check that ditches and culverts (ditches piped under gates and
roads) are not silted up or full of debris. If they are they should be
cleared in autumn, maintaining the original slope and intended depth

of the ditch as these will have been set up as appropriate to local soil conditions. Dispose of the spoil away from the ditch so it does not eventually wash back down into it. This may involve gaining access to a neighbour's land or even working with the neighbour, as your drain outfalls may be beyond your boundaries.

Ditches should be fenced off from horses and ponies, both for the animals' sake and to avoid hoof damage to the ditch walls. Care should be taken to ensure that the bottom rail of any fence is low enough to prevent small ponies and foals from rolling underneath and drowning or a foal injuring itself trying frantically to get back to mother.

(c) If you have a wet patch and suspect a drain tile may have fractured, you can dig down to replace it but fence off the area until it settles as the going in the dug area may be unsafe for a while.

(5) *Soil type* The actual chemical make-up or type of soil may well vary from field to field (often the reason for siting old boundary hedges) or within a field, or may exist over a vast area with very little variation.

General soil type refers to particle size and chemical composition and will affect the nutritional value of herbage grown on it, the 'going', the drainage and the general management. The main particles are clay, sand and humous (organic matter), all of which are likely to be present in a given area of land but to varying degrees. A mixture of *sand* and *clay* is referred to as *loam*, e.g. medium loam = 50% clay/50% sand, which is the most amenable soil type to manage. *Clay soils* and *clay loams* are referred to as *heavy soils* and *sand and sandy loams* as *light soils*. These will all contain some *humous*, but a highly organic soil is referred to as *peat* or *peaty soil*.

Basically clay-type, heavy soils tend to retain moisture and nutrients but are harder to drain and colder; peaty soils hold water like a sponge but when they do dry out can actually burn (hence the use of peat as a fuel in some areas) and tend to be of poor nutritional value; sandy, light soils drain well but are therefore prone to drought, and they do not retain nutrients well so tend to need more fertiliser.

The presence of humous (organic matter) in clay soils helps to keep it open and more freely drained, partly by encouraging the activities of beneficial soil flora and fauna (worms, micro-organisms); humous in sandy soils helps bind them together and retain moisture.

It is a good idea to check up on your soil type so you can anticipate any problems or benefits and management requirements this may impose.

(6) *Water sources, access, boundaries, field size and shape and shelter* These are all facilities which you may be able to influence to a greater

or lesser extent, and should certainly be considered when developing a new layout.

(a) *Water sources* Although natural water sources such as springs, ponds, streams and rivers sound like an attractive idea, they should only be considered if there is *absolutely* no possibility of pollution being carried from downstream or via ground water, and should be tested regularly to confirm this. The source of pollution could be many miles away, so take care. It is also important that the water is flowing and not stagnant, and that it has a gravelly bottom or sand may be ingested and accumulate in the gut, leading to sand colic; muddy water is obviously not a good idea either. Generally, piped water is a safer bet and you may be able to sink your own bore-hole, with the aid of a water diviner to locate a suitable water source. Whatever source you use, it is important that:

- Foals and youngstock can reach it (and see into but not fall into it!)
- Receptacles are clean and checked regularly (dustbins can be knocked over, buckets are inadequate and old baths downright dangerous)

Ice should be broken at least twice a day in winter; a major cause of colic in grass-kept animals in winter is dehydration. A large (unswallowable) ball, heavy enough not to blow away, bobbing in a trough will help prevent ice formation but *does not* replace regular checks.

(b) *Access, boundaries, field size and shape* These are all beyond the scope of this book, other than the obvious need for safety. Check hedges for poisonous plants (which may appear at different times of the year) and ensure that the overhanging boughs of any potentially poisonous trees and safely removed, as they may come down in a gale and, especially once the leaves have wilted, provide a very palatable, and lethal, snack.

(c) *Shelter* Provision of shelter, particularly against harsh sun (and flies) and wet, windy weather which horses hate, is essential and should be carefully sited, taking into consideration some horses' preference for standing outside the building in the lee of the shelter!

A very useful system to consider is that of open stabling with a 'loafing' area where horses can self-exercise, though still reasonably confined, and can have access to fresh air and be worked without the close confinement that stabling involves.

Confining horses to fields is *not* a natural system so you must ensure that you cater for all the horse's requirements, including those imposed by such confinement.

Managing your pasture

Why bother?

Time spent on basic pasture management, including upgrading if necessary, and regular weed control, liming and fertiliser application, topping, harrowing and other treatments, as and when necessary, and long-term attention to drains and soil structure, will all repay you in both the short and long-term in the health and performance of your competitive horses, whether they be the unborn foal in the womb, the international standard endurance horse competing off grass, or the event horse or show jumper having a daily airing or a seasonal break. Many jobs are routine, whether on a daily, weekly, monthly, seasonal or annual basis; others are one-off or occasional exercises, but it is worth spending a little time on planning and preparation.

Droppings

Daily collection of droppings is preferable from a parasite control viewpoint, though not by any means replacing the need for a regular and effective worming programme.

If collection is not possible, the field should be harrowed weekly with the *short-tined* or *flat* side of a reversible chain harrow, to spread and breakup the droppings. However, it is vital that this is *only* done on a dry day, preferably with a good drying wind to desiccate the worms. Some people feel that harrowing droppings can be a disadvantage, but on balance it is a good policy when performed under the right conditions. A car, Land Rover, ATV motorbike or some horses can be used for this job – in fact it can be a useful means of strengthening the back muscles (*Longissimus Dorsi*) in competition horses and brood mares, and a source of amusement for elderly horses properly introduced to such work.

Harrowing

You should also aim to thoroughly harrow the pasture, at least at the beginning of the season and preferably monthly through the growing season, with the *long-tined* side of a reversible chain harrow to rip up the grass mat and aerate the sward and encourage healthy grass growth. Cross harrowing – i.e. up and down one way, then across the other way at right angles – is especially effective in the spring.

Rolling

Rolling should be performed with reticence and definitely not overdone. It can be useful in spring to flatten puffy, frosted soil and break down poaching, but it can lead to compaction of the soil, especially if the field is badly-drained, so should only be performed if necessary and *not* as a matter of course.

Topping

The grass should be 'topped' regularly through the growing season to prevent growth of rank, unpalatable, un-nutritious grass and to promote 'tillering' of the grass plants – i.e. a form of branching to produce a dense, bushy sward which will help prevent weeds growing and develop a good 'bottom' to the sward, i.e. a tough but springy base which will stand up to considerable wear and tear from even unshod horses' hooves, while providing a resilient base that will reduce concussion to valuable limbs. Selection of low-growing grass species is also an aid to development of a good 'bottom'.

If you are topping for the first time when grass is lush, or at the end of the season, you may need to remove the cut material perhaps using a forage harvester, or even producing hay if it is suitable. Otherwise, once topping regularly, keep the grass down to about 15 cm (6 in) in height and never more than 25 cm (12 in) to encourage tillering and the production of fresh, palatable, nutritious grass and again to discourage weed growth. Many mini-tractors and ATV motorbikes can be used for mowing or topping, and on small areas a turk-scythe is very useful and not difficult to use.

Weed control

There are two main reasons for controlling weeds, the first being that they tend to rob the soil and therefore edible herbage and consequently your horse, of nutrients especially minerals, and to compete with pasture herbage, thereby reducing its yield.

The second and more pressing reason is that some of them are toxic. Poisonous trees such as yew and laburnum and weeds such as ragwort (*Senecio Spp.*) and horsetails (*Equisetum*) are sufficiently poisonous to kill in small quantities. Others may have an insidious, long-term toxic effect, often leading to liver damage and performance and temperament changes, including sluggishness and stumbling, hyper-activity and extreme nervousness, bad temper, or skin lesions. These may eventually prove fatal, or at least predispose the animal to other causes of premature death. Such plants include bracken (*Pterdium Spp.*), hard rush (*Juncus Spp.*), and even buttercups (*Ranunclulus Spp.*).

Many of these plants are also toxic in hay (except buttercups), and indeed may be more palatable when cut and wilted or dried. Horses will not usually graze on, say, ragwort, but this is no reason to be complacent, as a galloping horse may cut off plants with its hooves, which when wilted will be highly palatable – and *less than one plant* may well be sufficient to kill your valuable competition horse.

The other problem is that, though horses may not usually graze on buttercups or bracken, if their pasture is bare or unpalatable, or of poor nutritional value, they may well resort to these plants; I suspect this is a major reason for behaviour problems in ponies kept on such paddocks.

It is essential to dig up and remove ragwort (burning it away from the paddock), and then perhaps spray any regrowth in spring. 'Topping' or cutting the plants will only encourage them to grow more vigorously.

Other poisonous and non-poisonous weeds may be sprayed using either a tractor or spot treatment with a knapsack sprayer or wick-applicator. After spraying, horses must *not* have access to the paddock for at least three weeks. Be guided by your local agricultural merchant about suitable chemicals and how to use them, and *always* read and follow the label and dispose of empty containers properly. Conduct the whole exercise with due consideration to the environment, your neighbours and others in the countryside. Always spray on a still, dry day to avoid wind drift.

Most sprays will also kill herbs in your pasture (see below).

Other common and unsightly, but non-poisonous, weeds which can take over a horse paddock include docks, thistles and nettles. Some species of the first two are covered by the Injurious Weeds Order and the authorities are empowered to force you to deal with them.

Cut and wilted nettles are relished by some horses and can be a source of various minerals, but this does not really justify their existence in a horse paddock. Docks, thistles and nettles can only really be dealt with by spraying young plants or digging out older ones. If you are too late to spray young plants, some benefit may be gained from cutting older (green) plants and spraying the re-growth – but you will almost certainly need to spray again next season. Cutting and burning older growth, especially docks, before they drop thousands of seeds for next year is a good idea if you are sorting out a previously badly-managed pasture. You will then need to spray in the spring, and possibly the next autumn or following spring, to get them under control, as there will be a reservoir of dormant seeds in the soil.

Once you have eliminated the worst growth of weeds, persistent spot-spraying or digging-out of new growth, and attention to liming and fertiliser policy, will help minimise the problem in the long term. Where larger areas of weeds are killed, it may help to patch-up with some suitable grass seed, to help compete-out any newly-germinating weed seeds.

Other problem weeds include chickweed (*Stelleria media*); dandelion (*Taraxacum officionale*) a useful herb in small quantities but one that will take over in a badly managed pasture; plantain (*Plantago spp*); and in some instances clover (*Trifolium spp*) (if we take the definition of a weed as being 'a plant out of place') and unpalatable weed grasses such as couch (*Agropyron repens*) (wickens, twitch, etc.) and Yorkshire fog (*Holcus Lanatus*). Their specific control is beyond the scope of this book, but good fertiliser and topping practice and not over or under-grazing will help to control these potentially deleterious plants.

Fertiliser and liming policy

The presence of weeds and unpalatable rank grass is often an indication of poor liming and fertiliser policy.

Liming

Correction of the lime status or pH (acidity) of your paddock can often have a remarkable effect on the herbage, and even on poaching and other soil problems. Apart from benefiting the herbage and the horses eating it, in general terms, because liming materials are a source of calcium, correcting the lime status of your paddocks is vital for production and maintenance of healthy bones and other body systems.

You can get a rough idea of the lime status of your soil using an inexpensive lime-test kit from your local garden centre, and this is probably the most practical option for users of small acreages, who can then buy Cornish calcified seaweed (see below) by the bag to correct any imbalances.

For larger areas, many lime and fertiliser merchants will do a free or reasonably-priced test and give recommendations based on this, or you may use a Government agency (e.g. The State Extension Service in the USA) or a consultant who will charge a fee, such as members of the British Institute of Agricultural Consultants (BIAC) (such as myself) or the Agricultural Development and Advisory Service (ADAS).

The acidity or pH for optimum pasture growth needs to be in the order of pH 6.0 (5.3 on peat soils), 7.0 being neutral and below that acid and above it alkaline (e.g. chalky soils). Very alkaline soils can lead to locking-up of essential trace elements, which can lead to health and performance problems, so excessive liming can be as undesirable as inadequate treatment.

The most common treatment is to use limestone (chalk), which is usually applied by a contractor using heavy vehicles. It is best applied in autumn but when the ground is not too wet, or excessive damage from the vehicles may occur. The correct rate will be worked out on the basis of soil pH and Calcium Exchange Capacity (CEC), when it is analysed.

Applications will be needed every 3 to 5 years. Horses should be kept off the field until rain has washed the lime off the plants down into the soil. If the land has been very neglected and needs a high level of lime, it may be better to apply half in spring and half in autumn, or over two autumns if necessary.

An alternative material is especially convenient for small areas, being available in smaller quantities in bags, but is also very useful for any horse paddocks. It is called Cornish calcified seaweed and is in fact a ground high-calcium coral-like substance that is also rich in trace elements. It can be applied by hand if necessary, or via an appropriately calibrated farm fertiliser spreader, and horses may be grazed on treated land immediately afterwards. It has the added advantage of sweetening the grass, even in dunging areas, and making it more palatable, encouraging even grazing.

If you do not apply any other fertiliser to your field, it is vital that you keep the lime status in balance for your horse's sake, and monitor it every 3 to 5 years, acting accordingly.

Fertiliser

Many horse owners are reluctant to use fertiliser because they have witnessed problems relating to sudden flushes of grass growth induced by inorganic fertilisers, especially nitrates. However, judicious use of the appropriate products can ensure the production of a nutritious, healthy, palatable herbage, and help to reduce weed and clover growth.

Fertilisers are used to supply mainly nitrogen (N), phosphorus (P), (phosphate), and potassium (K), (potash), plus perhaps magnesium. The numbers on a sack of fertiliser refer to its content of N:P and K, so 20:10:10 fertiliser would contain 20 units of nitrogen (N_2) to 10 units of phosphate (P_2O_5) and 10 units of potash (K_2O), a unit being one per cent.

Ideally you should have your soil analysed on a regular basis (say every 2 years) to check on the specific requirement of your paddocks, but this may not be practical on smaller areas. You can get *some* idea of your soil status from a garden centre test kit, and on larger areas most fertiliser companies will do a free or reasonably-priced test or you can have an independent test done by a BIAC consultant or ADAS etc.

Used carefully, inorganic (artificial) fertilisers *can* be used on horse paddocks, but they tend to cause a sudden flush in growth (which may lead to scouring) or be leached (washed away) by heavy rain. Also, as they are in a relatively 'pure' form, they do not help to replenish trace element levels in the soil. They are usually in a 'prilled' form.

Semi-organic fertilisers on the other hand allow for a slow, gentler release of nutrients throughout the season, helping to iron out the peaks and troughs of the grass-growing season, *and* are a significant source of trace elements. Do check however that they do not contain human sewage, which can lead to a build-up of heavy metals in the soil, or pig slurry which contains too much copper for horse pastures.

A useful new product for horse paddocks in the UK is Palmers Four Seasons fertiliser, a 7:10:12 formulation with added sodium, as salt, (which improves pasture palatability) and magnesium. It is available in manageable 25 kg sacks from horse feed merchants and tack shops, and is ideal for smaller areas, applied at a rate of 3 to 6 bags/acre ($\frac{1}{2}$/Ha) once or twice a year, and can easily be spread by hand.

On larger areas it would probably be more cost effective to have the soil tested and use a more specific product if necessary.

One particular advantage of such products is that they can be applied late in the autumn (up to Christmas in the UK), as unlike inorganic fertilisers their nutrients will not be significantly leached away and will thus give an early start to spring grass in the paddock you want to use first – preferably a well-drained one.

When applying pelleted fertiliser with a spreader which has previously been used for a prilled product, you will need to re-calibrate it to ensure the correct rate of application is achieved.

If you do have a sudden flush of sappy grass, it is a good idea to feed some hay, oat straw or chaff to help avoid problems due to digestive disturbances such as scouring or laminitis.

Herbage seed mixtures for horses and pasture upgrading

Upgrading pasture

It is almost *never* a good idea to plough-up and reseed an existing horse pasture because this will remove the springy turf and 'bottom' to the pasture, which takes years to develop and is an important anti-concussion device for valuable limbs. Also, newly seeded grass cannot usually be grazed by horses until the second season because their sharp hooves will tear it up.

Cultivations for laying down a new pasture are beyond the scope of this book, but guidelines for seed mixtures are applicable.

If an existing pasture is in bad shape, with thin, patchy grass and few palatable species, it can be improved by slot-seeding or broadcasting appropriate seed mixtures, and establishing a suitable regime of liming, fertiliser usage, harrowing, topping and weed control, along with maintenance of the drains and ditches and not over or under-grazing.

Seed mixtures

Suggested seed mixtures for a horse pasture include:

(1)   *two* low-growing (prostrate) pasture perennial ryegrass (*Lolium perenne*) varieties to make up **50%** of the mixture
(2)   *two* creeping red fescues (*Festuca rubra*) to make up **25%** of the mixture
(3)   the remaining **25%** being made up of
    (a)   crested dog's tail (*Cynosurus cristatus*) **5–10%**
    (b)   rough stalked meadow grass (wet areas) (*Poa trivialis*) wet **5–10%**
    or
    smooth stalked meadow grass (dry areas) (*Poa pratensis*) dry **5–10%**
    (c)   a little wild white clover *if* you can be sure you can manage the pasture so it does not take over. Otherwise leave it out. **1–2%**
(4)   Herbs (e.g. dandelion, chicory, yarrow, plantain, burdock) *can* be added to the mix but *not* relied upon as a nutrient source for performance horses (some don't like them). They will also tend to take over, or disappear, in a badly-managed pasture, and will be killed by most herbicides. Better to feed a balanced ration and plant a separate herb strip if you wish.

If hay is to be taken, some timothy (*Phleum pratense*) may be desirable, and there are some increasingly palatable cocksfoot (*Dactylus Glomerata*) (USA – orchard grass) varieties becoming available, which could replace some of the perennial ryegrass.

A number of seed houses produce mixtures for horses, but these can be *very* expensive, so check with your local agricultural merchant for a price for a mixture as above, especially if you have a large area to deal with. Make sure he knows that it is for horses.

For patching-up, it is probably simplest to use either a proprietary mix of a suitable perennial ryegrass. A tough grass for around gateways, water troughs and exercise areas is *Agrostis* species, but again, as this is of poor nutritional value, it should not be allowed to take over.

Look after your pastures and your pastures will help look after your horses!

Shelter

Shelter is necessary but often overlooked. It is not a luxury. Lack of shelter stunts youngstock and uses up resources in keeping warm when they should be going towards development and growth. Mature horses also suffer from lack of shelter by this misuse of resources. Ideally, paddocks and stable yards should have the benefit of a natural shelter belt of trees and shrubbery on the windward side of the premises. Wherever the prevailing wind comes from in your area, that is where a shelter belt should be established. If there is no noticeable prevailing wind, your shelter belt should be to the north of your premises in the northern hemisphere or to the south in the southern hemisphere. In Britain, shelter on the east is also desirable; the eastern side of our small, island country is the coldest, receiving the brunt of the winds from Russia and Scandinavia.

Advantages should be taken of any sunshine in temperate climates, stable buildings of the conventional loose box type normally being best sited facing south, but in hot countries the reverse should be the case. Interior stabling such as American-type barn accomodation follows different rules. It is normally best to site such buildings with one short side to the prevailing wind so that as little of the building as possible is exposed to cold winds, yet in hot weather when a cooling draught is needed the large doors at that end can be left open, plus those at the opposite end, permitting a cooling breeze down the centre of the building.

For precise advice on shelter belts and suitable trees and shrubs, readers are referred to *Pasture Management for Horses and Ponies* by Gillian McCarthy. Whatever plants are chosen, it should be borne in mind that poisonous varieties should be avoided wherever horses might have access to them. Because trees and shrubs take time to become established, all suitable vegetation should be retained and not felled in too much of a hurry by a new owner – not until careful consideration has been given to shelter. Every effort should be made to provide natural shelter and to divide paddocks with hedges in time, rather than be satisfied with man-made fencing which provides no shelter at all. Some shelter is provided by the highly expensive, close-boarded fencing such as was used in stallion paddocks in the old days, and still is today where money is little object, but these people have not fully realised that stallions do better when they area able to see over their domain, rather than being shut away like wild animals.

Suitable trees for shelter belts include beech, a favourite with stud owners as it retains its dead leaves often until the following spring and, therefore, breaks the force of winter winds and rains better than leafless twigs and branches, which do, however, have a dissipating effect at least. Other species are oak (which, however, can be poisonous to horses, especially the acorns), planes, limes and various conifers. The latter are excellent for quick establishment (as are deciduous sycamores, and alder in wet areas). If you want a native conifer, there is only really Scots pine as our other native, yew, is highly poisonous to horses. Scots pine is not happy in the south, however. Shrubbery and smaller trees include hawthorn (excellent for hedges), quickthorn, hazel, holly (evergreen, of course) and birch. Copper beech gives an air of luxury to your establishment but is rather expensive.

One way of providing some shelter while waiting for plantings to mature is to erect very close-woven plastic mesh fencing as high as practicable. This will at least break the force of the wind somewhat.

Overhead shelter is also needed in extremes of weather – horses can suffer from sunstroke, as well as exposure and hypothermia in winter. There is sharply-divided opinion over allowing horses access to spinneys and wooded area. One school of thought says it is dangerous and that horses milling around in a wood are bound to bump into the trees and injure themselves. The other says that this natural shelter is much appreciated by horses and those used to having access to such a facility will not behave in such a way as to cause real problems. We cannot wrap our horses in cotton wool, anyway; the best we can do is eliminate as many practical problems and danger points as we can. Much depends on the nature of the wood. If it is full of poisonous plants, low branches and protruding roots, it is obviously best fenced off, but otherwise, and with correct management and maybe a little alteration here and there, it is a facility which horses will doubtless prefer to even the most spacious field shelter or run-in shed.

The latter, however, may be your only alternative. Where large numbers of horses are concerned, it may be hopelessly impractical or expensive to provide man-made sheds. If so, and there is no natural shelter either, you will have to face the fact that the premises are just not suitable for breeding horses, which do not do well in windswept areas, particularly those with any 'blood' such as the type of animal used for racing or competition today.

Sizes of shelters vary, but it is generally felt that one horse needs an area about the size of a normal stable, with half as much again for each additional horse. It is of great benefit, bearing in mind the social organisation of the horse family, to have several medium-size shelters on a stud, with two or more in each large paddock, rather than having one large one, because dominant horses invariably keep out subordinate ones no matter how large the shelter. With an alternative shelter there is somewhere for the latter to go and get away from the weather or the flies which will otherwise take their toll on its well-being and contentment.

Round or octagonal shelters, with a quarter of their circumference open for the entrance, are ideal for horses but rarely seen (Figure 6). They provide shelter on all sides, yet a cornered horse can simply run

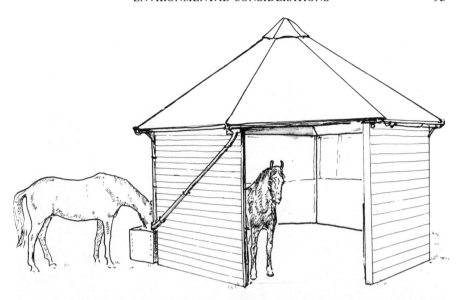

Fig. 6 A rounded or, for example, octagonal field shelter, like this, is very rarely seen, unfortunately, but is much safer than the normal square or rectangular sort. It is impossible for one bully horse to corner another inside so there is always an escape route as the less dominant horse can simply run round the wall to the exit. Also, no matter from which direction the wind is blowing the horses can find shelter from it and any rain it may bring with it, which is often not the case with rectangular shelters having the whole of one side open. This shelter has guttering (necessary in this design to prevent rain flowing down the entrance where horses often stand and look out) which directs the water to a trough. Owners who dislike this practice can equally well direct it to a drain or other outlet.

round the wall inside and will not become hemmed in by a bully, as can easily happen in a square building even if the whole of the front is open. The entrance should, of course, face away from the prevailing wind, and the building should be on the best drained part of the field with a clear space round it for horses simply to shelter behind it, if they prefer, and to give them room to escape from others if necessary.

Hedges should be established whenever possible. While they are maturing, some sort of boundary fence and maybe a windscreen will be needed depending on the location. The epitome of luxury in stud or equestrian establishment fencing is generally taken to be mature hedges within a 'lane' or double post and rail fence, in other words a post and rail fence on each side of the hedge. This obviously takes time to establish, not to mention money for the double fencing, but if you are proposing to make the enterprise a permanent one it is well worthwhile. While waiting for your hedge to mature, therefore, the fencing you erect on each side of it to protect it from inquisitive equine teeth will not be wasted in the future.

Plate 18 A hedge being professionally trimmed and laid. This type of barrier not only provides an effective means of keeping horses where they belong, provided it is high enough, but also a valuable source of shelter for which it should be on the windward side of the field depending on the direction of an area's prevailing wind. Once trimmed and laid, such a hedge will need little maintenance – mainly trimming every few years.

From a long term point of view, hedges undoubtedly do best if they are professionally laid once they reach a suitable stage of maturity (see Plate 18). The act of laying the trunks and branches diagonally encourages the hedge to throw up extra twigs and branches vertically from the bottom and this makes for a thick, interwoven hedge from ground level to the top, where the hedge will probably be finished off with a 'braid' of twigs all the way along to stabilise and toughen it.

Mature hedges should ideally be about a metre wide up to half-way, gradually tapering to an A shape. This shape has been found to be very beneficial for nesting birds and also for the absorption of light rays which are needed for photosynthesis – the process by which green plants manufacture their food from carbon dioxide and water; so by gradually trimming your hedges into this shape you benefit not only wildlife but the hedges themselves and ultimately your horses. As for height, two metres is not too high for horses and this should be stressed to the personnel who trim and lay your hedges. Whereas cattle tend to push through hedges, horses are prone to jumping over them! Once the hedge has been laid, it will require little attention in that regard for ten years or more, basic trimming being all that is needed (not decimating with a flail) about every two years, although a routine eye should be kept out for gaps.

Thick, high windbreaks and shelter belts, including woods and hedges, are felt to help prevent the spread of disease from outside the premises. Incidentally, the famous Italian racehorse breeder, Federico Tesio, was one of the first to incorporate this feature on his studs. Other authorities, however, claim that too much shelter in areas where wind is not a problem can lead to a 'stuffy' feel about as place and the actual development of disease, although this is a minority view.

It is interesting to note that experiments with wind flow and turbulence have shown that a 50 per cent permeable windbreak is the most effective, achieveable with vegetation of staggered heights, such as tall trees, shorter trees, shrubbery and hedges; such a windbreak on the windward or northern/eastern boundaries of an establishment is a very great advantage. Within the premises, high hedges will serve the same purpose. Obviously, solid structures such as brick or stone walls or close boarded fencing will not. They act as a complete barrier over which the wind blows. When it hits the barrier it doubles back and forms unpleasant eddies on the windward side. The wind blowing over the barrier similarly turns down and forms eddies in the paddock some distance from the wall, on the leeward side.

Apparently, a permeable windbreak (as opposed to a complete block) will reduce wind speed on its leeward side for a distance about 30 times its height, the maximum reduction occurring for a distance of ten times its height. Most horses and ponies really dislike wind so every effort should be made to create natural shelter facilities, wisely-placed, and to supplement them with man-made ones where necessary.

Fencing

The most suitable man-made fencing readily available in Britain is still wooden post and rail despite various other types having been introduced in recent years, although reinforced flexible (PVC or plastic) rail fencing is also excellent, as is reinforced rigid plastic railing. In fact, the latter also has the advantage that horses are not prone to chewing the rails as they are with post and rail made of wood (hardwood for the posts and softwood for the rails).

In America, small diamond mesh fencing in a wooden or plastic frame is justifiably popular on establishments where high-value stock are kept. Unlike much wire fencing, it is safe, reliable and highly effective. It is hard to come by in Britain, however.

Ordinary plain wire fencing strained on to hardwood or reinforced concrete posts is a much cheaper alternative to wooden post and rail fencing and is acceptable where economy is a major consideration. However, should a shod horse get a foot or leg over the wire there is always the chance that it will get a wire between its shoe and hoof which can cause panic, demolition of the fence and a badly torn foot. The main objection for stud stock is that such fencing simply cannot be seen well and youngstock can get tangled up on it. Although the wires will come loose if enough pressure is put on them, they are not prone to actually snapping and can badly snare up a horse. Wooden rails do at least break under the pressure a horse is likely to put on them if jumping the fence or colliding with it, although they should normally withstand the pressure of rubbing. Because of the propensity for rubbing, the rails should be fixed on to the insides of the posts so they cannot be pushed off.

The posts themselves should be pressure preservative treated (simply

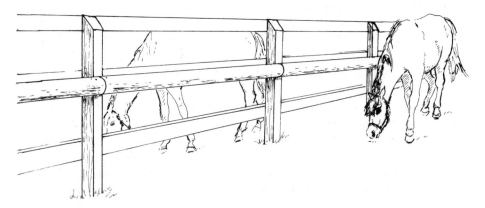

Fig. 7 Correct post and rail fencing for horses. The top rail is at least the height of the horses' backs and is flush with the tops of the posts so that there is no dangerous projection should a horse try to jump the fence or on which a headcollar could get caught. Three rails are used which is plenty for mature horses (two would do, four or more for breeding stock) and on the side of the fence where the posts project an extra rail (in this case rounded although this is not essential) has been run at shoulder height to prevent shoulder injuries from the posts on horses galloping along the fence line. This also discourages horses on the 'wrong' side of the fence from leaning on the rails and pushing them off the posts.

painting them with creosote, which is also poisonous, is not enough to preserve them for a long enough period to be economical). They should be dug and preferably concreted into the ground for one third their length for security.

The height of any fence should be about that of the back or withers of the tallest horse using the field, and the top rail should be flush with the tops of the posts so that headcollars cannot be caught on the posts and horses trying to jump out do not injure themselves on the post tops. The bottom rail (two are sufficient for adult horses) can be just above horse's knee height. For youngstock, three and preferably four rails must be used. The bottom rail should be about a foot from the ground with the others evenly spaced in between, otherwise foals can get through or roll under. If the bottom rail is *too* low, however, horse can more easily get their feet over and break the rail and possibly injure themselves trying to get free.

Gates should be sited along a run of fencing, not in a corner as this can create injuries should horses mill around and gather near the gate either waiting to be brought in or fed, or simply looking over for entertainment. Ideally, the insides of the gates should be covered with Weldmesh or something similar to prevent horses getting their legs through the gates. Strong tubular metal gates ready filled in are available from some suppliers. Most gates are hung too low and are too shallow. The gate must obviously comply with the same measurements as the fencing. They should be hung, for stud stock, so that the bottom is a foot off the ground and the top (with an extension fitted if necessary) level with the top of the fence, otherwise horses can be encouraged to try jumping out. Gate latches should be the recessed kind which horses will neither catch themselves on nor be able to undo.

It may sound obvious to those experienced with horses, but barbed wire must be avoided like the plague on equestrian establishments. Amazingly it is so often seen, and the owners of such premises seem to lead charmed lives with relatively few accidents. Unfortunately, apart from everyday scratches sustained on such fencing, when an accident does occur it can be very serious. I have know several young horses with great potential have their careers and future lives ruined by being caught up on barbed wire fencing as youngsters. The savage injuries caused not only blemish the animals probably for life but inflict injuries which the best veterinary treatment cannot always put right.

Adult horses do not seem to develop much respect for barbed wire fencing, in my experience, and as galloping horses do not appear to see well, the fact that they often collide with it or brush against it, ripping their sides and legs open, is ample evidence to justify its removal for *all* equines, not only stud stock.

Square mesh fencing, despite being marketed with small lower mesh sizes especially for horses, is also a poor alternative (even though substantially cheaper) to plastic or wooden rails on wooden or concrete posts.

Ideally, the rails or plain wire strands should run flush with the inside of the posts rather than be on the outside or running through the middle of the posts. This is to present as smooth a surface as possible to horses brushing or leaning against the fence. Shoulders can be badly bruised or even fractured by impact with a square wooden or reinforced concrete post. If rails or wires are to run through the posts, round posts are to be preferred to square ones. Although concrete posts are quite widely used on studs, many people feel they are too hard and strong for horses and keep to wooden ones.

Buildings and ventilation

The purpose of any building used for accomodating horses, from a simple basic field shelter to a complex, specially laid out stable yard or indoor barn, is mainly to shelter the animals from extremes of weather. Stabling also keeps horses handy for use or attention. There is no doubt that, given a suitably mild climate horses do much better when kept out all the time, as is common practice in, for example, New Zealand and parts of Australia. In Britain, although officially in a temperate zone, our climate is too chilly and wet on the whole for a completely outdoor existence for such animals as Thoroughbreds, Arabs, Anglo-Arabs and crosses with substantial amounts of such blood. These thin-skinned, sensitive types suffer not only from our cold, wet, windy winters and, perhaps surprisingly as they originate way back in hot countries, from too much sun and, particularly, flies. There are those who say it toughens up animals to make them 'rough it' by exposing them to extremes of weather, but there are limits to what horses can reasonably be expected to endure, even in Britain where the horse rescue charities can supply any number of dead or emaciated animals left to winter out without proper shelter or feeding. The attentions of flies in hot weather can, in extreme cases, cause badly ulcerated eyes, and at the least can cause constant irritation and mental anguish, jarred legs and damaged feet from galloping away from them.

The main problems with buildings are poor ventilation and associated respiratory disorders and inflamed mucous membranes in bad cases, and the stress of over-confinement in animals given insufficient freedom and exercise.

Most prefabricated loose boxes sold for horses are too low and the floor space recommended for given categories of equine too small – for reasons of economy, of course. Without going into technical details about air change and cubic airspace needed, from a practical point of view, the 3.5 m by 3.5 m (12 ft by 12 ft) floor area normally recommended for a 16 hands high horse is absolutely minimal, not good. A much more comfortable size for such a horse would be 4.5 m by 4.5 m (15 ft by 15 ft). As for height, a critical factor often overlooked, the stable inside should be nowhere lower than 3.5 m (12 ft) if it has a ridge roof, and 4 m (14 ft) if a single plane roof.

Outdoor loose boxes normally have the usual double-leaved doors and the top one is and should be kept firmly fixed open most of the time, not only for ventilation but to allow the horse to put its head out and feel less confined. There is usually a window on the same side as the door and it is recommended that the Sheringham type (opening up and in) is used, ostensibly to direct the flow of air up and over the horse's back. In practice, it does not matter whether this type is used or the type common at the Irish National Stud and other establishments, which opens down and out like an ordinary house window. What does matter is that the window should be way up above the horse's head at eaves height. Particularly with the Sheringham type, placed conventionally low, either the window or its guard forms a projection inside the box at about horse's head height which, it must be obvious, is a danger and a disadvantage.

Boxes should also have some means of letting warm, stale (risen) air out at the top of the box. Ridge roof ventilators, preferably running the whole length of the ridge, should be installed, louvres in gable ends and either louvres, windows or a simple wooden flap placed in the wall opposite the door to create a suitable cross flow, particularly in warm weather. These devices plus a sufficiently roomy, lofty stable, will help ensure truly adequate ventilation.

The airspace in stables is polluted not only with ammonia gas from decomposing organic matter (urine and droppings), which is the cause of inflamed eyes and mucous membranes leading to coughs and respiratory disease, but also fungi from even good samples of hay and straw, and general stable dust. The general atmosphere is also affected by the insulating qualities of the materials used to build the stabling. Only materials which are bad conductors of heat should be used (brick normally being best), otherwise insulating panels should be used to line walls and roofs to avoid the clammy, damp air caused by condensation. This is obviously greatly reduced by good ventilation.

Because the first pollutant mentioned, ammonia gas, is a heavy gas which settles largely in the lower half of the box (just where the horse's head, and therefore his nose, are when he is resting or sleeping) it is normally recommended that an air inlet is provided about 15 cms (6 ins) above floor level to help disperse the ammonia. However, bringing air in at low level does not mean that the ammonia gas will be removed, obviously. Also, low-level inlets do create floor draughts. The best course of action, I find, is to have no air inlets at low level and pay scrupulous attention to the state of the bedding and the drainage of the stable. Although this is not by any means a manual on basic stable management, it is my experience that insufficient attention is paid to truly clean, dry beds in most establishments, even some of the 'best', and I would stress that half the air pollution problems in stabling would vanish if (a) dust-free bedding such as paper or dust-extracted shavings were used, and (b) greater attention were paid to removing droppings and wet materials and to installing loose-weave asphalt or similar drainage floorings rather than the almost universal concrete floors so often seen, at least in Britain.

Further pollutants occur when hay is brought into the box, it having been shown that even what appears to be top quality hay has mould spores due to a natural, organic product being dead and starting to go through the normal decomposition process. Transferring to hayage or thoroughly soaking hay for at least 12 hours before feeding can do away with this problem.

Clean, pure air is so vital to horses that I feel there is an excellent case for putting *all* horses on a clean air regime (dust-free, clean bedding, proper ventilation indoors and hayage or soaked hay) whether or not they show a susceptibility to wind problems. It is felt by many veterinary surgeons and similarly qualified management authorities that any challenge to the system such as is imposed by dust, gases and moulds summons up the horse's finite energy resources in fighting it off, even if no symptoms are present. Resources should not be going on unnecessarily fighting off 'outside attacks', particularly in athletic horses who need them to reproduce, grow and work. This aspect of the horse's environment is starting to receive more attention in the light of research and the findings being brought to the attention of the horse industry.

American barn-type stabling complexes, used not only in America but also largely in Scandinavia and some other European countries and increasingly in Britain, have particular ventilation problems, surprisingly. Although the standard design of a large building with two or more rows of box stalls (indoor loose boxes) and large sliding doors at both ends of the aisles gives the impression, when the doors are all open, of ample ventilation, what in practice happens is that the pollutants accumulate and stay in the actual stables which are offset from the airflow down the aisles and, therefore, subject to still, muggy air.

In such a stabling complex, and some of them are very complex indeed, with whole facilities for riding and feed storage and so on, as well as actual horse accomodation, being sited under one roof, special attention must be paid to ventilation and air change. Each stable must have a high-level air outlet, or a continuous one running down a line of stables, and expert advice should be sought to ensure an adequate air change without draughts. Sometimes mechanical/electrical devices, even full air conditioning systems, may be needed, according to the size and complexity of the system and the regional or national climate. Whatever the circumstances, clean air is essential to working horses and is a major environmental consideration.

Horses tolerate cold, dry, still air very well. There is normally no need to heat stabling except in excessively cold areas. However, again considering the conservation of body resources, it is generally felt that the temperature in stables should not be allowed to fall below 4°C (40°F); this particularly applies to youngstock, especially foals, and clipped, working competition/race horses. Horses kept out, unclipped, well fed and with ample access to proper shelter facilities can withstand temperatures much colder than this provided the air is still and dry. A

Plate 19 This type of housing for horses allows them to socialise much more naturally than individual stables, permits freedom of movement (even enough room for a little canter and buck) and, if the building has large doors which open into a paddock like this one, the attendants have the facility of allowing the horses to come and go as they wish, or keeping them out or in as required. There is a great saving in labour and time taken in the maintenance of bedding, normally droppings only being removed regularly. Whether horses are working or resting, this kind of housing, provided compatible companions are selected, results in more contented, balanced and often healthier horses. (Photograph by Susan McBane.)

significant chill factor occurs, however, when wind and rain are present and a special eye must be kept on horses in those conditions.

Yarding

There is much to be said for the yarding or open stable system of keeping horses and it could be that in future labour and accommodation costs make its adoption almost a necessity. It is suitable not only for youngstock and store horses but for actively working/competing animals too. Horses are kept together in compatible groups in surfaced enclosures commonly called yards, usually partially roofed and often leading on to a grazing area but not necessarily. Because they are living in fairly natural social herd conditions they are often much more settled and calm. They can wander about at will, socialise naturally and do not suffer the stress of loneliness and confinement common in fully stabled animals. Clipped, working animals can be adequately rugged up with New Zealand-type rugs instead of conventional stable rugs, plus clip-in under blankets, and can come in and go out as they wish. Alternatively, when desired, outdoor access can be limited or prevented altogether, the horses staying together in the yard.

Droppings are regularly picked up but there is no time-consuming, labour-intensive mucking out to do, as we know it, unless it is felt desirable to stable the horses at night as some establishments do. Bulk feeds such as hay or silage are fed communally and often concentrates, too, in cattle-type feeding troughs running, say, the length of one wall, but a close eye needs to be kept on individuals to make sure they are neither over-eating nor being kept off their rations by bullies. If this happens, those concerned are simply fed separately, often in the yard from a bucket held by a groom who fends off 'enquirers'.

The floorings used in such yards seem to be almost anything – straw (not really recommended for athletic horses these days), shavings, sawdust, or a manège-type mixture of shavings, peat and sand. Anything firm, springy and resilient will do as the horses will obviously roll in and lie on it, as well as cavort about to some extent.

Stress

It is, of course, possible to keep horses in less than good conditions. However, experience has shown that horses do not thrive as well and this affects not only the finished product from the point of view of development and constitution but the price ultimately obtained for such stock.

It is known that youngstock deprived of, for example, adequate space and exercise (in other words who are over-stabled or kept in small paddocks) exhibit mental disorders, develop vices at a young age and do not develop physically as well as those with more or less unlimited access to space and exercise facilities. The body needs the stress of play and the activity and galloping about common to youngsters in order to respond and develop to a sufficient level of size and strength. Without the stimulus the response will not occur and stunted, weaker stock will be the result. Constantly having to use up physical resources fighting the challenges and stresses presented by poorly ventilated housing, humid, clammy conditions caused by poor insulation, overcrowding or lack of congenial company, less-than-clean bedding, poor quality, unbalanced diets and so on is an expensive waste, the bad results of which are never really overcome later in life. Such stock do not reach their potential or live such long, useful lives. Mature horses, too, are obviously at a considerable disadvantage when suffering stress and deprivation of their natural needs, often purely for physical convenience or because of the financial constraints of their owners or managers.

When producing any horses, but particularly valuable competition stock, if money is in such short supply as to cause lack of proper basic facilities, particularly feeding, shelter, company and space, then the enterprise should not be embarked upon as not only is it unfair to the horses but the financial rewards can only be disappointing.

Weaning

While on the subject of stress, either physical or emotional, it seems appropriate to mention one of the most stressful occurrences in the lives of most domestically-reared horses – that of weaning. Some professional stud managers make light of this process, others have a genuine feeling for both mare and foal while yet others, both professional and amateur, have a positive dread of it. In her excellent book *The Behaviour of Horses in Relation to Management and Training*, Dr Marthe Kiley-Worthington says on the subject:

'Frequently mare owners say to me, "Oh! I so dread weaning, I feel so hard-hearted and cruel." The answer is, "Why do it then?" Just bear in mind, if you *do* do it, that indeed you *are* being hard-hearted and if cruelty is defined as causing distress and suffering, yes, you are also being cruel. And this cruelty may well result in permanent scars in the form of behavioural problems for the foal later on.'

This puts it in a nutshell with more authority than *I* can muster. Dr Kiley-Worthington also points out: 'Weaning is, of course, a standard practice on most studs. Like many standard practices, whether or not it is either sensible or necessary is very rarely considered.' How very true!

Apart from recommending her book to readers of this one, particularly those actively involved in breeding, I should like to offer some alternatives to the usual, extremely traumatic process of weaning by means of a sudden and complete separation of mare and foal. It is acknowledged among breeders that weaning does normally set back foals because of the severe mental and emotional distress which can be suffered and which has physical effects: foals can lose significant condition (at a time of rapid growth and approaching cold weather when they can least afford to do so) and become nervous and depressed, the effects of which can be long-lasting and, many believe, permanent even after apparent recovery.

It must be remembered that in wild and feral conditions weaning is a long drawn out process with stallion, mares, foals and followers all living together in a herd. The youngest members are kept strictly in place by the older members of the herd, and foals left on their dams longer than the normal five or six months are better behaved ultimately than those weaned at that age.

In domesticity, experienced mares know when autumn comes round that they are going to be deprived (or relieved!) of their offspring before long and their behaviour, plus that of their foals, should dictate the age at which they are parted. It is true that some foals become a real mental and physical burden on their dams as they add the months to their ages and such dams are better off without their foals, to be left in peace to relax and calm down before the birth of their next offspring, assuming they are in foal again. Other mares are very tolerant of their demanding, boisterous foals and can not only keep on with their jobs very well but also act as a valuable disciplinary influence on the foal.

Early weaning is only to be recommended in cases where the mare is a bad mother and is uncaring or violent towards her foal. Where the mare is a good mother but unable to supply enough milk, it is better to supplement her supply and leave the foal on her rather than hand-rear it or put it on a foster mother. There might also be a case for separating the pair if the foal is unusually forward and/or is harassing the dam to such an extent that she gets no peace and is having a very unpleasant time. With today's advanced diets and nutritional knowledge, leaving a foal on its dam does not drain the mare of nutriment or put an unreasonable challenge on her by causing her to continue lactation while the birth of her next foal draws nearer, provided she is well-fed and sheltered.

Assuming that a suitable time for weaning has been decided upon, taking into consideration the relationship between mare and foal, the foal should be prepared by ensuring it is eating freely on its own. It should have been picking at its dam's rations from an early age and should, by weaning time, which will hopefully not be before six months of age and preferably later, be eating its own rations of hay and concentrates quite normally and confidently. If it is not feeding properly it is not ready to wean.

The mare's rations should be temporarily cut down and, if possible, her water supply reduced a little to inhibit the production of milk. The foal will have been reducing its own demands for milk as it grows older and the supply should be dwindling, anyway.

To help the foal's digestion over the changeover from part milk and concentrates to all concentrates plus hay, it is a good thing to start including milk products in the foal's rations for a month or two before the anticipated weaning time, and to continue them for some months past weaning. In the wild, yearlings may well still be suckling occasionally, so feeding a milk product until that age is not being over-cautious.

Having ensured that the foal is feeding freely and its diet is in order, next comes the decision on the actual method to be used and here we are only considering gradual methods, as being the least distressing and the nearest to nature. To suddenly separate foal and dam is akin to orphaning a child at three or four years of age or earlier and bringing it up with other children of that age, with no normal social contact with other humans of other ages and without the protection and support of a parent. Foals who have had stressful weanings can take a year to get over them physically and may never really do so mentally.

With gradual methods, mare and foal hardly notice increasing periods of separation, beginning, say, by leading the already obedient and fairly independent five-mouth-old foal and its dam in opposite directions in the field, by stabling the foal for short periods alone (with a top grille on the box) while the dam has her feet attended to, is groomed outside, maybe within sight, or goes for a short, gentle hack, and ultimately by stabling them separately at night after a day together in the paddock, maybe putting the foal with others. Over the months, they spend less and less time together as the next foaling date approaches until, about two months before the birth, dam and foal are stabled and grazed apart, but with other company.

Another good system is to put foals out to play in a properly fenced dirt yard or central paddock with loose boxes bordering directly on to it. Then they can play with each other and develop their own relationships, and can reach the dam's nose nuzzling down over the door but cannot reach the milk bar. Initially, the mares can be boxed in this way for an hour or so only and ultimately for half a day, after which they can be turned into a separate paddock from the foals, being reunited at night in their loose box.

Eventually they are separated completely with no ill effects. Obviously, this method should only be used from an age where the foals and mares are reasonably independent of each other, otherwise the mares may well injure themselves charging about the boxes and trying to get out. Should this occur in an isolated case, fit a grille to the top of the stable door so mare and foal can still see each other but the mare cannot attempt to jump out.

Having a carefully chosen nanny mare or friendly gelding has often worked well. The nanny (non-breeding/lactating if a mare) is turned into the field with the mares and foals a week before weaning and is left with the youngsters as the mares are gradually separated from them. The foals now have an adult to run to in times of trouble, someone familiar who will probably take an interest in them without fussing them, but they can obviously get no milk. The nanny also exerts a valuable disciplinary influence on increasingly boisterous youngstock and provides essential leadership to the young herd.

The herd influence is considerable with horses and I am sure that it is often the deprivation of a mixed adult/youngster herd environment as much as the removal of the foal's own dam which causes the stress at weaning time. For this reason, another gradual system which has been found satisfactory is to introduce the nanny and after a few days gradually remove the mares one or two at a time. The mare which should be first taken out is the dam of the most independent foal, the dam of the next most independent one being removed next day, and so on. In this way, the foals still have the presence of other adults and when eventually the last one is removed they barely notice that they are on their own apart from the nanny who can remain with them.

With this system it is important not to remove the dams of foals who are still very dependent on them, otherwise you can get considerable problems of 'orphan' foals trying to suckle other mares and usually not only being unhappy and confused but being battered about by unwilling 'foster' mothers. In a mixed herd there are usually foals of sometimes vastly differing ages, so it is obviously best to start with the dams of the oldest and taking as many weeks or months over the process as necessary.

When the time comes, under any system, for the foals to be stabled for the night without their dams' company, there is often an inclination on the part of breeders to put two foals together. However, even when great pains are taken to temperamentally match the pair, one will always come out boss and this can make the whole process even more unpleasant for the poor underling. It is probably best to box foals separately, if they cannot be yarded together, but with meshed holes in the dividing partitions so they can see and sniff their neighbours but are not actually able to get at them.

The humans involved should take every opportunity to make handling and talking to the foals at this time a top priority, rather than spending valuable time at a critical point in their charges' development sweeping the yard and doing other secondary 'support' tasks which do not directly affect the animals' well-being. Horses need the best possible start in life and this can best be accomplished by giving them moral support, leadership and kind, firm discipline at a most difficult time of their lives.

6
Selecting breeding stock

Selecting the stock with which to found your own personal line or family of competition horses is a very personal matter. Given good conformation and action, soundness, temperament and some evidence of ability in the field, if you put two breeders together with a selection of good potential stock they may well come up with quite different choices. It becomes largely a matter of taste at that point.

There is a well-worn saying in life which goes: 'You can't learn from other people's mistakes'. It may be true that the lesson is better learned if you make the mistake yourself, but it's certainly not a true saying as it stands. In fact, in the horse world you *have* to learn from other people's mistakes unless you are young and rich and therefore have the money and the time to learn from your own. Breeding horses and developing a line or family of your own creation, as it were, proven in all important respects, can be a lifetime's work. Most studs or breeders do not begin to attract the respect and patronage they deserve for at least ten years and it can take much longer, particularly outside racing. Competition horses, as opposed to racehorses, start work much later; they don't begin to make individual names for themselves until at least the age of six, which is still very young for a horse in these disciplines. Racehorses, on the other hand, often retire on the laurels of a two-year-old racing career; comparatively few race at four, particularly if they have won important races as three-year-olds, the year of the traditional Classics. If they survive the rigours of the racing world to come out with a reasonable record, they can be at stud and breeding before they have even stopped growing.

Not so with competition horses. For a start, most male competition horses are gelded, as are most point-to-pointers and steeplechasers, so their individual abilities cannot be passed on. Breeders wanting their bloodlines have to resort to their parents or near relatives. This applies less to warmbloods and maybe Arabs, but other categories of competition horse are commonly gelded before they have proved themselves in competition or even (and usually) before they are backed unless they seem to be outstanding, on the reputation of their parents, and are bought by someone interested in breeding.

Competition horses, particularly in the lower echelons where they are owned purely for fun by amateur owners in the truest sense, are felt easier to handle by such owners if they are gelded. Geldings are easier to sell to such a market than mares who can become 'mareish' or difficult when in season, which they are very frequently throughout spring and summer unless their seasons are artificially suppressed. Stallions are very rarely bought by such owners because of the obvious disadvantages, such as fear – real or imagined – of the horse himself, embarrassment if the horse should 'make advances' to a mare when out in public, problems of suitable turning-out facilities, refusal of many livery stable proprietors to accept stallions and so on.

Starting up

All these points add up to a general difficulty in establishing a successful line and the impossibility of doing so quickly. Because of this, it makes sense to start off with the very best stock – even if only a single mare – you can possibly find and afford. If you already possess a mare you wish to use as a foundation broodmare, the stallion you send her to must be, again, the best you can affort that is complementary to her.

It is difficult to assess a mare of your own honestly and objectively, particularly if you have owned her for years and are very fond of her. She may be a genuine swan but it is not a bad idea to get a (truly) knowledgeable friend to give you a no-holds-barred judgement – if you are prepared to risk the friendship! Your swan just may turn out to be a real goose, and equine geese rarely lay golden eggs.

Chapters 1 and 2 dealt with conformation and other specific characteristics required by different breeds and types of competition horse. Here we shall concentrate on breeding requirements.

There *are* ways in which you can cut corners when establishing your name as a breeder, the most obvious being to buy stock from an established stud and carry on their lines. The animals' reputations will be made and you can establish a line of your own concurrently alongside. By the time your own line is proving itself you should have sold some successful animals from your 'adopted' family and will be becoming established in your own right as being a good judge of potential competition horse stock, and this will brush off on to stock of unknown ability. If the relationships are suitable, you can, of course, cross the established line with the other so that at least one half of your offerings' bloodlines will be proven and favoured.

When choosing to establish your own breeding family, the best rule of thumb to go by is to buy only animals, mares and stallions, which have themselves been proven in competition. This way those proven successful genes will be well up in the pedigree with an excellent chance at being passed on to your home-bred stock. This is by far the most certain way of establishing yourself swiftly and surely, provided always that the animals complement each other, as discussed elsewhere.

Another, slightly less straightforward, approach is to use close relatives of proven performers – sires, dams, brothers, sisters, daughters or sons – as the genes are still quite close and likely to be present. Another good method is to use animals who, although they may not be proven in competition themselves for some reason (maybe they never competed), are known to consistently produce offspring which become good performers.

The above three categories of animals should reasonably certainly (in a risky and uncertain business) produce competent performers. When you start getting further away from those categories, for example using cousins, grandparents and so on, or a family with very few crosses of successful animals, your chances of producing the goods are much weaker. However, mention should be made of the common phenomenon of genes 'missing' a generation and coming good again in the third generation.

A stallion in the racing world who, for example, does not produce anything notable himself may find that his offspring do. He then becomes what is termed 'a broodmare sire', in other words he produces mares who produce winners. This is not, of course, confined to Thoroughbred bloodstock. A less used term for a stallion who produces sons who sire good performers is, predictably enough, 'stallion sire' or occasionally 'sire of sires'. Surprisingly, perhaps, mares who 'work' the same way receive less recognition, probably because they produce far fewer offspring in a lifetime than a stallion.

It cannot be overstressed that it is essential to really study bloodlines and families for their achievements – not easy in a country like the UK where performance records have not habitually been kept – so that you really know what a particular stallion produces, what an individual mare has produced and so on. It is time consuming and painstaking but essential and very worthwhile if you want to avoid wasted years, money and effort, not to mention dashed hopes.

One-mare owners may know she has won nothing of importance and for them it is even more important to go to a really well-known performance-producing or performance-proven stallion, otherwise what will there be to offer potential purchasers of the resulting foal? Many experts advise against breeding from such a mare, but as Henry Wynmalen points out in his classic book *Horse Breeding and Stud Management*, the mare must have *some* good points for you to have kept her so long and be fond of her. No one loves a lemon! She may have a particularly kind temperament, which *is* an asset, or undying stamina, an unflappable nature or be known to try her heart out under pressure. Whatever her good points are, write them down and play on them during your marketing operations. If, for example, she was brilliant across country in the hunting field, this can be a real bonus when selling her foals locally or regionally. She may be known and remembered, or you may be able to refer purchasers to people who do know her and recall how good she was. This is all important and counts.

Soundness

Soundness is a real bugbear. So many people breed from horses who were only retired because they became unsound and think it is quite all right and normal. What earthly use is a performance horse who doesn't remain sound? By breeding from unsound animals we are simply breeding into future generations the propensity for unsoundness. Although some of today's equestrian disciplines are very demanding on physique, particularly eventing with its drop fences and spreads, the fact is that inserting unsoundness into your breeding stock can be a recipe for disaster. You reputation will suffer very quickly.

If you know that the unsoundness was caused by a genuine accident, *not* having taken place during competition or training such as a breakdown, but was the result of an argument with a motor vehicle, the horse putting its leg in a rabbit hole in the field or something similar – in other words not caused by the demands of training and competition – this is a different matter. Unsoundnesses directly related to work should be avoided, no matter how much of a bargain the horse may appear to be. It is true they may be the result of unwise management, but you cannot be sure. If you want to be certain, only breed from sound stock.

Many breed societies and other registries have a list of unacceptable hereditary conditions which must be avoided, and which usually comprise the following:

bone spavin	ringbone (high and low)
cataract	roaring and whistling
defective genital organs	shivering
navicular disease	sidebone
parrot mouth	stringhalt

Obviously, from a practical point of view, mares must be free from these disorders as well as stallions – a fact which is often overlooked by some breeders – as they are just as capable of passing them on as stallions.

Both hereditary unsoundnesses and undesirable characteristics can soon be bred and fixed into a bloodline unless great care is taken to avoid them, particularly if pre-potent parents are being used. The result could be generation after generation of stock with the same defects, perpetuating them *ad infinitum*. Far better to avoid them assiduously in the first place. This may sound obvious but it is surprising how many people acquire breeding stock cheaply because of such a defect, believing that they will be able to 'breed it out', only to find that, once the damage is done, they have not been able to do so.

An example of such an undesirable defect not classed as an unsoundness is that of a sloping vulva in mares, which is becoming particularly widespread in Thoroughbreds and is obviously being transmitted to their crosses, but is present in other breeds and types too.

This malformation results in the mare's drawing in air through the vulva which can pass up to the uterus and, as it takes with it all sorts of micro-organisms, can easily start off an infection of the genital tract which can not only be difficult to cure but can result in abortion or resorption of a foetus. Also, because of the resulting 'set back' position of the anus, when the mare does a dropping some faeces will fall on the vulva, similarly setting up infection.

In natural conditions, this infection would probably result in the mare not producing offspring and so the malformation would rarely be passed on and would not be perpetuated. However, man, as so often happens, has found a way round this to thwart nature's survival mechanism whereby only the fittest (meaning the most suitable) survive. A veterinary surgeon can administer a local anaesthetic, cut down the sides of the vulva and stitch them together along the sloping part. After about two weeks the stitches are removed, the wound has healed and the sloping part of the vulva is no longer prone to taking in air and faeces. Problem solved. This is called Caslick's operation.

But this should not, of course, be necessary. The malformed mare will continue to breed and pass on the sloping vulva to who knows how many of her daughters and the ability to pass it on may be carried by her sons. It is not unreasonable to imagine that the defect will, consequently, become as common in Thoroughbreds and their crosses as hip dysplasia is in German Shepherd dogs – virtually universal. And once that happens, it may well be all but impossible to get rid of it.

This applies to other defects, too, of course. It may be said that as long as we can get round problems, why bother about the consequences if the animals concerned have other highly desirable qualities. We *should* both because we are not only purposely deforming the animals concerned but making trouble and expense for ourselves. It could, without much imagination, reach the stage where animals need all sorts of minor operations and other treatments before they can work. The familiar Hobday operation to relieve laryngeal hemiplegia, in which one vocal cord, usually the left, does not draw back to permit the passage of air during inspiration, is another case in point.

It is foolish and unnecessary, I feel, to breed from basically unsound stock like this. If there were no market for them breeders would try harder to eliminate the faults concerned by not breeding from affected animals no matter how good they may be otherwise.

Selection and assessment

When selecting a broodmare, or checking over your own for suitability for breeding, assuming her bloodlines, performance, temperament, action and general conformation are good, check her udder to see that it is free from lumps, thickened tissue or warts and that both teats appear normal and evenly-sized. Check the conformation of her vulva, as described, and if she is yours note any discharge she may have been exhibiting over the last few days or weeks. This is the most you can do personally to check her breeding organs; the rest is up to the veterinary surgeon who will be able to tell you whether or not she has any physical condition likely to prevent her from breeding, can take swabs for checking infection and do blood tests and profiles to check for general health, sub-clinical disease and infection and so on.

From a practical point of view, good broodmares are usually not too short in the back and are roomy and deep, giving plenty of room inside for a foal to develop. When a mare becomes heavily pregnant, any lameness she may have may make it very difficult for her to carry a foal successfully and the stress and discomfort, maybe even pain, she suffers can result in abortion. She may be prone to falling and to not being able to rise after rolling or lying down to sleep. Refusal, consequently, to lie down and get sufficient proper sleep obviously results in her not getting enough rest which can all bring her down in condition and affect the foal.

For the mare's sake, and to prevent possibly difficult births, it is usually wise not to use too-small mares for breeding competition horses, depending on your discipline. Some people use small mares and send them to big stallions with a view to increasing the size of the foal. This can result in a disappointingly small foal, a large foal born prematurely, an unnecessarily stressful foaling for the mare or maybe even the need for a caesarian operation, necessitating extra nursing for the mare (and again stress) and extra care for the foal whose dam may not be well enough to care for it properly for some time.

It is usually better to use a stallion no more than a hand bigger than the mare, although many will disagree with this. If you do have a small mare, aim to increase the size of your stock over two generations or more rather than all at once. The first generation, although smaller than you may ultimately want, will, all else being equal, be quite saleable for a teenager's mount, for endurance riding or, say, as a small hunter or hack, so it will not be wasted. If a filly, she can be put in foal to a larger stallion at three years (no earlier as this may stunt her growth), which is an age at which little can be done in the way of work, have one foal and then begin work herself. If you are in a relative hurry to build up your stock, this is one way of doing it, although it is really better to wait until a mare has fully matured before stressing her resources with a pregnancy.

Choosing a stallion for your mare, or to buy for your own stud, is basically the same procedure. You still want a horse you like, which has the bloodlines you want that are, perhaps, uncommon in your area – often a plus point. His conformation must be, as they say, very difficult to fault and he must look even better in action than when standing still.

His temperament and behaviour may be strongly influenced by his handlers but you cannot be certain. It is natural for him to be on his toes, but actual bad behaviour such as excessive rearing, screaming, refusal to show his paces, nipping repeatedly at his handler and the like should be viewed with suspicion. It may be that he has weak handlers or that he simply will not agree to behave and co-operate – this type of trait you do not want passing on to your own stock. Try to see him in his box first and note whether or not he seems calm but alert and interested with a pleasant expression in his eye, or whether he looks sour, bitter, nervous or even aggressive. Note how he greets you and his handler.

You may already know that he seems bad tempered but throws sweet-natured stock. In that case, bad handling is obviously the cause of his problems. If you have no such knowledge, however, do not take a chance. Do not use him. Even if his temperament *is* the result of inappropriate handling, that is not your concern if you have no proof. If those studs which mistreat their stallions found themselves with a declining clientele it might make them mend their ways and treat their stallions, who are the main advertisement for their stud, properly – kindly but with fair discipline.

When choosing a horse for your own stud, it is often a good idea to choose one that not only has fresh bloodlines for your area but is of a type not common there, or is proven in a discipline to which few other stallions in your district belong. There is no point in buying a repetition of what is already readily available. You will simply end up splitting whatever market there is. Create your own market by supplying what is wanted by local and regional mare owners but in a 'fresh package', as it were.

It may sound foolish, but many mare owners do send their mares to a local stallion just because he is nearby, not paying too much attention to whether or not he is the best husband for her. It is difficult to persuade them, it seems, that an extra few tens of pounds on travelling or a higher stud fee can mean hundreds on the price of the resulting foal or three-year-old when it comes to sale time.

Some mare owners, too, seem to feel that stallions are miracle workers and will throw superb stock from mediocre or downright sub-standard mares. The mare *is*, as explained previously, genetically half the foal. As a mare owner yourself you should use the best stallion, and the most suitable, you can possibly afford, but as a stud owner you will be wise to make your horse's mares 'approved' and state on his stud card 'approved mares only', so you can judge for yourself and select only those who will produce good stock to him and so enhance your stud's reputation.

Selecting youngstock for competition or as a cheaper, if longer drawn out way, of acquiring stud stock, can be extremely risky. Racehorses are selected as yearlings but those doing the selecting are extremely knowledgeable and experienced: even so they make mistakes. There are far more throw-outs than successes. For the less experienced, it is very wise to take along a truly experienced judge of the type of horseflesh in which you are interested.

From a general point of view, do not buy youngstock which is over-topped (overweight) as carrying excess weight on a young skeleton is a sure way of over-stressing it, particularly the legs, and, so starting off with an already weakened physique. It is good to buy well-behaved youngstock which has been well-handled and taught to lead in hand as well as basic stable manners and simple commands such as 'walk on', 'whoa', 'over' and so on; also to tolerate grooming and having the feet picked out. However, although this becomes more and more difficult the older and bigger, and therefore stronger, the animal is, it is not essential to have an immaculately behaved youngster if you are sure you can educate it or have someone else do so. There is some truth, however, in the belief that the longer it is before a youngster learns discipline, the more difficult the animal will be to train and handle during adulthood – witness some of the semi-wild youngsters found in a bog in western Ireland with never a hand laid on them at four years of age! They often do come to hand eventually but I feel sure they are never quite as reliable as those who 'started school' earlier in life – but I could be wrong!

Studying youngstock is also an excellent way of assessing just how pre-potent is any particular stallion in which you are interested. Bear in mind that if he is pre-potent there is a good chance his offspring may be, too, and this quality is definitely one you want for your stud if you want your stock to acquire a reputation of breeding true to type. If a horse's offspring are patchy in type with no family resemblance, or worse, all possessing a particular fault or faults, avoid that stallion.

Similarly with mares, try to see different years' offspring if you possibly can to see whether they tend to resemble her or their sire(s).

Youngstock from particular mares and stallions, who obviously all have some resemblance prove the pre-potency of their parents and are what you want for breeding purposes. When buying youngsters to bring on for sale or competition, reliable inheritance of particular features makes your job of judging them that much easier and gives you a clearer idea of how they will mature and how good they are likely to be in work, given good management and training. You'll also get an idea of whether or not a particular stallion or mare throws early-maturing, compact animals, say, or backward, rangy types who may need an extra year or so to come up in front (so that their withers are at least level with their croups) and generally mature and fill out. Those that are slow-maturing physically are usually so mentally, too, and often do not come into their own until at least six or later, but they tend to make up for the early wait by producing good work over a long lifetime, if properly managed.

Buying animals of any age from other people has two sides to the coin. It is often said that breeders will not be selling youngstock if they are any good (particularly warmbloods which have grading processes at particular ages), but, warmbloods apart then, breeders cannot keep all their animals or they would never make any money. They do breed to sell, and even if they sell what they consider are not their best, their 'seed corn', so long as the horse comes up to your expectations and meets your criteria, what does it matter?

Mature animals may be being sold, quite legitimately, to make room for younger ones or to reduce a particular bloodline, or maybe because the breeder has a policy of selling animals over, say, 15 years of age because their best years are behind them. With breeding stock, this is a moot point. Animals kept in good condition and breeding regularly may well have many years of production ahead of them, but because of their age they may be significantly cheaper than younger ones, so you may get some real bargains.

The important point is whether or not the animal concerned reaches the standards you have set, based not only on the horse as an individual but on your study of its near relatives, performance records and related youngstock.

Veterinary inspection

I feel that only a fool would buy an animal without a full veterinary examination, particularly with expensive competition horse stock expected to either perform or produce. Veterinary examinations are not cheap, particularly when travelling is added on top, but you can economise by only having vetted those horses you are seriously interested in buying. If, for example, you have narrowed your choice to three animals but want only one, the obvious course of action is to have only your first choice vetted and if the result is satisfactory buy it and forget the others. Despite the expense, it is surprising how many people have several horses vetted before making up their minds.

A veterinary surgeon will report on a horse's suitability for the purposes for which you have said you want to use it. Therefore, you must be completely honest about your intentions. If you want an eventer, it is pointless saying you only want a dressage horse (who may be expected never to leave the ground). This may sound obvious, but many people make this mistake and then try to blame the vet when the animal proves unfit for the job. If you buy a mare to show jump for a few years and then intend to breed from her later, tell the vet so he can examine her both as a jumper and as a potential broodmare. It would be most diasppointing to have a successful show jumping mare only to find out some years later that your intentions to breed from her are thwarted because of some physical fault not pointed out at the original inspection because you had never mentioned breeding from her. This is obviously particularly important if you are trying to establish a stud of performance-proven animals.

You can discuss with your veterinary surgeon the desirability of blood tests and other biological tests, and limb X-rays to be done as part of the examination. Some veterinary surgeons feel they are advisable and some do not. Some owners will not permit them and others will. It can be said that if an owner will not permit a blood test, which, skillfully done, upsets the horse only very slightly, there could well be something to hide such as pain-masking drugs or some other bodily disorder, so discuss this with your vet. Foot and limb X-rays are also the subject of disagreement, some vets believing they are unnecessary and not necessarily revealing of developing disorders, yet others almost insist on them for stock of the calibre we are considering in this book. Again, the pros and cons should be discussed and the significance of the lack of the information they could provide carefully weighed up.

As in all sections of the horse world, fashions in type and conformation come and go. As ever, fashion is often detrimental to the form and function of the animal although we have not yet, in the horse world, come to the stage of seeing grossly deformed and disabled animals in our showrings as has happened in the dog world. One fashion which is current at the time of writing, particularly in Quarter Horses and some breeds of warmblood, is that of producing animals with feet which are too small for the size and weight of the body they have to carry.

This fashion has apparently come about because of the desire for a horse to apper 'neat' and nimble, refined and full of quality, but it has been taken to extremes and foot problems can easily result from feet which are too small for the weight and size of body. The same amount of weight and force has to be borne on a smaller area, therefore the stress suffered by the feet is greater and so is the likelihood of tissue injuries, concussion, laminitis and navicular disease, among others.

Other fashions will doubtless come and go, and it can be difficult to ignore them when it is those animals of fashionable appearance which seem to be winning in the showring. As many breeders use the showring as their shop window this can be very worrying, but in the medium to longer term it is almost always those properly conformed animals which bring home the bacon when it comes to ability in the field, during *real* competition some would say. When a fashion appears to be harmful, as with small feet, it is far better to ignore it and stick to your principles. When it does not, as with today's requirement for swinging, elastic paces in dressage horses, by all means breed it into your stock if it does not mean compromising your ideals. It is soundness and ability which count in the long run and the bad effects of breeding for a particular, possibly harmful fashion will be apparent in your stock, and its effects felt, long after that fashion has flown out of the window.

If you use only sound animals (genuine accidents possibly excepted) of good conformation and athletic action, of good temperament and constitution as far as you can tell and preferably of individual proven ability or from a line or proven performers, you stand an excellent chance of acquiring or producing an animal which will cover itself in success and possibly glory in competition. These simple criteria do not seem so much to expect, and this combination of individual qualities and conformation, plus the record of the pedigree, provide the best practical guidelines from which to go on. If one element is missing your chances lessen significantly.

There *are* many good horses around for both breeding and performance. It costs as much to raise and keep a mediocre horse as a good one and it is always quality, not quantity, that counts. If you use the above criteria and stick to your principles, not allowing yourself to be too swayed by sentiment (difficult sometimes), and add good management and training on top, your success is (almost!) assured.

7
Dietary Management
by Gillian McCarthy

Appropriate feeding and nutrition is a major factor in achieving optimum health and performance in the competition horse. Devising a balanced and appropriate diet for the individual horse, combined with an informed and suitable training and conditioning programme, can enable the horse to achieve its maximum potential, both in an individual competition and over a lifetime of performance – from foalhood through competition and perhaps on to breeding to produce a future generation of top performers.

Though fine-tuning of the diet may not necessarily allow the horse to go faster or jump higher than a horse on an 'ordinary' or less than appropriate diet, it may well enable the horse to perform more often over its lifetime more effectively, and be less prone to illness and injury, especially stress and fatigue-related injuries. So, for example, it may enable the three-day eventer to avoid falling at the last fence or damaging a tendon through fatigue, or to get around the cross-country without time-faults and then go on to show jump on the final day without stiffness or lack of energy; and on the parts of the dressage horse it may prevent resistance and inaccuracy as the muscles become increasingly fatigued as a test or series of tests proceeds.

In fact, correct nutrition can have a particularly noticeable effect on stamina, and also on temperament and the possibility of accidents or time lost due to temperament problems – more on this later.

Many new or inexperienced competitors favour copying the dietary management of top riders; as the advertisers of compound horse feeds are well aware, and as they are obviously successful, there is a lot to be said for this.

However, there are two flaws in this approach. One is that the ultimate aim is presumably not just to emulate top performers, but to out-perform them! Equally, it is in the interests of those top performers to remain at the top, so while it is a good idea to stick to something that suits a particular horse, allowances must be made for changes in its requirements as it ages or is affected by the long-term stress of performing, illness or injuries. Sticking rigidly to a system for a horse at

12 years old because it worked when the horse was 8 may well shorten the career performance potential for that horse.

The other drawback with 'copying' the basic methods of another performer is that in fact, many top class competitors world-wide are feeding less than balanced diets, and while they may get away with it, or appear to, a less fit horse with less than ideal conformation, in the hands of a novice who may not recognise when to 'ease off', could have a disastrous result. The horse and its rider/handler is an individual unit and must be treated as such.

An example of this is a top class competitor who, having become aware that many European horses' diets are deficient in calcium, which can seriously reduce health and performance, has on the basis of 'a little knowledge is a dangerous thing' gone so overboard with calcium supplementation both in the feed and on the pastures that the horses in question *must* be receiving excessive levels of calcium. This must be out of balance with other nutrients and is almost certainly 'locking-up' vital trace elements which are involved both in bone strength and density and in other metabolic functions. So far, nothing obviously untoward has happened, but there is a risk of many problems such as sudden bone fractures, sore shins and less obvious loss of performance. However, as this is a top rider, expensive horses with superb conformation are involved.

But with the same diet fed to a less than perfect horse, subject to additional stresses due to conformational faults, perhaps inadequately fit and with a rider who does not know when enough is enough and how to wait to 'fight another day', at best a series of niggling injuries could prevent the horse competing; at worst, a serious accident could occur. This is just offered as one example of what could happen if:

(1)   The diet is unbalanced one way or another – more is not always better.
(2)   You place too much reliance on other people's methods.

A diet that is *balanced* and in correct quantities and palatable for two equivalent three-day eventers in adjoining stables may produce optimum performance from one and be totally *inappropriate* for the other, perhaps for reasons relating to management of the pregnant mother, the foal or youngster, genetic predisposition (including temperament), or previous illnesses and handling – all facets of individuality whose influences may be known or unknown, and which should all be considered when *devising*, *adapting* and *adjusting* a ration programme for the performance horse at all stages of its life and career.

Quantity, balance and suitability are the three major factors in deciding the make-up of a horse's diet, assuming reasonable availability of feed ingredients, and while to sustain life they are listed in order of importance, to sustain *maximum* performance each of the three aspects is probably of equivalent value.

What does the feed provide?

Obviously the feed provides *nutrients*, which in addition to water include carbohydrates, proteins, fats and oils (lipids), vitamins and minerals (including trace elements), along with roughage – an oft-neglected aspect – and 'amusement value', to prevent boredom and give a sense of repletion and contentment.

The *nutrients* are used to provide:

(1) *Energy* to fuel the body processes necessary for staying alive, to maintain body heat and weight, facilitate growth and lactation and provide the fuel for work.
(2) All the complex requirements for growth and repair, and maintenance of the horse's status quo.

The *roughage* or fibre in the diet has a number of roles whose importance is only now being recognised. Apart from keeping the horse occupied and amused, the roughage has an important physical role in exercising the gut, which must be kept 'fit' like other organs such as the heart and lungs in order to operate efficiently. It also provides a substrate on which billions of beneficial micro-organisms living in the gut (principally in the large intestine) can thrive.

The well-being of these micro-organisms can have a profound effect on the horse's health and well-being and is very largely influenced by the management of the horse by man. Researchers are beginning to find that a healthy microbial population is necessary for optimum and healthy growth and disease resistance, including to viruses and cancer. Obvious manifestations of a microbial population out of balance are scouring (diarrhoea), constipation, colic, nervousness and tempera-ment problems, lack of concentration, wood chewing, dung eating (coprophagy) and even filled legs and other irritating 'stable' problems.

Upsets are likely to occur at times of stress (weaning, sales, moving stables, competing, travelling, after illness or operations or after certain drugs, including antibiotics, have been administered) and also in early life before the normal gut flora and fauna (microbes) have been established (one of the reasons why foals often practice coprophagy is as a natural means of starting the population up using bugs from the mother's dung). Foal scours are common and traditional treatment often works *against* the microbial population, not *with* it. The use of probiotics in this context will be discussed below, but these will not replace good dietary management and provision of adequate fibre as a means of keeping the bugs happy!

Apart from their role in maintaining 'gut stability' and the general well-being of the horse, the microbes help it to digest fibrous feeds (as the horse possesses no enzymes of its own for this purpose) and so survive, if not actually thrive, on poor quality forages if necessary. Thus nutrients are released which would otherwise be wasted, producing protein, energy and various vitamins, especially of the B-group, some of which become available to the horse for its own use. As the fibre (bulk feed) levels in the diet decrease as the horse gets fitter, the bugs produce fewer vitamins, which is one reason why a performance horse is more likely to need additional supplements, quite apart from any increased requirement due to greater levels of activity.

Keeping the bugs happy is one reason why the horse benefits from being fed *little and often* (so as not to overload them) with *no sudden changes in the diet*. It can take the microbial population – a mixture of many different bugs – three weeks or more to acclimatise to a new diet, which is why horses often scour or at least have loose droppings when feed is changed or they are brought in/turned out too suddenly, or there is a sudden flush of rich grass. The use of a weekly bran mash is an undesirable 'sudden' change in feeding and has no place in the dietary management of the top performance horse as the gut flora and fauna will never reach optimum balance. *A little of each major ingredient should be fed at each feed*. Different bugs digest mainly different feed groups, and as each bug may live for only a few hours to a few days, they need a constant supply of their favourite food (substrate) or they may be swamped by more voracious feeders – which puts the population out of balance and may lead to serious problems.

Digestion of feeds

In order for the horse producer and competitor to be in a position to make informed decisions about their horses' dietary management and any addition or adjustments which are to be made to the diet, it is important to have an understanding of the process of digestion of feeds and how this may be influenced by the nature and quality of feedingstuffs, and of the specific nutrient requirements of the horse.

Throughout this chapter a number of apparently new concepts are discussed, although in fact many of these have been used for many centuries under various guises, but are only recently being scientifically recognised; this should not be regarded as a denigration of traditional feeding methods. In many instances these may be perfectly adequate, but horses are kept in rather different conditions from those of our forefathers, and particularly with the introduction of roads and air transport for horses, they are exposed to different stresses and disease challenges far more frequently than was previously the case; also feedingstuffs themselves have changed either for the better or in some cases for the worse over the years, and 'new' feedingstuffs have become available throughout the world, so it is possible to draw from the best aspects of traditional methods while applying our scientific and intuitive understanding of horse nutrition to the development of a specific dietary regime along the lines set out below. This may be more appropriate, particularly when considering the high performance horse.

The horse evolved as a free-ranging herbage eater, though a somewhat inefficient one when compared with the ruminant (cow, sheep, goat). Keeping a horse at grass, in captivity, cannot be really described as a natural system although it may be desirable. This aspect has been discussed further in the section on pasture management in Chapter 5.

If we are going to impose a system of management on horses in captivity we must take the responsibility of controlling that horse's environment with the object of maintaining health and well-being. In order to do that, we need a combination of stockmanship (horse sense or the 'art' of horse management) and technique or know-how ('the science'). Horse nutrition should no longer be described entirely as 'an art which defies arithmetic'. Much can be quantified scientifically.

Figure 8 shows the digestive system of the horse.

Basically, the digestive system consists of a long tube, varying in diameter, from mouth to anus, through which the food passes and is acted on physically (churning and squeezing), chemically (acids and enzymes) and microbially (fermentation by bacteria – gut *flora* – and protozoa – gut *fauna* – in the hind gut). This releases the nutrients that the food contains and enables them to be absorbed into the blood stream, for distribution to the various organs and tissues to provide for the maintenance of the status quo, growth, repair, reproduction and lactation.

A number of aspects about the digestive system should be borne in mind when developing a diet for your horses:

(1) Feed will not be broken down efficiently if it is inadequately chewed, so teeth require regular attention by your vet or equine dentist – *every 6 to 12 months*. Ideally any new horse in the yard should be checked on arrival, and then a routine of 6 monthly checks instituted. Severe problems may become apparent with head tossing and tilting, bolting, and quidding (dropping feed out of the mouth), but the situation should not be allowed to deteriorate to anything like this

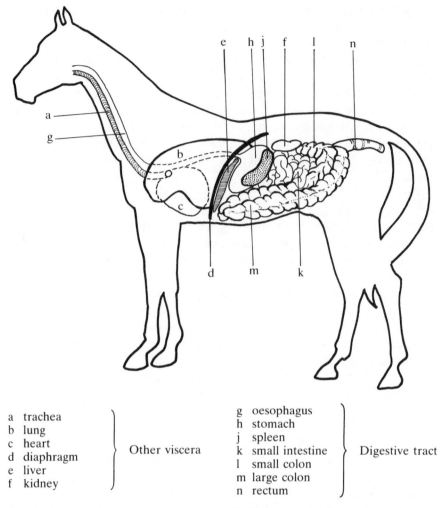

a	trachea	}	g	oesophagus	}
---	---------		---	------------	
b	lung		h	stomach	
c	heart	Other viscera	j	spleen	
d	diaphragm		k	small intestine	Digestive tract
e	liver		l	small colon	
f	kidney		m	large colon	
			n	rectum	

Fig. 8 The digestive system of the horse. Drawn by Isabella Whitworth; after Renwal Products inc. (1961), Smith (1971), Frandson (1974) and Codrington (1974).

extent if optimum performance is to be obtained from the horse.

(2)   Feed will be wasted (a) if parasites are eating a share of it, and (b) if parasites damage the gut wall and cause blockages, preventing maximum uptake of nutrients from the feed. Regular and frequent treatment with suitable anthelmintics (wormers) is vital, even in stabled horses. Be guided by your vet and remember that not all the wormers you can buy without prescription, e.g. at the tack shop, are active against all parasites, and particularly against immature larval stages

which can cause the most damage such as by blocking blood vessels supplying the gut. It has been suggested that as many as 90% of all colic cases can be related to worm damage, particularly that caused by migrating red worm larvae, and it is not unknown for horses to drop dead during moments of peak exertion, either in competition or at the stud, due to a blockage caused by an embolism resulting from migrating worm larvae. Apart from being rather distressing, this can obviously be highly dangerous to both horse and rider.

(3)   As described above, the relationship between the horse and its intestinal population of micro-organisms, particularly in the hind gut, is of utmost importance to its health and well-being. It is almost a case of 'look after the bugs and the horse will look after himself'!

Other management-orientated factors influencing gut stability, including gut motility and acidity, are also frequently man-made and may have a devastating effect on the harmony existing within the horse.

(4) Feed should be of the best physical as well as chemical (nutritional) quality available. Dust can cause coughing, and mould can cause both allergic responses such as broken wind (heaves, small airway disease SAD, and chronic obstructive pulmonary disease COPD) and, if mycotoxins are present, (poisons produced by rogue micro-organisms, particularly moulds and fungi on feeds) severe ill health which may result in death, or abortion in pregnant mares followed by infertility, or at the very least loss of performance. It is possible that mycotoxins on grass are responsible for or involved in, grass sickness.

Feedstuffs do not have to be visibly mouldy to the naked eye to contain mycotoxins. Remember that once cereals are rolled or crushed they are dead, and dead things decay. Plant a whole oat and it will grow – it is alive; plant a rolled one and it will rot – it is dead. Apart from this, vitamins are destroyed when air is allowed in by rolling. So, do not roll feedstuffs unless you have to, and only roll as much as you can use in two weeks (winter) or one week (summer). If you buy ready-rolled, check with your merchant that they are freshy rolled.

So, briefly, the digestive process by which nutrients are released from the feedstuffs for uptake into the horse's body (food in the digestive tract or 'tube' being effectively outside the body) is as follows:

(1)   Food is gathered into the mouth by the lips and bitten off and chewed by the teeth, physically exposing the chewed feed for action by saliva which starts in the mouth. It should be noted that the whiskers are sensory organs used to detect food, especially in the dark, and should *not* be cut or singed off, particularly with horses kept outdoors or with defective eyesight.

(2)   The bolus of food plus enzymes in the saliva is pushed down the oesophagus (or gullet) to the stomach by waves of muscular contraction called peristalsis.

(3)   In the stomach, which holds 8 to 15 litres ($1\frac{3}{4}$ to $3\frac{1}{4}$ galls) of material, the food is flooded with gastric juices which consist of water, mineral salts, mucous, hydrochloric acid and pepsinogen, and is churned by muscular stomach walls. It may stay in the stomach for as little as 20 minutes.

(4)   From the stomach the food passes into the small intestine (duodenum, jejenum and ileum) which holds 40 to 50 litres ($8\frac{3}{4}$ to 11 galls) of material and is some 20 to 30 metres long. Here, bile and pancreatic juices are secreted and further breakdown of the non-fibrous fraction occurs. The digested material takes some 20 to 90 minutes to reach the end of the ileum. Here proteins and glucose which have been released are absorbed into the blood stream.

(5)   The food then passes into the hind gut, which comprises the caecum, colon and rectum, where it may remain for from 1 to 3 hours up to 3 days.

This is where the fibre in the diet can be broken down by the gut micro-organisms which produce volatile fatty acids (VFAs), some of which are obsorbed by a horse and used as an energy source. This is a process of fermentation, and the fact that it occurs *after* the stomach and small intestine is a major flaw in the design of the equine digestive system for a herbivore. It is a posterior fermentor. In the ruminant, fermentation occurs in the rumen, a giant fermentation vat, *prior* to food passing into the stomach and small intestine, allowing for maximum utilisation of nutrients in the feed as the 'exposed' nutrients have the full length of the rest of the digestive tract to be absorbed in. It is an anterior fermentor.

However, the horse undeniably benefits from the fermentation process, even though it occurs near the end of the tract, as without it the horse would not benefit from grass, hay or bran, and as has been mentioned before, its relationship with the population of gut micro-organisms is vital to health. The products of microbial digestion include volatile fatty acids, water and electrolytes (tissue salts), as well as B vitamins and proteins.

The colon is rather badly designed in that it has a very narrow right-angled bend, or flexure, which can become blocked, leading to impacted colic. This can be avoided by supplying adequate water, and feeding frequent, regular, *small* feeds.

Any undigested or partly digested food is passed into the rectum and expelled from the anus, and all experienced horse keepers will be well aware of the importance of the consistency and amount of the droppings in evaluating the health of the horse.

The nutrient requirements of the horse

As mentioned above, the horse has a specific often scientifically measurable requirement for certain nutrients:

- water
- carbohydrates
- fats and oils
- proteins
- vitamins
- minerals

It also has a physical requirement for *fibre* as a source of roughage to exercise the gut and keep the ration open.

Water

Water is the most important nutrient. Over 50% of the horse's bodyweight (70–80% in foals) is made up of water in body fluids and tissues. Loss of 20% of body water will cause death rapidly. Water is needed to maintain the integrity or shape and form of every cell, including the bone, and is present in every body fluid. It is a carrier for substances into and out of the body e.g. saliva (in) and urine and sweat (out), and is vital for many digestive processes and metabolism. It plays an essential role in regulating body temperature, both due to ambient temperature and to the heat produced in muscles by work, or the lack of it through inactivity. The hotter the horse the more it sweats, and sweat is made up largely of water, which also carries waste products out via the skin.

Water is also a lubricant in joints and eyes, transports sounds, and carries nutrients around the body (blood/lymph), bathing cells. If the horse sweats excessively or has an inadequate supply of water, or both, it becomes dehydrated. As this happens it can overheat, and the blood supply to the muscles may be reduced as the blood becomes thicker (peripheral circulation) so waste products are not removed, and oxygen and nutrients are not delivered efficiently, leading to fatigue or cramp. *This is why it is bad practice to deprive the high-performance horse of water for extended periods before, during and after competitions.*

A horse will not drink to excess before competitive work provided it is not deprived of water for a period, and has a continuous supply. This is especially important if a horse is boxed long distances to a hunt or a competition, especially as it may lose considerable water as sweat on the journey, although it may arrive dry if a box or trailer is well ventilated. Be sure to arrive in ample time for the horse to drink its fill before the competition – at least one hour recovery period for every hour in transit in temperate climates. Stop to water on long journeys, and take you own water or add a little molasses to local water if necessary to encourage the horse to drink.

Do not deprive the horse of water for more than half an hour before exertion, and allow him to drink his fill whenever possible in endurance

Plate 20 The condition of the horse's gums are a good indicator of its state of health. They should be a pink or salmon pink colour; pale, insipid gums are a possible indicator of anaemia while yellowish ones, particularly in young foals, can indicate jaundice, In this photograph the gums are being tested for capillary refill time which is an indicator of whether or not the horse is dehydrated. (Photograph supplied by Gillian McCarthy.)

events, or hunting. However, between phases in horse trials he should not be offered more than 2 litres (4 pints). If he wants more than this after, say, the roads and tracks and steeplechase, he probably is not fit to go on the cross-country anyway.

Reduction of performance and delay of recovery afterwards is likely to be far greater if the horse is dehydrated, than if it drinks a reasonable amount (say up to 2 litres (4 pints)) before fast work. Ask your vet to show you how to do the 'pinch test' for dehydration. Colic after a competition or journey is more likely in the dehydrated horse.

Broodmares will also have an increased water requirements when lactating, for obvious reasons.

A typical stabled horse requires 20 to 40 litres (5 to 10 gallons) of water per day. *Change* the water frequently and scrub out buckets daily. If you just top-up, the water takes in ammonia from the atmosphere (from urine) and becomes stale, 'flat' and unpalatable, so even a thirsty horse may not drink its fill. If you are giving an electrolyte drink, (see below) always offer plain water at the same time. If he does not need the electrolytes but *does* need the water, he may go thirsty rather than drink the electrolyte drink. Human athletes say that electrolyte drinks taste like nectar when you need them and like canned sweat when you don't! So give him the choice so he can balance himself.

The force feeding of salt or electrolytes, including the use of paste electrolytes, is probably not a good idea under most circumstances, as it could in fact lead to further dehydration. However, if your horse consistently refuses electrolyte drinks, when you would logically expect him to require them, try a different brand as he may simply not like the taste of the brand you are using.

Carbohydrates

Carbohydrates, mainly in the form of starches and sugars, are needed as the major source of energy. The simpler carbohydrates, i.e. the starches and sugars, are mainly obtained from cereals, while fibre feeds contain far more complex carbohydrates, which must be released from their relatively indigestible state by the action of digestive micro-organisms. All carbohydrates are ultimately broken down to sugars, namely glucose, before they are utilised by the horse.

Fats and oils (lipids or lipins)

These are 2.25 times richer as a source of energy than carbohydrates, and also a source of fat-soluble vitamins (A,D,E and K) and essential fatty acids. A certain amount is present in most feedstuffs at low levels, but may be added as fish or vegetable oil. Use of high fat/oil diets in relation to the performance horse is discussed below.

Energy

Energy is not a nutrient as such, but is the vital component obtained by the burning or oxidising of nutrient fuels in the feed. These fuels are mainly carbohydrate, and to a lesser extent fats and oils, and in addition *excess* protein in the diet may be used as an (expensive and very inefficient) energy source.

It should be noted the term *protein* and *energy* are *not* interchangeable. Protein *can* be used as an energy source if excessive levels are fed, but energy can never be used as a protein, although it is needed for protein synthesis. Muscular activity is fuelled by energy *not* protein. Energy is used up by muscles in work, protein is not, so when work or performance levels increase so do energy requirements whereas for practical purposes protein requirements *do not*. Once a horse is mature it does *not* need extra protein for extra work. Protein requirements for wear and tear are comparatively extremely small, though they may become slightly higher in elderly animals that may be less efficient at utilising the protein in their diet due to old age and effects such as parasite damage of the gut.

So energy is required for virtually all life processes and is probably the most important consideration in the diet from a practical feeding point of view. Energy is necessary for the action of the heart and maintenance of blood pressure, the transmission of nerve impulses, the maintenance of muscle tone and activity, for growth, the maintenance of body temperature, for gut movements, the secretion of milk, for protein and fat synthesis and for transport of materials across membranes (i.e. nutrients, gases and waste products). It is the horse's *fuel* and without it the horse cannot function. The energy requirements for these life processes must be satisfied from the diet, before the horse can perform work or produce milk or offspring. The first priority of the horse's body is to keep itself alive.

Every horse requires a certain level of energy, or more specifically, *digestible energy*, for maintenance of the status quo. This is measured in joules, which are the metric form of calories – 1 calorie = 4.184 joules. You can measure whether your horse is receiving adequate energy for maintenance by monitoring its bodyweight and observing its behaviour and attitude. Assuming the horse is not working, if it is neither gaining nor losing weight it is receiving adequate energy for maintenance. This requirement will vary with the temperature and environment of the horse. Measurement of bodyweight and calculation of digestible energy requirements are discussed below under 'Rationing'.

Protein

Proteins are found in all living cells, where they are intimately involved in all the activities which sustain the life of the cell. Each tissue, organ or organism has its own particular type of protein. For instance, the protein in liver is different from that in milk, eggs, or grass and so on.

Protein is used to build up new tissues in the growing animal, and the foetus in pregnant mares and for replacing worn-out tissue, particularly in elderly or severely debilitated horses. In the healthy mature horse any additional protein requirement for this process will generally be covered by the normal diet, and as we shall see below, excessive levels of protein, which are in fact found in a number of compound horse feeds and vacuum-packed forages, could actually reduce performance.

Proteins are made up of *amino acids*, which may be likened to the pieces of a jig-saw puzzle, each type having a distinct 'shape' which fits in a particular place in the puzzle (protein), but the pieces may be used in different puzzles (proteins). There are 25 amino acids known in nature, 22 of which are known to be required by the horse. These 22 are sub-divided into two types. Twelve are referred to as *non-essential amino acids*, which can be synthesised by the horse itself and need not be present in the diet as such, as the horse can manufacture them as the body functions demand. In other words, though they are essential to the horse, they are non-essential in the diet.

However, the other 10 amino acids are described as *essential amino acids* because it is essential that they be present in the diet as they cannot be synthesised by the horse. So, for optimum health and performance, adequate levels of these 10 amino acids *must* be supplied in the diet.

In practice, it is fairly difficult to *under*feed 7 of these amino acids to a mature horse using reasonable quality feedstuffs, but three, called *methionine, tryptophan* and particularly *lysine*, are deficient or marginal in many diets, especially those based on cereals or cereal by-products (oats, barley, maize, wheat bran, etc.). These are referred to as *limiting amino acids*, and lysine is referred to as the *first limiting amino acid*. A fourth amino acid which *could* be involved in a horse's resistance to disease, particularly when under stress, is arginine, but this requires further investigation to confirm.

Provided that at least some of each essential amino acid is present in the diet, the total amount may not be crucial for the mature horse in light work, but it is increasingly necessary for performance horses, young animals and broodmares to receive the correct amount if optimum performance is to be achieved. For example, lysine deficiency may reduce performance, feed efficiency and growth; methionine deficiency may manifest itself as hoof and coat problems, and tryptophan as hyperexcitability.

It is not, therefore, just the *quantity* of protein in the diet that is important, but also the *quality* of that protein. A diet containing 8% crude protein (see below) with adequate levels of essential amino acids may be more effective than a 20% crude protein diet with unbalanced amino acids, and is almost certainly a good deal cheaper!

The protein level on the feed sack label is in fact the crude protein content, which is not a good measure of the usefulness of that protein to the horse as it is merely derived from a calculation based on the nitrogen content of the feed. Old leather boots have a high *crude protein* content, but are not renowned for their digestibility and value as a protein source for horses! We should also interest ourselves in the *digestible crude protein* in the diet. It may be more economical and better for the horse to feed a ration of 10% crude protein which is 80% digestible, than 14% crude protein which is only 40% digestible, particularly when high performance horses, are involved, including breedingstock and youngstock.

Current research and practical observation indicates that the desirable lysine content of the over-all diet is 0.7% for foals and weanlings, 0.6% for yearlings, 0.5% for 2-year-olds, and 0.25 to 0.4% for mature horses, depending on the level of performance. Elderly horses would probably benefit from a little more, say 0.6%, plus a good supply of methionine for coat and hoof condition. (Elderly horses do not *have* to look moth-eaten and scruffy.)

Mature horses and ponies require 8.5 to 10% (as fed) crude protein in the *total* diet, i.e. forage plus concentrates. The term 'as fed' refers

Table 1 Crude protein requirements of horses (as fed)

Horses	% required in total diet
Mares in the last 90 days of gestation	11
Lactating mares, first 3 months	14
Lactating mares, 3 months to weaning	12
Foal creep feed	18–20
Foal, 3 months of age	18–20
Weanling, 6 months of age	16
Yearling, 12 months of age	13.5
Long yealing, 18 months of age	11
Two-year-old	10
Mature horse – light work	8.5
– moderate work	8.5
– hard work	8.5
Elderly horse, 16 years plus	12–14 (probably – be guided by health and condition)

to the feed in the condition it is in store (i.e. it would refer to unsoaked sugar beet, although this would be soaked before feeding), whereas analysis of feed on a 'dry matter' basis facilitates comparison of apparently widely different feeds, e.g. fresh grass and hay, as it refers to the feed value of those feeds with all the water removed. So you can compare like with like. There is also a limit to the total dry matter intake of the horse, which is one reason why a high performance horse in fast work cannot be fed an unconcentrated (e.g. forage) feed as its sole nutrient source.

It is particularly important that the nutrient requirements of young-stock destined to race as two-year-olds are fully met by the diet so that the animals are sufficiently mature to go into training.

For the average mature horse doing medium work, no high crude protein supplement (soya, linseed, fish meal, skim milk) is necessary, although additional lysine may well be beneficial, especially in hard work. Linseed is a particularly poor source of lysine compared with other high protein feeds.

In fact, excess protein may be counter-productive, increasing sweating, causing 'breaking-out' after work, higher pulse and respiration rates (particularly undesirable for endurance horses), unnecessary stress, and in the long term may cause kidney damage. Frothy, sticky sweat is a particular indication of excess protein. As the horse sweats and urinates more in order to get rid of the by-products of the excess protein, it is likely to become dehydrated, particularly if traditional watering methods in competition are used, (i.e. inadequate water). As a result the blood becomes thicker and flows less well, particularly in the peripheral (muscular) circulation, which means that oxygen and nutrients are delivered less efficiently to the muscles, and waste products such as lactic acid are not carried away as effectively and may pool in the muscles. The result of this at best may be the early onset of fatigue, and at worst may be an accident due to less sufficient operation of the muscles, and even 'tying up' or other muscle myopathies.

High protein feeds tend to be more expensive and it is foolish to over feed them. Work out the energy levels first for the diet, and then adjust the protein as necessary to achieve the optimum levels described above.

Vitamins

Vitamins are vital substances concerned in many metabolic or life processes. They are required in minute amounts but are vitally important to the health and welfare of the horse.

There are two types: *fat soluble* and *water soluble*. The *fat soluble vitamins* are A, D, E and K. A precursor of vitamin A, beta-carotene, is also thought to be necessary in its own right, especially for unimpaired fertility of breedingstock. Fresh or dried grass, alfalfa (lucerne) and carrots are all rich in beta-carotene.

The *fat soluble vitamins* can be stored in the fat storage depots (adipose tissue) of the body, and a grass-kept horse or pony on *good pasture* should store at least enough to see him through until Christmas. However, supplementation may be desirable after this time, until the spring flush of grass appears. Stabled horses are likely to benefit from some degree of supplementation throughout the year, especially when in hard work.

Additional megadoses of vitamin E have been found by some horse owners to be beneficial for nervous horses, and up to 7000 iu/day of vitamin E with selenium may be given for 5 to 7 days before an important competition. If you do not see any obvious result from this, there is no point in continuing such high (and expensive) doses. Other aspects of the diet may be contributing to the horse's nervousness, including inadequate fibre or de-stabilised digestive micro-organisms producing toxins which cause excitability or nervousness and can be corrected by a probiotic, or sodium montmerrillonite (e.g. Thrive), and in some cases increased doses of vitamin B_1 and the amino acid tryptophan. However, expert guidance should be sought before attempting dietary manipulation other than vitamin E, fibre, probiotics or Thrive. In fact a combination of these factors may be involved, or of course the horse may have an unalterable nervous disposition! A predisposition to nervousness may be hereditary, but can often be exacerbated to some degree by dietary manipulation.

The role of addition vitamin E for breedingstock has not in my opinion been satisfactorily proven, but 1 to 2000 iu/day is fed by some stud owners around covering time as a precaution. This, however, cannot possibly replace the feeding of an over-all balanced diet, which is often neglected, and vitamin E or any other supplements cannot be regarded as a magic dust which will cure any fundamental inadequacies in the over-all diet.

Horses on high fat diets (over 3% oil), such as endurance horses, require an addition 5 mg vitamin E per kg of feed for each 1% above 3% of oil in the total diet. So on a 6% oil diet, $6 - 3 = 3$; 3×5 mg = 15 mg/kg of feed of *extra* vitamin E to be fed.

Horses being fed proprionic acid-treated cereals, hay or silage should be receiving at least 1000 iu/day of vitamin E. However, there are many new and more effective feed preservatives on the market now which may not require any additional vitamin E. Check with the preservative manufacturer.

The other, larger, group of vitamins are the *water soluble* ones, which cannot be stored by the horse and which it requires on a daily basis. Many, particularly with a high fibre diet, are adequately synthesised in the gut by the gut micro-organisms, but if these micro-organisms are upset (such as by antibiotics or a sudden change in the diet), or if the horse is on a lower fibre diet or has higher requirements than normal (e.g. the high performance horse), additional levels may be required. There is, however, little to be gained from feeding excessive levels as these generally cannot be stored and the horse must waste metabolic effort in disposing of them, which may be crucial in high performance situations. The possible exceptions are folic acid, which some horses seem to require high levels of; biotin, again under-utilised by some horses and needed at higher levels to maintain the integrity of the hoof and coat (usually for 3 to 9 months, then a drop to normal levels can be introduced); and *possibly* vitamin C in some disease situations.

The water soluble vitamins then are the B vitamins, which are thiamine, riboflavin, niacin (nicotinic acid), pantothenic acid, folic acid, pyridoxine and cobalamin (B_{12}). Biotin, choline and inositol are also sometimes considered as B vitamins and are water soluble, and vitamin C (ascorbic acid) is also water soluble. Vitamin K, the fat soluble vitamin, also comes in the synthetic water soluble form.

Vitamins are destroyed by heating and cooking and by exposure to air, light, damp and moulds. So add vitamin supplements *after* hot or cooked feeds have cooled, always re-seal supplement containers and store in a cool, day place, and ensure that your supplier does the same, i.e. do not purchase buckets or bags of supplements which have been in store adjacent to radiators, shop lights, or in a shop window. You should also avoid rolling or otherwise processing (i.e. damaging) more feedstuffs at a time than you have to; cooking or boiling feeds will also destroy vitamins and other nutrients. Likewise, feeds which need to be soaked should be prepared in very small quantities using cold water, and for example with sugar beet, the water should also be fed as it will contain soluble nutrients. However, hay which is soaked for horses with wind problems should have the water discarded, as it will also contain large quantities of dust and mould, and this water should be changed very frequently. Incidently, steaming such forages will neither adequately swell mould spores to prevent them having an allergic effect, nor remove dust; it will simply destroy vitamins and so is really rather a waste of time and effort.

Minerals

Minerals are another essential constituent of a balanced ration for horses. They form the major constituent of bones and teeth, as well as being ubiquitous in tissues and fluids and playing a vital role in biochemical reactions. The total mineral content of a feed roughly equates to the 'ash' content on feed bag labels. However, this figure does not actually tell us anything about the quality of the feed, unless it is exceptionally low or high, because it does not tell us which minerals make up the ash, and what form they are in – i.e. whether they are available to the horse.

The minerals are usually sub-divided into *major or macro minerals*, required in relatively large amounts, and *trace or micro minerals*, required in minute traces but no less important than other nutrients. Other terms include trace elements and trace nutrients.

The major minerals are:

- calcium (Ca)
- phosphorus (P)
- sodium (Na)
- potassium (K)
- chlorine (Cl)
- sulphur (S)

Assuming the diet contains adequate levels of forage (which is rich in potassium), the only ones you may have to consider adding separately to your horse's diet are calcium, phosphorus, and sodium chloride (salt). Very few diets are adequate in these for working horses, and although cubes may contain sufficient levels, vitamin/mineral supplements rarely do as it would be virtually impossible for the manufacturers to get the levels right for all horses in all situations.

Lack of calcium or phosphorus, or an imbalance, can manifest itself with brittle bones, sore shins (star fractures of the cannon bone) and poor bone growth (metabolic bone disorders – MBDs) in youngstock e.g. epiphysitis, caused by lack of minerals, *not* high protein levels, provided protein is not excessive. In severe cases rickets or osteomalacia may occur as well as loss of teeth. Muscle function may also be impaired. High performance horses, especially endurance horses and eventers, deficient in calcium (and possibly potassium) may suffer from the 'thumps' (synchronous diaphragmatic flutter). This can be avoided by practising balanced nutritional and conditioning techniques, and taking due consideration of heat and humidity conditions and the wind chill factor during competitions and hard training.

The *ratio* of calcium to phosphorus is important, apart from the actual amount. For mature horses it should be between 1.1:1 and 1.6:1, *never* less than 1.1 and preferably no more than 2.5:1. Diets containing high levels of cereal products, especially wheatbran, are likely to have an unbalanced calcium to phosphorus ratio, and they also contain a substance, phytin (phytate, phytic acid) which 'locks-up' calcium in the rest of the diet. This can be alleviated by:

(1)   Feeding up to 50 g of limestone/kg wheatbran (for mature horses), less if sugar beet pulp or alfalfa is fed.

(2)   Using chaff (chop) instead of bran (a *much* better idea).

(3)   Always feeding sugar beet, or lucerne/alfalfa nuts or to a lesser extent grass meal/nuts, when large amounts of cereals, particularly wheatbran, are being fed.

Vitamin D is also important in the utilisation of calcium and phosphorus, and if the horse is not fed on fresh grass or regularly exposed to sunlight, he should be fed supplementary vitamin D. Animals at risk include those kept out but wearing a New Zealand rug in winter, and all stabled horses, especially those exercised in an exercise sheet or in the early morning before the sun is out or has clouded over.

As well as there being little vitamin D in feed, including hay, stored for more than six months, animals which have stored vitamin D at grazing over the summer are likely to have depleted their reserves significantly by mid-winter, especially if the pasture was of poor quality.

You can easily add calcium (e.g. as a feed-grade limestone-flour) or calcium and phosphorus (for youngstock and horses fed large amounts of alfalfa (lucerne)) as dicalcium phosphate. Bone meal flour also provides calcium and phosphorus, but you should be absolutely certain that your supplier has correctly treated it, to prevent the possibility of disease (salmonella). I personally prefer not to use it. Skimmed milk powder and milk pellets also contain calcium, but are not especially rich in it, and rarely provide enough to balance large amounts of cereals. Correct proportions of sugar beet feed or alfalfa/lucerne meal/cubes/chaff are probably a better source of *available* calcium.

Salt supplementation is quite simple. A simple salt lick, trace mineralised as appropriate for the area in which your horse is grazing, is usually sufficient for non-working horses in the field or stable, but not for lactating broodmares or horses in hard work, when it may be necessary to add 25 to 100 g (approximately 1 to 4 tablespoons) of salt/*day* to the rations, *plus* keep a salt lick or loose-salt box available for insurance at all times. Working and lactating horses cannot obtain their full salt requirements simply from a salt lick, and some horses either do not like, or find it difficult to use, a salt lick. Sugar beet is again a good source of salt, and where this forms a significant proportion of the diet, slightly less salt needs to be added. Fish meal also provides significant quantities of salt, as do most compound feeds.

The rule-of-thumb for salt is that it should be 0.5 to 1% of the total diet by weight. However, be guided by the degree of hard work and ambient temperature and humidity. Salt-deficient horses may become dehydrated, and will at least suffer from reduced appetite and performance. (See also electrolytes below.)

Chlorine is supplied with the salt (use iodised table salt *not* dishwasher salt), and magnesium is not likely to be a problem in most practical situations as most horses obtain sufficient levels in their normal diet. However, problems with magnesium supply may be implicated in certain muscular and nervous problems.

The *trace minerals* usually considered are copper (Cu), cobalt (Co), iron (Fe), manganese (Mn), zinc (Zn), and selenium (Se), and there is increasing interest in the possible requirement for germanium (Ge). These will generally be in adequate supply for grazing horses and those in light to medium work, if a trace-mineralised salt lick is used, although some horses benefit from additional zinc (especially in terms of improved hoof, skin and coat condition – and this may be particularly true for ponies prone to sweet-itch). Added selenium may be of value in some areas of the country (e.g. Devon/Cornwall, Welsh Mountains, Scottish Highlands, i.e. areas where selenium is noted for being deficient in the soil), or if high vitamin E levels are being fed. Problems of selenium deficiency, and conversely toxicity, occur over wide areas in Africa, North America, Australia and New Zealand, and it is important to ascertain which type of area you are in before changing the feed supplementation.

Further levels may be required for stabled horses in hard work – see vitamins/minerals supplements below.

Many other trace elements are required in *minute* amounts, but are not likely to be deficient in diets based on normal feedstuffs.

Electrolytes or tissue salts (also called blood salts)

These are minerals and trace elements in their salt form, which is how they are present in the body fluids. *Electrolyte drinks* and pastes are a mixture of tissue salts and usually glucose or another high-energy, palatable carrier, which can be mixed with drinking water and given to a dehydrated horse which has lost salts through sweating and exertion. They can be useful after, or even during, a competition (e.g. eventing, endurance riding); or as a pick-me-up after a hard day's hunting – far more beneficial than oatmeal gruel or hay-tea (a primitive electrolyte drink itself); or after a long journey, especially in hot weather. Remember a horse in a trailer may sweat profusely but appear dry on arrival as the air movement in the trailer can dry it rapidly.

There is *nothing* to be gained from force-feeding electrolytes or salt before a competition as they cannot be stored by the horse. The horse will know if it needs them. Always offer plain water alongside as the horse will know whether it requires salts, water or both, and should not be forced to drink electrolytes it does not need through sheer thirst, or to actually go thirsty because it simply doesn't want to drink electrolytes.

The use of electrolytes in paste form, which is another form of force-feeding, should be very carefully considered before being undertaken, as should adding electrolyte powders or liquids, normally destined to be mixed up as drinks, to the feed (even if the manufacturer's label suggests this) in addition to other vitamin/mineral supplements and salt. Although the electrolytes are intended to *prevent* dehydration, over-dosing can actually *cause* various dehydration and other problems. Let your horse be the best judge, although be prepared to try different brands if a horse that fairly obviously is in need of electrolytes refuses to take them, as he may not happen to like the taste of the brand you have chosen.

Molasses, especially beet molasses (rather than cane molasses), mixed with water, can be a useful and very palatable simple electrolyte drink, and a means of encouraging horses to drink. There will always be the individual horse who refuses to drink even though he plainly needs to, or has to be given perhaps a paste electrolyte because he will not take a drink, again when he plainly needs one, but these are very much the exception rather than the rule and these methods should be used as a last resort. (Check for dehydration using the skin-pinch test, or by checking capillary refill time on the gums. Ask your vet to show you how.)

Many horses who are boxed-up and driven home too soon after competing or hunting, before they have rested and drunk their fill, will colic on reaching home due to dehydration. Too often, the owner fails to make the connection between his bad management and his horse's colic attack and does the same thing again next time out!

I prefer *not* to use electrolyte drinks containing glucose or dextrose for endurance horses, and probably eventers, as they prevent the horses from mobilising their own energy resources, and can lead to hypoglycaemia (low blood sugar), when the system floods with insulin to 'mop up' the unprecedented levels of sugar and may cause a temporary drop in blood-sugar levels, which manifests itself as fatigue. This would obviously cause problems if these drinks were being given *during* a competition, including between days or phases, but such glucose-containing drinks would be acceptable *after* a competition when no further work is required. (*Dextrose* is another name for glucose.)

If your horse is on a well-balanced diet, is fit and is not deprived of feed for more than four hours before strenuous performance, glucose is more likely to hinder rather than help it. If you are looking for an instant energy source, it is far better to use fructose (fruit sugar) or a suitable carbohydrate polymer such as Carbo-Booster, Equine Energizer or HySpeed H. These can safely be given immediately before competition, to provide readily available energy without lowering blood glucose levels (because they are utilised without the intervention of insulin); thus they prolong glycogen reserves and delay the onset of fatigue, and they may also be given between phases to eventers, between classes to show jumpers, and *en route* to endurance horses for the same purpose. They are also extremely useful as a pick-me-up after strenuous activity.

It can take up to three weeks for muscle glycogen (the energy store of the muscles) reserves to be replenished after strenuous activity, so if a horse is competing more often than this, over the season its reserves will be depleted with the possible result that it will become fatigued more easily, and will be more prone to illness and injury as its resistance is low. Therefore judicious use of fructose or suitable carbohydrate polymers for the high performance horse can be extremely useful indeed. It will never replace a correctly balanced diet, however, but could well be a means of giving a top class horse an additional 'edge', all other things being equal.

When you consider that at some levels of competition the horse may use up more muscle glycogen in the journey to the competition in a horsebox than in the competition itself, and that a horse is rarely given a normal feed prior to competition and quite often goes very long periods indeed without feed on competition day, the use of such products in the appropriate circumstances obviously makes sense. I have also noted that horses that will not normally eat for some time after competing, almost certainly due to severe fatigue, will eat up readily and so recover more quickly when given a carbohydrate polymer, either mixed with a normal feed or small feed, or even just with a little sugar beet pulp or as a drink. If you are happy that your horse readily accepts appropriate levels of electrolytes, you can safely mix a carbohydrate polymer with his electrolyte drink.

Vitamin/mineral supplements

In preparing a balanced diet, it is important not to fall into the trap of considering individual vitamins and minerals in isolation. There are complicated interactions between them, and between other nutrients, many of which are not as yet clearly understood or identified. Well-known ones are the interactions between vitamin D and calcium and phosphorus, and between vitamin E and selenium.

The perceived wisdom on the subject of supplementation is continuously changing and developing. There are no hard and fast rules, as not only is each horse an individual but all feedstuffs are variable in feeding value. One cannot state categorically which commercial vitamin/mineral supplement is the best one without knowing exactly what it is to be fed with, or what type of horse is being fed.

Whether to feed a supplement or not is the next question. Some people flatly refuse to use one at all; some use several different ones (somewhat ill-advisedly); some people feed them daily and others every now and again. The following are the rules-of-thumb I use when deciding whether or not to use a supplement, and when selecting which brand to use. I use these in conjunction with a unique equine ration formulation program on a computer, but the basic rules hold good whether or not you have access to such sophisticated techniques.

(1)   Horses and ponies at grass are likely to have depleted their stores of fat soluble vitamins, which are laid down during the summer, by mid-winter, or even before then if poor grass quality is prevalent. The simplest way to correct this is to feed stabilised cod liver oil until the spring flush of grass. *Do not* overfeed cod liver oil – follow the instructions on the pack.

(2)   Be aware of any specific mineral deficiences in the soil in your area, for example selenium, and choose a supplement accordingly. You should also be aware that different grazing and forage plants, as well as hard feeds, tend to be deficient in different minerals. For example, while horses on a grass/grass hay based diet are likely to require some form of calcium supplementation, those grazing legumes such as clover and alfalfa/lucerne, are more likely to require phosphorus.

(3)   For the grass-kept animal at rest or in light work, a trace mineralised salt lick should provide adequate mineral nutrition. However, if the land is poor (e.g. very sandy) or has some other significant characteristic (e.g. very chalky – the chalk locks up the trace elements), and you are not giving concentrate feeds, consider using feed blocks (range blocks) for protein, energy, vitamins and minerals. Alternatively, you could feed a vitamin/mineral biscuit, for example the Salvina Briquette, which can be fed by hand when you catch the horse to check it over. Adequate water and forage should be available when such blocks are used.

Vitamin injections are discussed below.

(4)   For the stabled animal whose feed intake is being controlled by you, you should consider:

(a)   which of his nutrient needs may be missing or low in the feeds you are providing: e.g. vitamin D, most of which has gone from stored hay after 6 months; calcium on grass hay and cereal diets; amino acid, lysine on most diets; salt, etc.

(b) are any nutrients affected by treatment of the feed e.g. cooking destroys vitamins; proprionic acid treatment while preserving some nutrients, increases vitamin E requirement; and rolling, cracking or crushing will eventually reduce vitamin levels as these become oxidised.

(c)   whether the type of diet may reduce the horse's capacity to synthesise its own B vitamins, e.g. a high performance horse on a low forage diet *may* not be producing adequate supplies of B vitamins,

(d)   whether the horse's requirements are increased by its level of performance (work, breeding or growth). Requirements of salt are obviously increased, and I would expect a high performance horse to have a salt lick *plus* 25 to 100 g (1 to 4 oz) of salt added to the diet. It also seems likely that the high performance horse has an increased requirement for B vitamins, especially on a carbohydrate-enriched diet (i.e. one rich in cereals).

I generally give a supplement to high performance horses, especially on a high-cereal diet. They will probably be given salt, calcium (unless the diet contains significant amounts of sugar beet or dried alfalfa cubes which are rich in calcium) and a good quality vitamin/mineral/amino acid supplement. Such a product would not necessarily be the one with the longest list of ingredients, or with the longest quantities of individual ingredients. I want a balanced product with no gimmicks at an economic price. A few pence a day is not much as an insurance when feeding a high performance horse into which a great deal of time, effort and money may have been invested. The performance horse may be perfectly well without a supplement, but may not thrive or perform at peak levels. Very cheap supplements often contain nutrients in an unavailable form and can be a waste of money.

For the stabled horse in light to medium work, a less complex supplement may be required. Alternatively, a trace mineralised salt lick, calcium or sugar beet/dried alfalfa and possibly cod liver oil may be all that is needed. In fact, if the diet is composed of a balanced selection of feedstuffs and especially if cereals are balanced with non-cereals, plus a salt lick, no further supplement should be required.

However, it should be borne in mind that after certain illnesses, for perhaps a few weeks or even for the rest of the horse's life, its ability to utilise certain nutrients may be altered and its feed requirements changed. Likewise, after severe worm damage to the gut problems may arise, and also if the horse has poor teeth.

The requirements of the elderly horse for supplementation are also frequently neglected, which is probably why so many elderly horses look moth-eaten and miserable. I have seen many retired elderly horses about to be put down for various reasons, including continuous scouring and general poor health, who with their diet adjusted to a more easily digested form, and perhaps soaked if teeth are a problem, and with perhaps inclusion of probiotics and other forms of dietary manipulation, have not only gone on to lead a happy and healthy life for several years, but have in a number of cases gone back into quite hard work. If an elderly horse appears to be grinding to a halt under your present system of management, consider adjusting that management to take into account the problems of old age before writing off your old friend for good.

(5)   Broodmares and youngstock almost certainly require salt, calcium and phosphorus, and benefit from a good broad spectrum vitamin/ mineral supplement and a good quality amino acid source. The requirements of the broodmare are particularly important prior to and approximately 18 to 30 days after service, for the last three months of pregnancy, and during lactation particularly in the first three months. Supplementation of young foals is often neglected, and those fed solely on mare's milk are frequently anaemic (think of veal calves).

Adequate and balanced nutrition early on, with careful steps taken to avoid such problems as foal scours, including the use of probiotics immediately after birth, are likely to set the potential performance horse up for a long and successful competitive life. Neglect at this stage (including the unborn foal) can do initially invisible, but potentially permanent, damage to heart, lungs, and the digestive system not to mention the skeleton. Such damage may not manifest itself until well into the horse's competitive career, particularly as it strives for absolute peak performance or as it becomes older. Alternatively, the youngster's career may end before it starts, as it fails to train on due to injury. This is especially true of two-year-old racehorses, but they are by no means unique.

Again, sugar beet and dried alfalfa are useful vitamin and mineral sources. Both have a particularly important role on the stud, as they are good sources of calcium, phosphorus, sodium, potassium, various vitamins including beta-carotene and folic acid – which are of particular importance to the broodmare – and trace elements including copper, a deficiency of which may well be implicated in joint problems and other metabolic bone disorders in youngstock. They are also a useful source of protein and energy for growth, pregnancy and lactation, as well as providing digestible fibre.

(6)   If one scoop of supplement is good, two scoops are not necessarily twice as good. Follow the feeding instructions and if possible feed by bodyweight. *Do not* feed more than one broad-spectrum supplement at a time. Also, be wary of feeding a supplement with compound cubes or coarse mixes (sweetfeeds) which have already been supplemented, although in some cases judicious additional supplementation may well

be beneficial. Conversely, diluting a supplemented compound with bran, oats or other ingredients will also dilute its supplement so you may need to add a *proportionate* dose of a *compatible* proprietory supplement. Do not pour hot water on to a feed, particularly after the supplement has been added, as you will destroy the vitamins.

Giving more than the recommended rate of a supplement can be counter-productive. For example, many people are obsessed by feeding high iron levels to 'raise the blood count'. You *cannot* raise the blood count above the *normal* for a horse by giving extra iron. You are more likely to make the horse dull and lethargic.

Manipulation of vitamin levels in the diet occasionally appears to benefit some horses, e.g. mega-doses of vitamin E, thiamine, folic acid or biotin, and possibly vitamin C, but these should only be used with expert professional (vet or *qualified* nutritionist) guidance in specific circumstances. Biotin is not a cure-all, *per se*, for every hoof problem, nor vitamin E or thiamine for nervousness, nor folic acid for anaemia. They all have their role to play but should be used in a balanced fashion.

(7)   Heat, air and moisture can all damage feed supplements, so store in a cool, dry place and *always* re-seal the container. If you have a very large container, or one that is difficult to open and close, decant some into a clean, dry, labelled ice-cream tub or smaller *correctly labelled* supplement bucket. Avoid buying supplements that have been stored in a shop window or next to hot lights or radiators. Also ensure that they are not past their sell-by or use-by date. If you are cooking feed such as a mash, add the supplement *after* it is cooled. Do not buy more than you can use in three months at the most; the product will deteriorate. If you have a supplement left from a previous year, the minerals will still be there but the vitamins will have deteriorated, and it will probably do your roses more good than your horses!

(8)   *Vitamin injections* Except in veterinary emergencies, or in the case of broodmares turned on to the mountain and moorland and unhandled for months on end, use of injections as a means of supplying vitamins is quite nonsensical. A shot of B_{12} before an event will not 'raise the blood count' unless the animal is deficient in B_{12}; if this is the case then the horse is not fit to compete and you should get your diets right to eliminate the problem. If is in fact more likely that flooding the system with a nutrient that it is not geared up or trained to metabolise, is more likely to reduce performance than enhance it. Steer well clear of vets and trainers who give vitamin shots habitually; there is something seriously wrong with their stable management and feeding if this is necessary, and unnecessary expense and stress to the horse result if it is not. Oddly enough, horses with problems of anaemia are more likely to respond to correction of the folic acid, and possibly even biotin, levels,

than B_{12} which is in fact rarely a problem! Unfortunately, even after blood-testing, the wrong vitamins and/or minerals are frequently prescribed.

Feedstuffs

Before looking at the specifics of ration formulation, and feed-related health problems in the performance horse, it is worthwhile discussing the attributes of particular feedstuffs and considerations which should be taken into account when using them.

Assessing the nutritional value and quality of feedstuffs

The *only* way in which you can ascertain the feeding value, or chemical analysis (nutrient content), of a feedstuff is to have it analysed in greater or lesser detail, and unless you are buying compound feeds with known feed value, for the performance horse this is most certainly a very worthwhile expenditure. Some idea of whether feedstuffs are as good as you expect them to be may be obtained from monitoring your horse's bodyweight, condition and performance, but this is necessarily an historical method, as you will not know something is wrong until after it has happened. You may then waste valuable training and competing time bringing the horse back to peak.

However, you *can* make an informed guess about certain aspects of feed quality, and you can certainly judge by its physical appearance whether it is clean and in a suitable condition to feed to a certain extent, and its probable palatability by examining it carefully with regard to appearance, smell and texture, and how 'clean' it is.

The nutritional value of any feedstuff will be affected by:

(1)   The soil in which it is grown.
(2)   Type and quantity of fertiliser application, and control of pests and diseases in the growing crop.
(3)   The standard of farming.
(4)   Weather conditions during the growing season *and* when the crop is harvested.
(5)   Storage conditions.

Physical quality can to a great extent be judged by eye, nose and feel. Poor quality feed should never be bought and feed which has deteriorated in store should not be used.

Both forages and grain are now often treated with preservatives, a number of which are perfectly acceptable for use on horse feed and are used to prevent formation of undesirable moulds and bacteria. A number of these products are based on natural materials which are found in the digestive system of the horse, unlike many of the unnatural preservatives used in foodstuffs for humans, whose long-term effects over the longer life of the human are a relatively unknown quantity. The object of these preservatives is to prevent the formation and proliferation of undesirable moulds and bacteria, and to reduce deterioration due to moisture and oxidation. Feedstuffs treated with such materials as proprionic acid will have a decreased vitamin E content, but the over-all feed value will be well preserved. With such treated feedstuffs, additional vitamin E in the diet may be advisable (see above).

However, this slight disadvantage will be greatly outweighed by the loss of all vitamins and soluble nutrients in a badly preserved and stored feed sample.

Feedstuffs are generally divided into forages and concentrates. The concentrates may be home-mixed using 'straights' or compounded by a manufacturer (nuts/cubes/pellets/course mixes (sweetfeeds)), or a home-mixed blend of the two. The 'straights' may be divided into cereal concentrates and non-cereal concentrates, and ideally to achieve a balanced ration a mixture of materials from the two groups is necessary.

Forage

The forage includes bulky feeds such as fresh grazed herbage, hay, feeding straw, silage, tower hayage, moist vacuum-packed forage (MVPF) – either fermented (e.g. Horsehage, Propack) or non-fermented (Hygrass) – and silage (pickled grass!). Chaff or chop may also be considered part of the forage ration, as can treated nutritionally improved straw (NIS) cubes (e.g. Viton), dried grass, and dried alfalfa (lucerne), although the last two are more usually considered with concentrates.

Hay

Hay is dried forage, usually grasses and legumes, cut at a relatively mature stage so that although the yield may be high, maturity of the plant means that much of the nutrient content is unavailable as it is trapped by the woody fibre. This is in comparison to grazed grass, when it is fresh, silage and hayage which are cut at a much less mature stage, and also grass meal and cubes and alfalfa meal and cubes (lucerne) which are also cut at a highly nutritious stage, but differ from fresh herbage and silages in that they are then dried down so that they are as dry as, if not drier than, hay. This has the effect of considerably concentrating the nutrients.

Hay should be sweet-smelling, crisp to touch and of a good green to golden colour. There should be no patches of visible mould or dust. It is essential to check the centre of the bale for such signs. To obtain the best results, hay should be cut before the grass is in full flower. This is unfortunately dependent on the weather unless the crop is to be barn-dried (see below).

Hay which has been mow-burnt (rained on and then dried again before baling) will be sweet-smelling and a varying shade of brown, and this may also occur if the hay is baled before the sap in the grass has dried, leading to overheating of the bales sometimes to the extent that the stack will catch fire. Horses will often relish *slightly* mow-burnt hay for its sweet taste, but its nutritional value has been spoilt.

Baling the hay after it has rained and before it has been thoroughly dried will result in a white and mouldy centre to the bale, although the outer surface may often smell and feel of good quality. Rain-washed hay will lose its colour and soluble nutrients. Colour and nutrients can also be bleached out by too much sun, the resultant hay usually being pale yellow. There will be less damage (nutrient loss) if hay is rained-on *immediately* after cutting, then if it has partially dried.

Barn-dried hay is usually of superior feeding quality as its production is less dependent on weather conditions, and this should of course be taken into account when balancing the ration. In fact, in most years, particularly in the UK, barn-dried hay is probably the product of choice for performance horses, as there is rarely a sufficient quantity of traditionally cured hay of the best feed value available on the market. However, bran-dried hay can be rather dusty, and some loss of leaf material may occur as it is dried.

When choosing hay, it is worth considering that the majority of the available nutrients are in the leaf material and *not* the stems, which basically provide roughage, and they are a substrate for digestive micro-organisms to act upon. Although this roughage is essential, if one has a horse with a limited appetite it makes sense to use hay of the highest possible nutritional value. However, legume hays, which can in fact be of a very high feed value, actually tend to contain too much protein for mature performance horses, and are also difficult to cure without problems of mouldiness because the stems are so thick, which means that the stems and the leaves dry at a very different rate. This is also a problem with mixed grass and legume hays. Generally for performance horses, a 'ley' hay of ryegrasses or timothy, or a *good quality* leafy meadow hay, are the preferred products. Meadow hays may also include beneficial herbs, but particular care should be taken to ensure that no potentially poisonous plants are present, such as ragwort, mare's tails or bracken.

Two year old hay is often sold as 'horse hay'. It should be noted that it is likely to be worthless in terms of vitamin content, and will almost certainly contain moulds which may be invisible to the naked eye and inevitably a certain level of dust. It is generally preferable to choose one of the other forages mentioned below, rather than accept 'old' hay. Such 'horse hay' is probably just a useful way for hay merchants to unload unsold and unwanted hay to unsuspecting horse owners!

Although dust can cause coughing, the major problem is the presence of mould spores which can actually cause allergy problems either on their own, or as an aftermath of other respiratory problems such as colds and influenza. Such problems, including chronic obstructive pulmonary disease, are discussed below, but it is obviously not a good idea to subject a valuable high performance horse to an unnecessary respiratory challenge when the health and action of the lungs is of such vital importance to the performance of that horse. Soaking hay for $1\frac{1}{2}$ to 4 hours will in fact swell the mould spores so that they cannot reach the site in the lungs where they cause the allergic reaction, making them safer for both horses and humans, but this should not be used as an excuse to feed inferior hay. If this method is practised, it is important that the water is changed regularly and that the hay is fed while it is still wet, otherwise the spores may well shrink again. It should also be noted that there is almost certainly a loss of soluble nutrients, including vitamins, minerals and sugars (energy) from the hay, which must be compensated for in the rest of the diet, although the actual amount of this loss has not been quantified as yet. However, the better quality the hay in the first place, the greater the loss of nutrient value that is likely to occur on soaking it.

New-crop hay should not be fed if possible until it is a few weeks old, as the hay is still alive and various life processes are still going on. However, if this is not possible, spread it out in an empty stable or barn to 'crisp' before feeding, and *always* mix new crop with old material which a horse is used to, i.e. make no sudden changes in feeding. If necessary, feed a probiotic to help with this transition.

Make sure to use safe hay-feeding equipment. Tie hay nets so they will be above the level of the top of the horse's leg when empty. It should not be necessary to mention this in a book addressed to people with high performance horses, but it is quite astonishing how many valuable competitive horses and youngstock are injured every year due to getting a foot caught in a hay net or other feeding equipment. An ideal method for feeding hay to stabled horses – which avoids the problem of hay seeds falling in the eyes as occurs with hay racks, and wastage when feeding on the floor – is to use a 'hay corner' type of feeder.

Ensure horses using field racks cannot get a foot caught if the rack legs cross over as part of their construction, or cannot bang their heads in a circular feeder.

Tower hayage

Hayage, which is cut before grass for hay and is a moister product, can be fed to horses kept on farms with a tower silo, but the main disadvantage is that it cannot easily be sampled for laboratory analysis before use. This material is often called Haylage, which is in fact the brand name of hayage produced in *Howard Harvestore* towers.

Moist vacuum-packed forage (MVPF)

These are of two kinds: fermented and non-fermented. The fermented products can vary in feed value somewhat, and the vacuum must be maintained in the bag to prevent spoilage. It is therefore essential that the bags are not punctured or gnawed by rodents. Although such products can be exceedingly useful for horses with respiratory problems, they tend to have a very high protein content, which applies especially to the lucerne/alfalfa types, but also includes many of the grass ones. This has, in fact, been found to cause a number of problems with horses, apart from taking the over-all protein content of the diet too high for performance horses, and very careful consideration should be given before selecting such a product as the main forage source for the performance horse. Some of the more enlightened manufacturers are now marketing a lower protein product, although they are aiming this at ponies rather than performance horse in their marketing. Do not let this put you off buying it for your performance horse; they are merely pandering to the ill-informed horseowner's quest for 'more protein' and it has nothing to do with the suitability of the product. The possible problems which might be incurred from overfeeding protein have been outlined earlier, and physiotherapists and a number of other experts have noted an above-average number of horses suffering from tying-up when fed large amounts of high protein MVPs, (probably in fact due to the concurrent high levels of soluble carbohydrate). In any case, as they are low in fibre and tend to be eaten quickly, although they have a very high feeding value which quickly satisfies the animals nutritional requirements, many horses tend to get bored and feel unsatisfied, so it is a good idea to feed another dust-free forage to 'dilute' the bagged forage. A useful example would be a molassed chaff if it is essential that it be dust-free.

The other type of moist package forage, which may or may not be vacuum packed but is usually packaged in some sort of plastic bag, is the non-fermented material. This tends to be of a more consistent feed value and a lower protein content, which I find ideal for performance horses as it combines the benefits of reduced 'respiratory challenge' of moulds and dust, which accrue from using a moist forage, without the potential disadvantages of excessive protein levels. Avoiding sub-clinical respiratory stress is one way in which you can ensure that your performance horse has the best possible opportunity to achieve its maximum potential.

In general, both types of packaged moist forage should be fed within four days of opening in winter, and two days of opening in hot weather.

All these products are of high feeding value, and it is often possible to reduce concentrate feeds somewhat if they are used, but it is a good idea, as I have mentioned above, to find some other way of satisfying the horse's requirement for bulk. You should also be aware that if you are reducing the total feed intake, you may also be reducing the intake of vitamins and minerals and this should be taken into account.

Silage

This is effectively 'pickled grass' and has been made since Roman times. Silage is cut much earlier than grass for hay, and at a more nutritious stage, although it is much wetter. It is important that the acidity (pH) is as low as possible to prevent spoilage, and that air is effectively excluded while it is made and stored. Wilted silage, i.e. silage which has been wilted after cutting in the field before collecting, is usually drier and of a higher feed value than non-wilted. Additives may be used to help preserve the crop, and trials have shown that proprionic acid ones are safe for horses if used with care, and provided the vitamin E level in the diet is adequate. Some of the newer additives which have recently come on to the market, including biological ones that are related to probiotics, may be even more suited to silage destined for horse feeding.

Silage may be made in clamps which can either be cut and carted to the horse, or eaten dried off a self-feed face. If the horses are self-feeding, care should be taken that they do not over-eat, such as by restricting access, and if they are yarded with cattle that the horse does not prevent the cattle from eating! Horses and ponies can get very possessive about silage and find it extremely palatable once they are used to it.

With big-baled silage, which tends to be drier, it is again essential that air is excluded and the bags protected from mechanical damage or damage by vermin. However, because it is harder than in a clamp to exclude all the air, it is probably advisable always to use a preservative. If in doubt, have the material analysed and check that the pH (acidity) is below 5.5, so that diseases such as botulism, which have resulted in the death of horses fed unpreserved silage in the past, can be avoided. Provided the pH is below 5.5 throughout the clamp or bales, the botulism organism cannot survive in a state in which it can produce the toxins causing the disease. Therefore clamp silage must be evenly compacted, and bales carefully made, with preservatives evenly applied, to avoid pockets of higher pH.

In any event, if you buy forage from a farmer, it is quite likely that he will have it analysed and tell you the exact feed value and pH if appropriate. It is to be hoped that forage merchants will increasingly follow suit and price their products according to the analysis. It is in the interest of horse owners to be prepared to pay a premium for forages which are *known* to be of a good feed value, whereas at present many so-called good hays and so forth, while they might be clean, are on analysis of a very low nutritional value and considerably overpriced.

Introduce silage gradually, like any new feed. Many horses find it unpalatable at first, but once they are used to it they may be reluctant to go back to hay. If they have a mix of hay and silage, they will usually eat the silage first.

As silage is a very moist material, in most cases it is a good idea to 'dilute' it with hay or feeding straw (oat or barley), or chaff, or in the case of broken-winded horses, NIS straw cubes, grass or alfalfa cubes, or molassed chaff.

Silage may be of grass, grass and clover, oat and vetch, and even whole-crop cereals including maize, or brewers' grains. All can safely be fed to horses *provided* they are introduced carefully *and* are part of a balanced diet.

Straw, NIS straw cubes

Straw can be a useful feed for horses provided it is free of visible moulds and dust, although for the performance horse it is most likely to be used to provide a source of additional roughage, perhaps as chaff, and a forage source when the horse is not actually working. It is important that it is free from visible moulds and dust.

Oat straw from spring grown oats is preferable as it has a higher feeding value, and in fact is quite often better than some so-called horse hays that appear on the market; barley straw may also be used provided it is not full of awns. Wheat straw is not generally fed on its own, although it may be used in compound cubes to increase the fibre level and 'dilute' the ingredients if they are too rich. Some horse owners may complain if they see straw listed as an ingredient in cubes, but it is in fact quite often necessary to dilute cubes in the interest of good feeding practice.

NIS or nutritionally improved straw cubes (e.g. Viton), are also a useful horse feed, particularly for children's ponies and resting horses, and they are most likely to be fed to performance horses either as an ingredient of cubes – in which case the compounder will re-grind them and mix them with the other ingredients – or as one of the ingredients in a coarse mixture. Basically they are made of ground straw which has been treated to release the nutrients ground up in the fibre of the straw so that the horse can digest them. Some types also contain urea to increase the crude protein levels. Urea *can* be fed to horses *provided* it is carefully introduced – in fact it is safer for horses than cattle but *should not* be overfed or rapidly introduced. If it is being used, it is also important to ensure that the horse is getting adequate supplies of the limiting amino acids (see above).

Dried grass, dried alfalfa/lucerne, molassed alfalfa chaff

Available as meal, cubes, molassed chaff, and in some areas wafers, these are highly nutritious and if used as a forage source, usually need 'diluting' with chaff. Available in various grades, the meals are sometimes more palatable, though dustier, than cubes, but cubes are usually accepted if they are *lightly* soaked before feeding at first, this being phased out once the horses are eating them.

These materials, when diluted, form a useful alternative forage for horses with respiratory problems or when the usual forage sources are of poor quality or in short supply, and they are also extremely useful when mixed with the concentrate ration for balancing cereals, as they tend to balance out a number of vitamin and mineral deficiencies in cereals while providing protein of a reasonable quality and a good source of energy. It is a good idea to use a supplier who specialises in the horse market, as they tend to take more care in the manufacture of the product, avoiding overheating which may reduce the nutritional value and cause palatability problems; a number now produce cubes and pellets in sizes specifically suited to horse consumption. Some imported products are of poor or variable quality.

Both dried grass and dried alfalfa cubes are often found incorporated both as an ingredient in compound horse feeds which have been cubed, and as a loose ingredient in coarse mixes. They are especially useful for feeding to breedingstock because of their high beta-carotene and folic acid levels, and the alfalfa is a very good source of calcium and has the added advantage that very little nitrate fertiliser is used in its production. Youngstock will also benefit from the high levels of copper and other trace elements. In fact I would go so far as to suggest that there is a place for good quality alfalfa cubes, either as a forage supplement or in the concentrates in the diets, on most stud farms at some time of the year if not all the time.

Grass cubes and alfalfa cubes can both be fed on free access out of doors when grazing is of poor quality, to top up the feeding value. Both can also be used with sugar beet to make a nutritious mash which is infinitely more beneficial than an indigestible, unbalanced bran mash, and may be particularly useful for convalescent horses and broodmares after foaling, when a bran mash which is short of calcium could actually be detrimental.

Concentrates (hard feed, corn feed)

Concentrates are hard feed providing a more concentrated energy (mainly starch) source for horses in hard work, or in cold weather, or with impaired digestion (e.g. some elderly horses) or with a limited appetite, (finicky feeders). For the high performance horse, even on good grazing or forage, some form of concentrate feeding will almost certainly be necessary. This is because concentrate feeds contain less fibre than forage feeds, and while a certain amount of fibre is highly desirable, when the horse's nutrient requirements increase, particularly the energy requirements, the nutrients in forages are 'padded out' to too great a degree to allow the horse, which has a limited appetite, to obtain sufficient energy within the amount of feed (dry matter) it can reasonably eat. Also, although the forage level fed to the performance horse is in many stables much too limited – leading to various digestive and temperament problems and other metabolic disorders including filled legs – even if the horse's appetite allowed it, it would not be desirable for the high performance horse to eat too much bulk as this would spend a considerable time in the digestive system and may press against the heart and lungs thus impairing their performance.

The most commonly used concentrate feeds for horses are cereals, i.e. oats, barley, maize (corn), wheat products (micronized wheat, breadmeal, wheatbran, wheet feed), sorghum (milo), various rice products, and even millet. Which cereal is used will depend to a great extent on which part of the world you are in, but the most widely-fed cereal to horses worldwide is probably maize (corn), although some would argue that sorghum way lay claim to this. However, as far as performance horses are concerned, it is probably correct to say that maize is the most widely-fed, with oats coming a close second in the western hemisphere.

Non-cereal concentrates include sugar beet feed, dried grass or alfalfa (discussed under forages above), legumes and pulses such as soya, peas and beans, by-products which are mainly included in compound feeds, including oil meals and cakes such as palm kernel meal, locust bean meal, cotton seed cake, ground nut cake, rape seed and canola meal, linseed cake, soya bean meal (all of which are the meals and cakes left after various plant oils have been extracted) and other materials such as dried apple pomace which is quite widely used in some areas, along with linseed, vegetable oils, tallow, meat and bone meal, and fish meal.

In general, healthy, mature horses on reasonable quality forage do not require the high protein soya, peas, beans, linseed, meat and bone meal or fish meal although these may be necessary for broodmares in late pregnancy and early lactation, and youngstock. Specific amino acid supplementation combined with a lower crude protein diet is probably more appropriate to the horse in hard work.

Many of these concentrates are processed in some way, usually in an attempt to make them more digestible, or in the case of whole (full fat) soya or linseed, rendering them safe to feed. They may be rolled, flaked, micronised (gelatinised) extruded or boiled, and in future may also be irradiated, though there are a number of questions to be answered about the safety of this technique.

Rolling, to crack the seed coat and let in the digestive juices, is necessary for barley but not for oats or maize which can be fed whole. Any benefits from rolling may be lost as rolled cereals rapidly deteriorate in feed value. Remember if you have a whole oat and plant it, it will grow; it is still alive. A rolled oat is dead and dead things decay, letting in mould which can cause allergies or produce mycotoxins, and air which destroys vitamins. However, very young or very elderly horses may have difficulty in chewing whole oats or maize. Never buy more flaked, rolled, bruised or crushed cereals than you can use in two weeks, and always buy them freshly rolled, or in larger yards consider rolling them on the premises every day or so.

Micronising (gelatinising) is a way of cooking feeds rather like popcorn and they are then rolled before feeding. In general, it increases feed value and may increase digestibility by 3 to 20%, so micronised feed should never be fed weight for weight with the same material non-micronised. It is important that they are fed as part of a balanced diet. They may be particularly useful for finicky feeders where it is difficult to get enough feed into them, or elderly horses or any animal with impared digestibility or appetite.

Extruded feeds are cooked to a porridge and flash dried, and sometimes processed into particular shapes. They may be individual feed ingredients, or a mixed feed to form a new way of producing a compound as an alternative to pelleting. We are likely to see a lot more of them in the horse market in the future (e.g. Horse Pearls in the USA). Again, this process tends to increase the digestibility of the ingredients, but they also have the advantage that they are eaten more slowly than other concentrates, thus resulting in fewer digestive upsets and problems with boredom. They may be particularly useful if concentrates are being fed on a free-access basis in yards or paddocks, to prevent greedy animals bolting their feed.

Both micronising and extrusion render full-fat soya safe to feed, and whole wheat can also be fed in this way. Both processes may affect the vitamin levels during the cooking process (continued research is needed to establish the precise details) and can render amino acids, including lysine, more available.

Boiling cereals, e.g. barley, is generally a waste of time. There is little increase in digestibility, and if boiled feed is not given at every feed it constitutes a 'sudden change in feeding', because boiling changes some of the constituents. Barley can more easily be fed rolled and is preferable in this form. Think how indigestible porridge can be before you inflict boiled barley on a tired or sick horse.

Cereal concentrates

Oats

A favoured feed for horses, oat grains should be large, plump, dry and clean, and of even size in a sample, which will tend to mean that they have dried evenly and there is less likelihood of spoiled and mouldy grain. Clipped oats have a lower fibre content, because some of the husks have been removed, but they are only economical if the value of the digestible energy content is raised by more than the cost of the clipping. Imported oats are usually of good quality but barely justify the expense and may be contaminated in transit with 'prohibited substances' which could cause problems for the performance horse. If you cannot easily obtain a good sample of nice, clean, heavy oats, you should consider using an alternative such as a compound, or rolled barley, or a combination of other concentrates.

Oats are not 'God's gift to horses', although because they are slightly diluted compared with other cereals because of their high fibre content, they tend to be more 'idiot proof' than other cereals. However, they can tend to have a 'heating' effect on some horses which is possibly an allergic response to a protein unique to oats, or a combination of proteins. It is dangerous and counter-productive to persist in feeding oats to a horse that becomes temperamental and hyper-active when they are fed, as it wastes the horse's and the rider's energy, and the horse will tend to concentrate less on the job in hand, which could lead to poor performance ane even accidents. Feeding an additive containing sodium montmerrillonite (e.g. Thrive), can help to alleviate this effect; probably it 'mops up' toxins produced due to this allergy (in fact more correctly referred to as a *feed intolerance*), but if you have a horse with this type of problem you should seriously consider using an alternative energy source.

Oats can be fed whole, cracked, cut, lightly rolled, micronised or extruded. While they are a good source of energy in the form of starch, and have particularly digestible fibre as cereals go, they are very low in amino acid lysine and calcium, with a poor calcium to phosphorus ratio, and contain phytate which will lock up calcium in the rest of the diet. The higher oil content than barley means that oats spoil (go rancid) faster when rolled than barley. The pronouncements by various horse owners in the past that horses must have oats when they are in fast work, and cannot do fast work on barley and other cereals, is merely an indication that those horse owners were unable to produce a balanced ration, and has nothing whatsoever to do with any special qualities which might be ascribed to oats.

Barley

Barley can be fed cracked, rolled, cut, steam-flaked, micronised, extruded or boiled but *not whole*. It is preferred by many horse owners to oats because it is much easier to buy a good sample of barley, as more is grown than oats, and it tends to be less 'heating'. Barley has a slightly higher digestible energy content than oats, so should not be substituted on a weight by weight basis, but should be incorporated into a balanced diet. The fibrous husk is much harder and less digestible than in oats, which is why barley cannot be fed whole; the superstition that barley can cause liver or kidney problems is an old wives' tale, for which there is no evidence whatsoever looking back in records and scientific trials for many hundreds of years. Again, as a cereal, barley is low in lysine, and it has a poor calcium content and a poor calcium to phosphorus ratio, and because of its lower digestible fibre content it is probably a good idea to break-up the concentrate ration with chaff, dried alfalfa or sugar beet. This is a good idea in any case, even with oats, but is perhaps more important with barley, wheat and breadmeal and maize, which have increasingly low levels of fibre.

Wheat

Wheat is not usually fed untreated as it tends to form a glutinous mass in the stomach which can cause colic. However, it has been widely used particularly for cavalry horses, and if used it is a good idea to feed the ration well-mixed with chaff to break it up.

Wheat is increasingly available both micronised or extruded, hence it can safely be fed, preferably with chaff. Higher in protein and energy than oats and barley, it should be introduced with care and the ration balanced appropriately. As with all cereals it is low in calcium and the calcium to phosphorus ratio is poor.

Wheat products

(1) *Wheatbran* As flour mills have become more efficient at extracting the flour, bran has diminished in feed value over the years. This is one reason why strict adherance to traditional feeding methods will not achieve the same results that it did in the past, and modification of the diets is necessary on an informed basis.

Wheatbran is a source of very indigestible fibre and unfortunately has a *very* poor calcium:phosphorus ratio, and contains particularly high levels of phytin which can lock-up calcium from the diet making it a very unbalanced feed source. For this reason, I prefer not to feed it to broodmares and youngstock, and consider chaff a much better balanced and more desirable roughage source; even this may not be necessary if the diet contains reasonable levels of grass/alfalfa meal/cubes and/or sugar beet.

Because of bran's highly fibrous nature, bran mashes are highly indigestible and should not be necessary if the over-all diet is balanced and in-keeping with the level of work. They are also very unbalanced and unless fed at each feed constitute an undesirable 'sudden change in feeding'. For sick horses, or those laid off due to snow, increase the forage ration, and if you are already feeding dried grass/alfalfa and/or sugar beet, you can make a nutritious, palatable (revolting-looking) mash from these. For sick horses in particular, a bran mash, rather than being an aid to recovery, is in many cases at the very least likely to prolong the road to recovery. It is rather like whipping the nutritional carpet out from under the horse's feet, just when the sickened or tired horse most needs it. If you feel you *must* feed a bran mash, make sure that you add 50 g of limestone for each kg of bran, to rebalance the calcium levels, and that you add a suitable vitamin/mineral supplement *after* the mash has cooled, so that the heat does not destroy the vitamins.

If horses are expected to go back to work after a rest-day or bad weather, give a little of each of the other working-ration ingredients at each feed to keep the appropriate digestive micro-organisms and enzymes ticking over.

For normal working horses, on a rest-day, if for example you are normally feeding three feeds per day, cut out the *amount* of one feed but *do not* cut out a feed entirely – spread the remainder over the three feeds. You can also increase the forage allowance. For a Sunday rest-day, ideally you would start this 24 hour reduction on the Saturday night's feed, and go back to a normal feed on the Sunday night, though if the horse has worked hard (e.g. hunted) on the Saturday, give a normal feed that night to replenish muscle glycogen.

With regard to broodmares, the common practice of giving a bran mash immediately after foaling is again likely to cause problems in some cases, as this is just the time when the broodmare is in particular need of easily available calcium in her bloodstream. A mashed feed containing her usual ingredients, or if she is used to them a mixture of alfalfa meal/cubes and sugar beet, with her usual vitamin/mineral supplement, will help her to recover rapidly and ensure that the milk produced is of the best possible quality for the foal.

Horses fed too much wheatbran, wheat feed, wheatings, sharps or middlings, without added calcium, may sufer serious, mysterious multi-focal lameness, epiphysitis in youngstock (big knees), bone fractures (including sore shins) and even nutritional secondary hypo-parathyroidism – i.e. Big-head or Miller's disease – giving character-istic fibrous swelling of the progressively de-mineralised bones of the face.

It is also possible that calcium deficiency, for whatever reason, will help to turn an acutely laminitic pony into a chronic sufferer, so a bran mash is the last thing you should give to a pony with laminitis. Starving laminitis-prone horses can also have a similar effect, as the resulting mineral deficiencies can lead to hormonal imbalances which may prolong the laminitis. Bran mashes will also further upset the digestive micro-organisms whose disarray has led to an attack in the first place. As a rule-of-thumb, if you *must* feed bran, and are not giving significant amounts of calcium-rich feeds such as dried alfalfa cubes, alfalfa hay/chaff or sugar beet feed, you will need to add 50 g of limestone per kg of bran for adult horses, and more for youngstock.

(2) *Breadmeal* Breadmeal is marketed in the UK under the proprie-tory name of Baileys No. 1 Meal and Baileys No. 4 Cubes (cubed breadmeal and molasses for palatibility, with some added minerals), and is also popular, particularly in showing circles, in Australia and other parts of the world.

It is an excellent source of 'non-heating' energy, probably because the wheat is cooked. It contains more protein than other cereals and has a higher lysine content. Again, the calcium:phosphorus ratio usually needs balancing, and as it is low in fibre it is usually a good idea to feed it with chaff, dried grass or alfalfa, NIS cubes or sugar beet feed.

It is safe to feed to children's ponies if they require additional digestible energy, as it does not appear to 'hot them up', and at the same time is an excellent concentrated energy source for high performance horses. There is absolutely no reason why a performance horse cannot have breadmeal as its sole cereal-energy source. Although a horse which is psychologically (to humans) 'jumping out of its skin' appears to have a lot of energy, in fact this is often a manifestation of nervous tension (the startle reflex), and may well mean that the horse is not concentrating on the job in hand. It will therefore waste valuable energy in messing about, running backwards at the start, and fighting the rider, who is also wasting energy, which may become particularly crucial when riding cross-country or for long periods in endurance riding. This will have the knock-on effect that the tired rider will further tire the horse. The aim should be to supply energy and other nutrients in a form which will enable the horse to concentrate on the job in hand and utilise the maximum amount of energy in the diet for performance.

Some horses are not keen on the taste of breadmeal, so molassed pellets can be fed to them instead. Breadmeal/cubes is *not* a compound feed which has been balanced, and should be considered as a cereal source along with oats, barley and maize. It cannot be compared in isolation with any form of horse and pony nuts, competition cubes and so on, either nutritionally or on a price basis.

(3) *Maize (corn)* Sometimes fed in the USA on-the-cob, which increases the fibre level and is therefore safer, the grain may be fed whole, steam-flaked, micronised or extruded. For the world-wide horse population as a whole, it probably vies with sorghum as the most widely fed cereal.

Maize contains more digestible energy than either oats or barley, and is lower in fibre so it should be introduced very gradually, and preferably fed mixed with a fibre source such as chaff. Many people misunderstanding the concept of balanced rations, say that maize puts weight on. It will only do this if it is fed on a weight for weight basis with lower energy feedstuffs such as oats or barley. If the total ration is formulated to contain the same amount of digestible energy (i.e. is isoenergetic) as an oat or barley-based diet, it will not cause any additional weight gain.

Some varieties of maize contain more lysine than other cereals, but again the calcium and calcium:phosphorus levels are poor. However, it is a very good source of concentrated (starch) energy.

(4) *Sorghum (milo)* Not widely available in the UK, except as an

ingredient for concentrates, but fed as an ingredient of home mixed rations in various parts of the world, sorghum can certainly be included in the diets of performance horses. Its feeding characteristics are similar to those of maize.

Non-cereal concentrates

Molassed sugar beet feed

A very under-utilised feed in the horse world, molassed sugar beet feed is often only used to 'damp the feeds', when in fact it can be used as a significant digestible energy source. It is particularly useful for competition horses as the molasses give an immediate release of energy, while the digestible fibre acts as a slow-release energy source, which may be especially important for endurance horses and eventers.

Molassed sugar beet feed is rich in salt (sodium) and potassium and is an excellent source of calcium, apart from the physical advantages of damping down the ration. The supply of water to the performance horse is important, and incorporation of a reasonable level into the concentrate feed in this way will help prevent the problems of dehydration. At normal feeding levels, soaked sugar beet will not cause problems due to bulkiness.

Up to 2.5 kg (5½ lbs) per day may be fed, especially if there is a shortage of good forage, although for horses the usual maximum level is 1.5 kg per day (unsoaked weight). The shred or pulp should be soaked in *twice its weight* of cold water for *12 to 18 hours* before feeding; the nuts must be soaked for *24 hours* in *three times their weight* of *cold* water. Where sugar beet is used as a significant source of digestible energy in the diet of the performance horse, it may be noted that the droppings are smaller. This is perfectly all right, and is simply because the fibre is more digestible than in most other feedstuffs given to horses, so while the horse is gaining the benefit from the physical qualities of the fibre as it passes through the gut, it is also able to obtain nutrients from the fibre during its passage. However, this means that there is less material left at the end to form the droppings.

Do not use hot water to soak sugar beet pulp or nuts as the destruction of nutrients, and even dangerous fermentation, may result. The use of hot water *does not* speed up soaking time. Likewise do not soak more than you can use in one day, especially in hot weather. In freezing weather, if leaving beet to soak, you should attempt to prevent it from freezing, otherwise incomplete water absorption may occur.

Do feed any spare liquid as it will contain soluble nutrients and is very nutritious. It will also help to make the ration more palatable.

As has been mentioned above, when making up a ration based on cereals it is a good idea to include some molassed sugar beet feed and/or dried alfalfa to improve protein quality and calcium levels, and dried grass or chaff to 'keep the ration open' and maintain fibre levels. Chaff may be deducted from the forage amount if you are rationing accurately.

The benefits of the available potassium levels and other salts in sugar beet should not be ignored, and may be particularly useful to horses who are prone to tying-up syndrome.

Soya beans and soya bean meal

Full-fat soya beans cannot be fed to horses in the raw form, as they contain a toxin. However, with the advent of micronisation and extrusion processes, it is now possible to use full-fat soya and it is included in a number of coarse mixes and compounds. Having said this, however, unless the rest of the ingredients are of *very* poor quality indeed, it is unlikely that mature performance horses will benefit to any great extent from the use of full-fat soya, which is expensive and very rich in protein – excessively so for such animals, as other sources of concentrated energy, such as vegetable oils, may be used without the possible disadvantage of drastically raising the crude protein content of the over-all diet. Although soya *is* a good source of lysine and other amino acids, as small quantities are used to avoid over-feeding crude protein, these do not make a significant contribution to the diet and if enough is fed to put the amino acid level right, then the crude protein content of the diet will be too high. I would therefore prefer to use an alternative amino acid source.

Soya bean meal is the by-product which is left after most of the oil has been extracted, so it is lower in energy content than full-fat soya (although still relatively high compared to cereals), but very high in crude protein content.

There is however quite often a case for feeding particularly soya bean meal to broodmares, and particularly to very young animals, as part of the balanced ration, as their crude protein requirements are somewhat higher than the mature horse. Care should be taken to ensure that the diet is balanced, as this is particularly crucial for youngstock. If necessary, expert guidance should be sought from a *qualified* animal nutritionist as it is very easy to push a ration out of balance, or to continue feeding a ration which may be balanced for a 6 month old youngster, but completely wrong once it has reached 9 months or 12 months old.

Having said this, I prefer to use as little soya as possible on the stud, as there are certain anti-nutritional factors in it which *may* (and this is purely informed conjecture at this stage) be one of the reasons why the fertility levels in equine breeding stock are so poor in comparison to other domestic livestock. I therefore look for the bulk of my protein from such materials as dried alfalfa cubes and other amino acids sources, and then if necessary top up with small amounts of soya. I should be more than happy to change this policy if it can be *proven* that the factors mentioned above are not in fact causing any problems.

Linseed and linseed cake (flakes)

Linseed is seed of the flax plant. It contains a fairly high level of rather poor quality protein (i.e it is very deficient in limiting amino acids, including lysine), and is rich in oil and mucilage. The flakes are again the by-product after much of the oil has been extracted. They are best soaked before feeding.

As a protein source it is not very desirable, but the oil can enhance coat condition. However, as linseed *must* be cooked before feeding, it is far easier to obtain the protein from a better-balanced source and feed 25 to 100 ml *(1 to 4 tablespoons) of corn oil* or other vegetable oil per day to enhance coat condition. In fact, purified feed grade linseed-oil may form part or all of this allowance.

Linseed must *never* be fed raw as it may contain hydrogen cyanide (prussic acid), a deadly poison. However, this is destroyed by first soaking the linseed for 24 hours, then boiling vigorously for a couple of minutes and finally simmering for a couple of hours. (A great deal of time and effort for not much benefit!) 225 g (8 oz) of linseed requires around 2 litres (4 pints) of water. Alternatively, it may be covered with water and cooked in a microwave oven for 20 minutes. One enterprising manufacturer is now marketing ready-cooked linseed (Xlint) in the horse market, so if you are particularly keen to use linseed, and can justify it economically, this is perhaps the simplest method.

After cooking, the resulting linseed jelly and tea should be fed, and the tea can be further diluted to make it go further.

Feeding a linseed mash once a week is a 'sudden change in feeding', and therefore undesirable. It should be fed daily or not at all. Many people like to give their horses a change but it must be remembered that horses are not humans and do not have the same priorities when it comes to feeding. The odd Polo mint, carrot or apple is one thing, but major dietary changes such as mashes are quite another.

Salt, limestone, dicalcium phosphate, vitamin/mineral supplement

Try to divide these between each feed for most effective utilisation, but at least feed on a daily basis. Feeding any of these supplements once or twice a week is largely a waste of money, and although the horse will derive some small benefit, it would hardly constitute a balanced rationing programme.

For endurance horses only some competitors have found it beneficial to cut out limestone for five days prior to competition, which is thought to encourage the horse to mobilise its own resources when dietary resources would normally run out over very long distances, and recommence immediately after. I would only expect this to be worthwhile for 75 to 100 mile events. *Do not* cut vitamins, other minerals and salt as these should be given daily right up to the competition.

Other feeds

Supplements such as carrots and apples are a welcome treat to stabled horses. Carrots should be cut lengthways and apples quartered. Mangolds may also be used and are especially useful for horses with a tendency towards vices through boredom, as they can be suspended from the ceiling for the horse to play with. Eggs are not really suitable as they contain avidin which 'locks up' biotin. If you do feed them, do not give more than three per week and feed the shell (crushed) as well.

One material which has not been mentioned is hydroponic cereals (barley grass), an extremely useful source of succulent feed which is suitable for performance horses and may be fed roots and all in the mats in which it is grown, or put through a chaff cutter and added to the concentrate feed. I would like to see consideration given in the future to adding micro-nutrients to the water in which hydroponic cereals are grown, to enhance their feeding value.

Compound feeds

Compound feeds are rations which are manufactured by a feed compounder and are balanced to a greater or lesser extent, depending on the knowledge and back-up facilities of the manufacturer and how reliable he is. They may be in the form of coarse mix (sweetfeeds), or cubes/nuts/pellets which are similar to the coarse mix, but the ingredients are ground and formed into pellets. A new development is formed feeds made up of extruded ingredients; these are already available widely in the USA and are likely to become increasingly available in other parts of the world. Coarse mixes and sweetfeeds do not keep as well as pellets, as their ingredients are more exposed to oxidation by air. They are also more prone to separate out in the sack, and should be carefully mixed to ensure that each feed contains the full range of ingredients.

People often say they do not like compound feeds because they cannot see what is in them, but in fact you cannot see what is in an oat, nutritionally speaking, and unless you are having all your feed ingredients analysed it is far more likely that the compound feeds will be better balanced than the majority of home-mixed rations. This is partly because, even if the home-mixer has a reasonable understanding of a balanced diet, unless ingredients are being analysed he cannot compensate for variations in different batches. For example, one sack of oats may be 6% protein, while the next sack, even of home grown oats, may be 16%! If both are fed at the same rate, fluctuations in performance will be inevitable. Because of his greater facilities the feed manufacturer has the ability to adjust the ingredients in the ration to compensate for variation, or even turn away batches of ingredients that do not match up to the standards he requires. The example of the two different oats may look remarkably similar, so the only way to be really sure would be a laboratory appraisal.

Complete diet cubes

Here the whole diet, forage and concentrates are pelleted together, although in practice they are usually fed with a little chaff (molassed for COPD-affected horses) or long forage (MVPF for COPD horses) to prevent boredom. They may be useful for horses in transit, for competition horses being moved around a lot, and especially for COPD-affected horses; they are however, somewhat inflexible and it may be more appropriate to use a combination of dried grass, dried alfalfa and NIS straw cubes, and molassed chaff for forage, or an MVPF, and the appropriate grade of concentrate cubes for performance or in feeding a COPD horse.

Concentrate cubes/coarse mixes

These are generally formulated to be fed safely along with hay, and diluting them with anything other than chaff or molassed chaff, which has been subtracted from the forage allowance, will unbalance them. Examples are horse and pony, hunter, competition, stud and racehorse cubes (or coarse mixes).

If they are diluted with oats, barley, bran, sugar beet, etc., the carefully balanced vitamins, minerals including calcium, and salt they contain will also be diluted. Diluting compounds is not normally good practice, but the *least* disturbing dilutant is molassed sugar beet feed. Likewise, adding a few cubes to a cereal mix will not balance the ration as many people seem to believe.

Always read the manufacturer's instructions as different brands of the same type have different nutritional densities and so should be fed at different rates. Bear this in mind when evaluating the cost of different brands. Although most brands will contain added vitamins and minerals, their levels may vary considerably from the absolute basic level which the manufacturer can reasonably get away with, up to the maximum expected levels required by performance horses (rare).

Virtually all manufacturers will claim that it is not necessary to add a vitamin/mineral supplement when feeding their product. However, when feeding the high performance horse, there *is* sometimes a case for feeding if not a broad-spectrum supplement possibly specific vitamins and minerals for a specific purpose. However, this should only be done with full knowledge of what is in the proposed supplement, and what is contained in the compound, and you should take qualified expert advice before doing this. Although the staff of some feed manufacturers may be perfectly capable of giving you this advice, be very selective about who you believe and who you do not, and consider consulting an independent nutritonist who is not trying to sell you something. Some veterinary practioners are also sufficiently knowledgeable on the subject of equine nutrition to give this sort of advice, but do not assume that they all are. Check that any adviser calling him or herself a nutritionist is actually qualified specifically as such.

The compound concentrate cubes can be particularly useful for elderly horses with missing or damaged teeth, as they can be fed soaked.

Protein concentrates

Protein concentrates are compounds specially designed to be fed as a cereal balancer. Most contain around 26% crude protein, and for a mature horse using this type of product, 0.5 kg/day with oats is ample (e.g. Natural Animal Feeds Bloodstock Conditioner). Others include Red Mills Bloodstock Conditioner, Ranvet's Amino Plus and Stud Grow, and Horse Health Product's Equalizer. Those recommended for use at 25% of the concentrate ration, if they have a 26% crude protein content, usually give excessive protein levels in the diet.

Protein concentrates are a very useful idea, and it is to be hoped that an 'energy balancer' such as Bloodstock Conditioner, with less emphasis on the protein, will become more widely used. This type of product is usually designed to balance the calcium, phosphorus, vitamins, minerals and possibly salt for the whole ration. Read the manufacturer's instructions for the brand you choose, however, as some may in fact suggest inclusion of a separate vitamin/mineral supplement.

Such products are extremely useful and flexible for performance horses, and they are particularly useful on the stud because in general terms most brands when introduced at a constant level to youngstock, but balanced with increasing amounts of cereals and other ingredients, will ensure a balanced ration throughout the growth period without complicated adjustments to the ration being required. Provided the entire regime is set up initially in the balanced ration, and the quality of the ingredients such as cereals and forages is checked on a regular basis, these products can provide a versatile and reliable means of ensuring optimum nutrition on the stud.

Herbs and other 'natural' supplements

There has been a resurgence of interest in the feeding of various herbs and spices in recent years, some of which certainly have a place in the diet of the performance horse and on the stud.

Comfrey has for many years been popular fed, cut and wilted, on Thoroughbred studs, and is a very useful source of vitamins, minerals and proteins for youngstock; it is also beneficial for mature, and particularly elderly, horses. It is thought to have certain therapeutic effects where digestive and arthritic conditions occur, and from practical observations it has certainly been my experience that this can be the case. I have seen a number of animals who have been condemned to finish their lives on a variety of anti-inflammatory drugs and painkillers, actually coming off these drugs and resuming work when fed on combinations of comfrey and garlic, and would certainly consider using these with a problem horse. However, they are certainly not a cure-all and should be used judiciously. Dried comfrey is also available for winter use, and year-round if you do not grow your own. (How to do this is covered in detail in *Pasture Management for Horses and Ponies* by Gillian McCarthy.)

Garlic Garlic oil and whole plant garlic have also been used as an expectorant, which when fed loosens the mucous and can be most helpful after coughs and colds, and for COPD (chronic obstructive pulmonary disease) horses. There are a number of brands on the market, and many owners have commented to me that they have found the more expensive brands appear to be more effective, and using a cheap product is false economy. I am inclined to think that garlic oil is probably more effective than whole plant garlic. Garlic oil has also been prescribed by doctors in the past to patients with circulatory problems because it helps to keep the blood more 'slippery', and this may well be beneficial to horses with problems where the circulation is affected, including laminitis and navicular disease. Again, this has not been scientifically proven in horses, but many owners are convinced that they have seen an improvement when such products have been used.

An added benefit is that feeding garlic seems to help keep flies away! This may be particularly useful for show animals and dressage horses, and also for any animal prone to sweet itch, or who has an open wound of some sort. Again, I have seen this work in practice but would not necessarily expect it to work for every animal.

Raspberry leaf The only other herb I have used with any regularity is raspberry leaf, usually made into a tea and poured on to the feed or added to the drinking water (if the horse will take it). It is useful for feeding to broodmares for a month or so before foaling, to help relax the muscles and to facilitate an easy parturition. Many human mothers swear by this, and stud managers have remarked that it has been beneficial for mares who are prone to difficult foalings for certain reasons.

Having said this, I would be very reluctant to consider herbs in general as cure-alls and I am also rather concerned that they are often presented as being particularly safe because they are natural. It should be remembered that many drugs are either derived from plants or are synthetic copies of plant materials, and that some herbs contain very concentrated ingredients indeed. They should therefore only be used in an informed fashion and care should be taken when adding them to other feed ingredients with which they may well clash. Some herbal remedies contain the deadliest poisons known to man, so horse owners should beware of a false sense of security. There are many self-styled experts in the herb-law field, many of which gained their experience dealing with humans and are not qualified to prescribe herbs for horses who may metabolise them in a completely different fashion. Many herbs offered for horses have a diuretic action (i.e. they make the horse urinate), and for the performance horse this may be very undesirable as it could lead to dehydration in competition and consequent problems. However, I am fully satisfied that both comfrey and garlic can be fed in reasonably large quantities to the majority of horses with impunity, whether specifically for therapeutic reasons or as part of the balanced ration.

With regard to other 'natural' supplements, many of the above comments apply to such materials as seaweed, wheatgerm and brewer's yeast, and it may, despite what it may say in the manufacturers instructions, be possible to overfeed these materials; they certainly should not be fed as well as a full dose of a broad spectrum vitamin/ mineral supplement, as overdosing will occur. I do not really see them as a viable alternative to a broad spectrum-balanced supplement for the performance horse, as their feeding value may fluctuate considerably depending on the time of year, which is rather unspecific when one is trying to obtain peak performance from a horse.

Always make any transitions from home-mixed rations to compounds, or one brand or batch of compounds to another, gradually. Then wait until you run out before ordering a new lot. If necessary, you can combine types of compounds e.g. Horse and Pony with Racehorse, but check with the manufacturers first.

Neutralisers and buffers

These additives are sometimes used for hores prone to tying-up and acidosis, though it is usually possible to adjust the diet and management so as to render them unnecessary. However, they can be useful if the cause of the problem cannot be identified.

It is most important that alkalis, such as biocarbonate of soda, should *not* be given to long-distance horses, who are more likely to suffer from alkalosis than acidosis.

Sugars

Glucose (dextrose) and sucrose (table sugar) are *not* a suitable instant energy source for performance horses as they are more likely to *lower* blood sugar, contrary to popular belief, although fructose (fruit sugar) and certain carbohydrate polymers (see above) can usefully be given for this purpose. Di-methyl glycine is also used in some products as an energy source for performance horses.

Working out a ration

The following method has been adapted from the American National Research Council method by Jeremy Houghton-Brown and is reproduced, with some updates and amendments by Gillian McCarthy, with his kind permission. Be prepared to sit down with a simple calculator for half an hour. Time spent doing this will save time and money later.

Rationing in nine steps

Step 1

How big is the horse or pony? Estimate the horse's bodyweight.
Method A Tape measure and table To estimate your horse or pony's bodyweight, take the girth measurement at a quiet time, right around the barrel. The tape should lie in the girth groove and just behind the

Table 2 Ponies

Girth in inches	40	42.5	45	47.5	50	52.5	55	57.5
Girth in cm	101	108	114	120	127	133	140	146
Bodyweight in lb	100	172	235	296	368	430	502	362
Bodyweight in kg	45	77	104	132	164	192	234	252

Table 3 Horses

Girth in inches	55	57.5	60	62.5	65	67.5	70	72.5	75	77.5	80	82.5
Girth in cm	140	146	152	159	165	171	178	184	190	199	203	206
Bodyweight in lb	538	613	688	776	851	926	1014	1090	1165	1278	1328	1369
Bodyweight in kg	240	274	307	346	380	414	453	486	520	570	593	611

(Tables 1 and 2 based on work of Glushanok, Rochlitz & Skay, 1981)

withers. Read off the measurement when the animal finishes breathing out.

The following tables are offered as guidelines; it is best to check cob-types against the tables on a public weighbridge to find which table applies to them. Tables 2 and 3 illustrate that just $1.23\,cm$ ($\frac{1}{2}$ in) change in girth can mean a 5 to 6 kg (14 to 15 lb) change in bodyweight, which may not be visible to the naked eye.

Once your horse or pony is fit, you should feed to maintain bodyweight throughout the season.

Method B Weigh Tape e.g. Equitape.

You read an estimation of weight directly off the tape.

Method C Weighbridge

Remember to deduct the weight of tack and handler.

Measure in kg (50 kg = 112 lb).

Methods A and B are less accurate for broodmares and youngstock but will at least give a guide to any changes.

Step 2

How much hay a day? As a rule-of-thumb, the usual ratios of forage to concentrates by weight, are as shown in the following Tables.

Mature horses in work

Type of work	% concentrates/forage
Light (to medium)	25/75
Medium	50/50
Hard	60/40
Hard, fast	75/25

25% forage by weight is the absolute minimum for healthy gut function. In cold weather increase concentrate levels. If forage is of low nutritional value, concentrate levels will also need to be increased to balance the ration.

Broodmares

Time	% concentrates/forage
First 3 months after foaling	55/45
Third month to weaning	40/60
Weaning to 90 days before foaling	25/75
Last 90 days of pregnancy	Gradual rise from 25% to 55% after foaling/Gradual decrease from 75% to 45% after foaling

Youngstock

Age	Youngstock destined to race at 2/3 yrs	All other youngstock
	% concentrates/forage	
Creep feed	100% plus milk	100% plus milk
3 month foal	80/20	75/25
6 month weanling	70/30	65/30
12 month yearling	55/45	45/55
18 month long yearling	40/60	30/70
2-year-old	40/60	30/70

Step 3

Work out energy requirement for *maintenance*.

$$\text{Energy} = 18\,\text{MJ} + \frac{\text{Bodyweight in kg}}{10\,\text{kg}}$$

So, for our 500 kg horse $= 18 + \dfrac{500}{10} = 68\,\text{MJ/day}$

Step 4

Work out energy requirement for *production*.
For work per day, for each 50 kg of bodyweight add MJ of digestible energy (DE):

Light work	+ 1 e.g. one hour walking
	+ 2 e.g. walking and trotting

Medium work   + 3 e.g. some cantering

  + 4 e.g. schooling, dressage and jumping

Hard work   + 5 e.g. hunting 1 day/week

  + 6 e.g. hunting 2 days/week

Fast work   + 7 e.g. three-day eventing

  + 8 e.g. racing

For lactation per day, for each 50 kg bodyweight add:

For first 3 months + $4\frac{1}{2}$ MJ of DE
For next 3 months + $3\frac{1}{2}$ MJ of DE

NB. All diet changes must be gradual, particularly for lactating and pregnant broodmares.

For pregnancy per day, add:

12% for the final $\frac{1}{3}$ of gestation or the last 3 months.

For growth per day, add:

Up to 1 year provide 13 MJ of DE per kg of feed, and feed to capacity. For youngstock over 1 year, feed at maintenance ration for their expected weight at maturity.

Example

We have worked out that the total daily energy requirement for a horse is 128 MJ DE/day in mid-training.
From the table we know that 8.75 kg of our 9 MJ hay will supply $9 \times 8.75 = 78.75$ MJ DE (say 79).
So our concentrate needs to supply $128 - 79$ MJ DE = 49 MJ DE.

We have decided to give 1 kg/day (unsoaked weight) of sugar beet, which has a DE content of 13 MJ (as fed but before soaking). So after 1 kg of sugar beet, our concentrates need to supply:
$49 - 13 = 36$ MJ DE.

Say we want to use oats and our sample has a DE of 12.5 (as fed), $36 \div 12.5 = 2.88$ kg of oats.

Step 5

Adjust the ration.
We now have a ration of:
8.75 kg of hay rounded to 9 kg
1.00 kg of sugar beet (unsoaked weight)
2.88 kg of oats rounded to 2.75 kg
In practice, I would round this up or down to give manageable amounts, then find the percentages these represent:

9 kg of hay	=	9 ÷ 12.75 (total feed) %	=	70.68% of total ration
1 kg sugar beet	=	1 ÷ 12.75 (total feed) %	=	7.8% of total ration
2.75 kg oats	=	2.75 ÷ 12.75 (total feed) %	=	21.6% of total ration
Total				100.0%

This supplies 128 MJ DE/day.
If your calculator has a memory, you only need to key in 12.75 once (into the memory), then press:
wt of hay (e.g. 9) ÷ memory % =
On many calculators you will not need to press the equals key.

Step 6

Check the protein level.
Find the protein level of your feedstuffs by laboratory analysis or from tables, then:

crude protein % of feedstuff × weight of feedstuff = protein contribution of that feedstuff to the ration.

For our example, say our hay is 8% crude protein, sugar beet 11% and oats 10.9%. On the calculator:

Hay 8 × 70.6%	= 5.6	CP from hay
Sugar beet 11 × 7.8%	= 0.86	CP from sugar beet
Oats 10.9 × 21.6%	= 2.35	CP from oats
Total CP in diet	8.8%	

This is reasonably near our target of 8.5%.

Step 7

In the same way, you should at least check the calcium, phosphorus and lysine levels, and as many other nutrients as you have time for or are concerned about. I cheat a little and use a computer to assess all the known nutrient requirements of each individual horse (including all the vitamins, minerals and several amino acids) but by hand that would take an inordinately long time. Of course, if you don't want to get bogged down you could always feed hay and cubes, as guidelines for their ration levels will have been worked out for you by the feed compounder – or you could consult a nutritionist who can work all this out for you and give a detailed programme specifically for your horse's work programme and individual requirements and characteristics.

Table 4 Analysis of commonly used feedstuffs (as fed)

These are average analyses and will vary from batch to batch of feed. These figures are offered as a guidelines only.

	DE MJ/Kg	Crude protein %	Crude fibre %	Calcium %	Phosphorus %	Ca:P ratio	Lysine %
Hay – meadow	10.24	8.5	32.8	0.41	0.15	2.70:1	–
Good hay	11.00	10.0	30.0	0.45	0.20	2.25:1	–
Average hay	8.50	3.0–8.0	38.0	0.20	0.30	0.66:1	–
Barley straw	7.07	3.7	48.8	0.24	0.05	4.80:1	–
Oat straw	8.17	3.4	39.4	0.25	0.07	3.60:1	–
Hygrass (hayage)	11.58	13.1	39.2	1.00	0.30	3.00:1	0.16
		Other hayages vary considerably in CP, but tend to have a lower DCP value					
Dried grass meal/nuts 14% CP	10.66	14.0	26.0	0.90	0.30	3.00:1	0.80
Dried alfalfa 16% CP	9.70	16.0	24.0	1.40	0.20	7.00:1	0.64
Chaff (see hay/straw)							
Sugar beet*	15.43	10.6	14.4	0.80	0.08	10.00:1	0.66
Oats	14.02	10.9	12.1	0.07	0.37	0.19:1	–
Barley	15.73	10.8	5.3	0.05	0.37	0.14:1	0.48
Maize	17.31	9.8	2.4	0.05	0.60	0.08:1	0.30
Breadmeal (Bailey's No. 1)	14.90	15.0	1.3	0.24	0.28	0.86:1	0.30
Wheatbran	12.31	17.0	11.4	0.12	1.43	0.08:1	0.68
Non-heating H & P cubes**	12.50	12.2	14.8	0.45	0.20	2.25:1	0.36
H & P nut from a national compounder**	10.00	10.5	16.0	1.40	0.65	2.15:1	0.25

* *Must* be soaked before feeding (shreds – 12 hrs, pulp – 18 hrs, nuts/pellets – 24 hrs. Do not soak longer, especially in hot weather, as fermentation may occur).
** Compare these two and you will see how important it is to follow the individual manufacturer's instructions.

Step 8

Don't forget salt, and consider the vitamin/mineral supplement.

Table 4 shows a sample of nutrient levels in various feedstuffs, as an example.

It is preferable to have your main inputs, i.e. forage and, say, oats, analysed for their actual feed values as they can vary enormously. I have asked 'experts' to pick out samples of good horse hay and the analysis has ranged from 3 to 15% crude protein! Oats can vary by nearly as much. People who will not buy cubes because they cannot see what is in them mystify me. You cannot see what is *in* oats i.e. you cannot judge their feed analysis just by looking at them. You can just see whether they are a clean sample!

Step 9

Monitor the horse's bodyweight, attitude and performance and amend feeding accordingly.

If the horse is overweight, work out the ration requirements for 5 to 10 kg (11 to 22 lbs) (no more) less than actual weight. When he has lost that amount, re-calculate the ration. Excessively rapid weight loss is not good for the horse, and 'starvation' slimming can precipitate hyperlipaemia, chronic laminitis, protein, vitamin and mineral deficiencies (requirements for these for maintenance remain virtually the same so when you cut down digestible energy for weight loss, make sure you are not underfeeding the other nutrients), and hormonal disturbances e.g. causing a tendency to put on weight even more easily (human slimmers should also be encouraged to avoid 'crash' diets for this reason), and again possibly causing chronic laminitis.

Keep weight loss steady and slow, and do not waste a winter slimming campaign by letting the horse put it all back on if he is turned out in the summer. However, if you weigh a performance horse on a weighbridge, bear in mind that protein weighs twice as much as fat.

8
Prohibited Substances
by Gillian McCarthy

Essentially, prohibited substances are chemicals which may be intentionally or inadvertently administered to the competition or racehorse
and which are deemed by the ruling bodies of the sport concerned to
have a potential for altering the performance of that horse in a manner
which would be unfair to other competitors and/or potentially harmful
to the welfare/performance of the horse.

For example, while painkillers may, when administered at a low
level, dull pain to a certain extent and enable, for example, an event
horse to proceed in a bold fashion and not be deterred by the odd
knocks and bumps, at a higher dosage they may allow the horse to
proceed when it is suffering from a relatively serious injury or disorder
which may well result in the horse being crippled, or even in an
accident fatal to horse and/or rider as the injured part gives way under
the stress of competition. Obviously the drugging of a horse in this way
is unfair to both the horse, the rider and other competitors.

Other substances which may be administered are those which can act
as a stimulant, theoretically increasing the horse's ability to perform by
'hyping' it up or increasing its 'aggressiveness', and therefore (theoretically) its competitiveness. The so-called benefits of substances of this
type are highly debatable as are such materials as anabolic steroids
which also build muscle, as there is little correlation between muscle
mass and athletic performance (you do not see many weightlifters
winning races!). The other side of this coin is the type of substance
which slows down the horse's reactions, reducing speed and/or stamina
and making it sluggish and dopey.

As a nutritionist, it is my experience that an awful lot of competition
horses are being either over-stimulated or rendered dopey due to
unbalanced feeding and an ill-informed fitness programme, but that is
another subject. Both chemical stimulants and chemical depressants
may be administered intentionally by the connections of a competition
horse, but what we are most concerned with in this section is giving
some guidelines to horse managers to enable them to avoid the
inadvertent administration of such materials.

I didn't mean it!

It is useful to remember that most drugs in use today are either derived from plant material or are synthetic copies of chemicals from plants in a purified form. It is not, therefore, surprising to find that an awful lot of stimulants and depressants and other pharmacologically-active chemicals occur naturally in plants which we may then feed to our horses or apply to them in some other way, for example as ointments, poultices or even inhalants. The horse may also inadvertently ingest such materials himself when he licks paintwork, chews fences which have been treated with preservatives, eats various plants which contain pharmacologically-active chemicals (including alkaloids and glycosides) or gets loose and comes into contact with materials which he would not normally be exposed to (drugs, slug pellets, pesticides, even ornamental plants).

The problem with many of these materials is that the rules governing their appearance in the urine and/or blood of the competition horse were formulated when international doping was becoming a major problem and analytical techniques were relatively crude. Basically, the Jockey Club of the UK decided that certain proscribed substances should simply not be present in these body fluids and that racehorses should not be fed any substances which could not be defined as 'normal and ordinary feeding' (which they described as oats, bran and hay only, if you pressed them hard enough for a definition). The Federation Equestre International (FEI) and, in fact, governing bodies of many equestrian sports in many countries, then adopted these rules.

This was all very well at first, but gradually two things were happening. First of all, different feedingstuffs were being moved around the world, particularly for use in compound cattle feeds, and as a result of this both compound and horse feed and straights (oats, barley etc.) were becoming contaminated – either at the feed mill or while being transported in ships and lorries – with materials (for example cocoa bean meal) which contained prohibited substances such as the stimulants caffeine and theobromine; so these were, quite inadvertently, turning up in racehorse feeds and, of course, those of other competition horses.

This meant that increasing numbers of positives were being called with the presence of either caffeine or theobromine and, to a lesser extent, other substances, when in fact it was quite probable that the amounts concerned were insufficient to stimulate a mouse let alone a thumping great Thoroughbred!

While big, bad feed compounders were continuously being blamed for this problem, trying to find contaminants of this order of magnitude is rather like trying to find a pinch of snuff in a haystack (sometimes literally as nicotine is a prohibited substance), and although many of them spent a great deal of money and completely reorganised their mills and transport, positives were still occurring. They also took out some pretty hefty insurance policies but the main result of all this frenzied activity was probably to increase the price of the feed and little else.

Also, as a wider range of feedstuffs was becoming available to the horse owner, many of which were capable of producing a far more appropriate ration for the high performance horse, it was becoming questionable whether it was reasonable to expect people to stick to an oats/bran/hay guideline or 'be prepared to suffer the consequences', especially after a number of oat samples were analysed as positive!

The second aspect of this was that as time went on, the analytical techniques being used were becoming increasingly sophisticated, which generally meant that they could detect smaller and smaller amounts of various substances and, even more significantly, were picking up other substances which nobody had thought to worry about previously.

A combination of these two factors meant that more and more feed-related positives were being called over the years, causing problems in the industry and a bad press in the eyes of the general public.

Recently, both the Jockey Club and the FEI have introduced an arbitrary minimum level of theobromine to try and weed out the insignificant, inadvertently-administered theobromine positives, so it is to be hoped that the industry can be less paranoid about caffeine and theobromine, although good mill and transport hygiene will still be important (particularly in view of the fact that the higher levels of these chemicals can, indeed, be harmful). It should also be remembered that, in particular, human foodstuffs including tea, coffee, cocoa and chocolate, should not be available to the competition horse. This does not just mean you do not feed Mars Bars to your competition horse, but you should not be dispensing powdered coffee or eating chocolate flakes in the vicinity of feed bins, and it may not be a bad idea to wash your hands after handling such materials. This may sound silly to many people but even with the minimum levels set by the ruling bodies, we are dealing with such trace amounts that it is quite possible for a horse to lick a chocolate-covered toddler and then show up as a positive and lose its Olympic medal. Make the stable yard a chocolate/coffee/cocoa/cattle feed-free zone.

Precautions

Before we leave the subject of inadvertently-administered prohibited substances in feedstuffs, there are one or two other measures which the competitive rider can implement which could be well worthwhile.

(1)   Buy compound horse feeds only from manufacturers and merchants who operate a 'clean mill' policy, and who are aware of the problems with prohibited substances and take these into account both in their manufacturing and their transport of raw materials and finished products. Ask them for a written guarantee of this and keep it somewhere safe.

(2)   The above also applies to the purchase of straights including oats, both from the feed compounders and neighbouring farmers who should not store them adjacent to cattle feed which might contain prohibited substances, or indeed pig, poultry and cattle feed which may well contain substances which are both prohibited and dangerous to the horse, including various growth promoters and so forth.

From about one month before the commencement of the competitive season, and thereafter until the results of any tests taken are known, it is well worth taking about 0.5 kg (1 lb) sample from each batch of feed purchased and marking it with the number of the delivery note, plus any bag labels with batch numbers available, so that if a positive is called you have your own reference sample of feed should any legal action ensue, and you can also be seen to be taking steps to avoid the problem if a decision has to be made about your culpability and how to penalise you.

(3)   Apart from the points about coffee and chocolate and so forth in the feed room and where feed is being dispensed or fed, points about feed storage in relation to farms supplying hay and cereals should also be borne in mind.

(4)   You should also be aware that certain pasture and hedgerow weeds can contain narcotic substances (and, of course, these may also appear in conserved forages), and you should do your best to eliminate these as they may not only show up as a positive in a dope test, but also they can, of course, be extremely dangerous to the horse. (See comprehensive tables in *Pasture Management for Horses and Ponies* by Gillian McCarthy.)

(5)   Discourage visitors to field and stables from giving titbits, not only of the coffee/chocolate nature but also various types of mints (see reference to menthol below).

(6)   Keep small samples of any supplements and additives you give as per point (2), including those given by syringe or in water, as it is quite likely in the future that increasing numbers of positives will be called not because of caffeine and theobromine but because of substances used as preservatives, flavourings or colourants in various feedstuffs (see below).

Apart from materials administered in feed, there is a whole range of substances which the horse may have applied to it or injected into it which can lead to a positive dope test. In general, 'clearance times', i.e.

the time it takes for a drug to clear out of a horse's system, have been worked out for many drugs which may be prescribed for horses but as horses may vary significantly in their metabolic make-up and as many of these tests are performed on resting ponies and not fit competition horses, these figures are not always reliable and it is advisable, if possible, to extend the period allowed before competing with a horse given such a substance.

It is, of course, vital that the vet is made aware that you are planning to compete in any way with a horse he or she is treating, so that he or she can modify any drug therapy programme, if possible, or at least ensure that you are aware of the potential problem.

Many horse owners will be aware that certain substances which are applied as ointments can end up in the bloodstream and result in a positive being called. However, there are many ointments which are known not to pass into the bloodstream and are often considered to be safe. The problem is that ointments do not just have to pass through the *skin* into the bloodstream. For example, the horse may lick the area which has been treated, or even rub against the stable or a fence post and then lick or chew that, so unless steps are being taken to prevent this happening you cannot assume that any ointment which contains a prohibited substance is safe for use on the competition horse.

Just what can you use?

Before attempting to answer that question, perhaps I might digress slightly to explain that one major problem in this whole field is that, although these substances may appear in the blood or urine of the horse, they may not be present in the same form in the material which has caused them to appear: that is to say that various chemicals which a horse might ingest or have applied to it in some way, may then be acted on during various metabolic processes in the body, and as a by-product, or even direct end product of these processes, other chemicals may appear (metabolites) which are prohibited substances. A number of glycocides (a type of plant chemical) fall into this category.

Basically, this means that you can analyse the feed, ointment, drug powder or whatever until you are blue in the face, but unless you are aware of all the possible metabolites (maybe thousands) of all the chemicals in the original substance, you have very little hope of predicting whether the prohibited substance is going to turn up in the blood or urine. This means that the manufacturer or producer of whatever material you want to feed to or apply to your horse may well be able to screen for such substances as caffeine and theobromine, but there are many others which you simply cannot test for, and neither can the authorities, which makes it very hard to advise the poor horse owner.

For the few substances which might be tested for their metabolites, again this is likely to occur in resting ponies due to the expense of conducting experiments and the natural reluctance of owners and trainers to subject valuable animals to tests which may even exclude them from competitive work if a positive comes up. There is a world of difference between the metabolites produced by a resting pony and those of a fit performance horse, and even between a resting, fit performance horse tested prior to competition and one tested immediately after competing, when its urine becomes more acid resulting in various glycocides showing up which would not otherwise appear. (This latter point raises interesting questions about dietary manipulation which can have significant effects on urine acidity and may well be a further benefit of fine-tuning the diets of performance horses.)

What all this means in practice to the competition horse owner is that while a limited amount of data is available with reference to proscribed *drugs* (although a lot of advice relating to this is on the basis of 'we do not really know so *do not* take a chance and use it), many people are becoming increasingly aware that there is a large number of herbal materials, particularly ointments but increasingly feed additives and supplements, which can have a highly beneficial effect on all manner of problems ranging from wounds and swellings and bruising to respiratory disorders.

Many people take the view that if it is herbal it is harmless but, as I said at the beginning of this section, very many drugs are plant derivatives and they have powerful pharmacological effects. I fear quite a number of them fall into the category of those materials which will not appear when the herb, ointment or whatever is tested, but could well turn up as metabolites which are proscribed substances in blood and urine testing.

I discussed this matter with the authorities – the Jockey Club and the ruling bodies of various equestrian sports – all of whom referred me to the FEI. The latter, while as helpful as it could be, said that while we know so little about these materials it is not possible to say that any of the possible 'home treatments' are safe from the prohibited substances point of view. Sadly, this means that the excellent arnica and calendula creams, even homeopathic ones, are out, although extensive use over the years of comfrey as a feedstuff, ointment and even poultice seems to indicate that this is safe provided other ingredients (e.g. of ointments) are inert in this context. Raspberry leaf has, in my experience, also been used to relax horses who have been subjected to testing and so far none of them have come up as a positive.

However, due to the changing nature of the machinery used for testing, a substance which is safe today could well find itself causing a positive to be called in the future. The best advice I can give is that you should not assume just because something is 'natural' that it is safe in this context, and you should check with the manufacturers of any material you wish to use. Do your best to research any natural ingredients, including herbs, which you wish to utilise, as well as keeping abreast of developments as they occur and consulting the ruling body of your sport if you are in doubt. I am aware that this is not terribly helpful, but if you are at least aware of the nature of the problem both from the viewpoint of the ruling bodies, manufacturers of various products used, and yourself and your horse, I hope it will help you make reasoned decisions on this matter.

An example of the confusion which can arise is a well-publicised problem in the racing world in 1989 involving a positive call for what proved to be camphor, an ingredient in many ointments, leg-washes and inhalants not to mention cough sweets and certain mints and other confectionery often given as titbits. The amounts contained in most of the above mentioned items would probably not affect your horse's performance and many people would wonder why this is considered to be a prohibited substance at all. However, Mr M.A. Atock, Head of the Veterinary Department of the FEI, points out that camphor has been used by certain unscrupulous people in the show jumping world to make their horses' shins more sensitive and, thereby, encourage them to pick up their feet, and as camphor applied in this way would appear in the bloodstream it *is* necessary for them to test for this. Unfortunately, it has not yet been possible to set appropriate minimum levels which, strictly speaking, means under current rules many of the leg washes, ointments and other material gaily splashed about as a matter of course before, during and after competition in many competitive spheres could, in fact, lead to a positive dope test and should, in the light of current knowledge, be avoided completely. It is rather unfortunate as many of these materials must be extremely refreshing to the horse, although it is true that even this benefit could, I suppose, be considered to have a potential to affect the horse's performance by changing its attitude and willingness to work. However, it is pretty sad if the tired competition horse cannot be indulged in the equestrian equivalent of 'relaxing in a Radox bath'!

It is probably a good idea to avoid using such materials prior to competition and between days of events such as horse trials and endurance rides, or during show jumping competitions, and reserve them for the end of the show provided another will not be following within less than seven to ten days, although a safe clearance time for most materials is about three weeks. One practice which people sometimes use when travelling several horses together is to apply Vick or something similar to their muzzles to discourage them from nuzzling each other and possibly subsequently fighting. As Vick is a source of camphor, obviously this practice should be avoided.

It is also important to remember that two ointments containing the same active ingredients may vary in their degree of absorption through the skin. If one contains, for example, DMSO or MSM – only the latter of which is innocuous from a prohibited substances viewpoint – this may well increase the degree of absorption into the bloodstream of an active substance and lead to a positive being called.

Currently there is a number of topical preparations (such as sprays, ointments, creams and lotions) which contain disinfectants and which may be used without contravening the rules of racing as they stand at the present time. These include proflavin, centrimide, chlorhexidine, chloroxylenol, gentian violet and fentichlor (an anti-fungal agent). Good old salt and water is also an extremely useful disinfectant.

With regard to homeopathic treatments, many of which seem to be very effective for a number of disorders (although strictly speaking in some dilutions no molecules of the active ingredient appear to be present), an independent analyst has indicated that it would be unwise to give a racehorse or competition horse any homeopathic treatment within less than four or five days of racing or competing, including treatment in the form of a plaster or ointment.

To put this section into perspective, the FEI had 96 positives from 1981 to 1988, of which 76 were for drugs, and it is suggested that many of these may well have been due to inadequate withdrawal periods being allowed. A spokesman for the National Trainers Federation has pointed out that most of the recent positives in racing 'have arisen from substances in common use in stables such as leg washes, harness cleaners and disinfectants'.

If you have spent months, or indeed years, getting horses ready for a top class competition, whether it be the Olympic three-day-event competition, a 100-mile endurance ride or a Grand Prix show jumping final, it is obviously a disastrous end to a long campaign to be disqualified and possibly penalised further due to a positive dope test. With this in mind, it has to make sense to do everything in your power to avoid inadvertent administration of prohibited substances, and, of course, intentional administration!

It is to be hoped that in time a sufficient body of data will have been collected to enable us to begin to know which materials must be avoided and what we can safely use, and that the list of the latter will include some of the many useful herbal ointments and creams available for topical application to minor scratches and bruises. In the meantime, much can be done in fine-tuning the diet and in dietary manipulation of specific nutrients, to improve the temperament and ultimately the performance of the horse in particular when combined with an appropriate fitness programme. A number of minor disorders are, in fact, better treated using various nutrients and other feed additives including probiotics, sodium montmerrillonite and organic feed sources such as MSM (methyl sulphonyl methane), without contravening any rules or compromising the horse's health and welfare; in fact, such techniques are more likely to enhance the latter than compromise it.

For those who wish to look into this subject in greater detail, the standard work on the subject is still *Drugs and the Performance Horse* by Thomas Tobin, although as this has not been updated since 1981 it should not be taken as the sole source of reference.

9
Management Topics

Any experienced competitor will tell you that competitions are won at home, and that management plays equally as vital a role in producing a horse capable of winning as schooling and actually competing. There does come a point where you can do no more at home, when the horse needs the actual hands-on experience of competition to bring it on even if you are not riding to win, but the competition, like any performance, is only the very tip of the iceberg. If the horse is not schooled to the required standard and sufficiently fit, well and happy within himself it is a waste of time entering.

The trainer/manager's job will be made much easier if his or her material, the horse, is of sound stock to start with, as mentioned earlier. It is as well to buy only from breeders and producers who are known *not* to overdo their youngsters right from the beginning as irreparable damage can be done to the skeletal system and musculature by having youngstock too fat. In the racing world there are still problems with legs, such as epiphysitis and so-called contracted tendons which are, in fact, tendons failing to keep up in growth with fast-growing leg bones.

In other areas of the horse world, including the performance horse sector, the main problem is over-fatness. Unfortunately, many young competition horses are shown from foals onwards in various in-hand classes to get them worldly-wise if nothing else, but partly to show them off in suitable shop windows to potential future buyers. The standard practice in the showing world is still, despite many erudite and often hard-hitting articles in the equestrian press, to show in-hand stock of most types overweight because judges do seem on the whole, to their everlasting shame in my opinion, to consistently put up fat animals, even in potential performance horse classes.

The exhibitors, for their part, believe that a bit of fat here and there can cover up a multitude of sins and purposely pile on the blubber. Others know their sleek, healthy animal will not stand a chance against the overtopped competition and feel they have no choice but to produce *their* animals too fat, as well.

The problem is that getting an animal too fat in the body – particularly when its skeleton is still developing and the bones, therefore, are still 'soft' with the epipyses (growth plates between the long leg bones in particular) still 'open' and gristly – puts undue stress on those immature bones and causes actual physical, mechanical damage to the bones which may never fully heal. This obviously puts the horse at a serious disadvantage when it comes under the often severe stress of a life in competition, and the unfortunate new owner is faced with a horse who may well not be able to stand up to training and competition but is frequently out of action due to lameness and back problems.

The horse matures, generally speaking, from the ground up. The long leg bones may be mature for normal movement (i.e. *not* carrying a rider or working in circles or at fast paces or 'popping' poles) by the time the horse is two years of age, but the shoulders and pelvic region mature later than this, at three to four years of age depending on breed, and it is often not realised that the horse's spine does not mature until it is five or sometimes even six years of age. Slower maturing breeds such as those of Arab or warmblood breeding, particularly the large types of warmbloods we are seeing now, fall into the latter category. Those of mainly Thoroughbred blood may mature earlier but not as early as the racing world would have us believe, as is evidenced by tremendous wastage in two-year-old racing.

Lumps, bumps, 'hot' joints and laminitis can all be the result of overfeeding, 'forcing', youngstock in an attempt to make them look well advanced when sale time comes. Particularly in the warmblood sector, this is even more pointless as their performance testing and selling age is not, as in the racing world, at yearling stage. It has been shown that animals pushed when very young have no advantage as regards physical appearance over those allowed to grow more naturally by the time the animals are three years of age, and the former may well have acquired permanently enlarged joints or other 'leg jewellery' by that age through overfeeding and, as is quite common, too much protein and a severely unbalanced calcium:phosphorous ratio in the diet. (At the time of writing research seems to be showing that a ratio of 1.5:1 should be aimed at.)

So starting off with properly reared youngsters is more than half the battle in keeping competition horses sound. With this solid foundation, what else can be done to maintain soundness?

Probably the two big 'killers' as regards management are lameness and wind problems. Lameness is partly a work/training problem and wind disorders stem almost entirely from poor management.

Lameness

The horse is nature's most specialised running machine, with its single digit foot, long legs, anti-fatigue design (no muscles below knee and hock) and its tremendous respiratory and circulatory capability. It is specialised for moderate-speed long-distance running over varied terrain, barefoot and able to pop the occasional obstacle if necessary with no trouble. We, of course, ask much more of it and have developed some pretty effective fitness-producing techniques to enable it to comply. When properly fit and working in a physically co-ordinated way, the horse stays amazingly sound. But being flesh and blood there are times when the machine breaks down and the horse

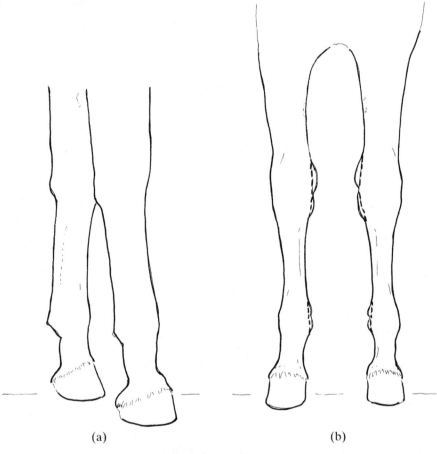

(a)   (b)

Fig. 9 Limb disorders which can be caused by faulty nutrition: (a) So-called contracted tendons producing an upright pastern and knuckling-over of the fetlocks; (b) Epiphysitis or 'bumpy joints'. Hot, painful bumps can also appear on the outside of joints.

sustains an injury due to overstress (i.e. overstrain, not stepping on a stone or tearing its skin on wire). Such injuries almost always occur due to fatigue and lack of co-ordination or because mental concentration is lost and the horse takes a mis-step which, because the smooth co-ordination and stride mechanics are interrupted, means some part receives more force than it can take, and injury is the result.

How can we prevent lameness? Basically by working the horse only when truly fit for the work being asked and by avoiding situations and manoeuvres which are over-demanding. Fitness and its attainment and management is very well covered in *Getting Horses Fit* by Sarah Pilliner, and will not be dealt with significantly here. It is enough to say that even today, with our increasingly-advanced knowledge of exercise physiology, we still see, and not always at the lower levels of competition, horses competing in various disciplines when they are patently *unfit* and, sadly, thier connections are rarely penalised. They usually simply receive a polite dressing-down and advice to improve 'for the good name of the sport' if nothing else. Meanwhile their horses have suffered untold distress, mental and physical, all in the name of recreation. *There is no excuse today for horses appearing in any discipline when not sufficiently fit to do so.* The only reasons for it happening are that the trainer does not truly understand the principles of achieving fitness and how to test it, and winning or even just 'having a go' are considered by the person actually competing to be more important than the horse's welfare. There is more danger of the latter reason applying when the combination concerned are part of a team ('we mustn't let the team down') but it does also happen when competing as an individual. I should like to see much more severe penalties and eliminations *on course* in such sustained disciplines as eventing, long distance riding, carriage driving and marathons etc., and proper checks between such classes as gymkhanas (yes, ponies suffer particularly) and show jumping. Severe cash penalties, suspension from future competition for a significantly painful period and the bad publicity would soon rectify matters in this area.

Conditions which can overstress animals include hard ground with the more severe concussion it transmits to limbs, high speeds when tendons and ligaments and their associated muscles are working at concert pitch, very soft ground which necessitates considerable muscular effort and subsequent stress on tendons, drop fences which similarly stretch tendons and ligaments to their limits, tight turns and circles, high and wide fences which invite spinal stress and injury, landing from a jump on to an uphill slope (tendon overstress again) and rough going. Readers may well be able to think of others but these are the main ones. They cannot be avoided altogether in modern-day competition but if riders bear in mind their dangers and moderate the frequency and extent of their demands accordingly much lameness will be avoided.

Protecting the horse's legs with boots or bandages and the feet with hoof pads only scratches the surface of physical problems. Boots and conventionally applied exercise bandages protect, especially when put on over padding, against knocks and scrapes, as do padded bandages such as the Bonner bandage. They do *not* enhance the strength or function of the tendons – in other words they do not support the tendons, *unless they restrict the action of the joints* and therefore the movement of the tendons. If they do restrict the action of the joints they are unsuitable for active work where free movement is necessary. Support bandages, air casts, plaster casts and so on do restrict joint movement and are used in severe tendon and ligament injuries, not for work.

What boots and bandages over padding can do is lessen somewhat the jarring effects of work particularly on hard ground, but that is all. The vibrations which occur during work can be lessened and, likewise, their effects on the structures of the legs.

Pads between shoe and hoof, and sometimes covering the whole frog/sole area, may offer some immediate protection from bruised soles and suchlike and may or may not significantly reduce the effects of concussion, depending on which expert you ask! Some feel that they encourage shoes to work loose.

Liniments still form a part of most stables' first aid kits, yet most of them are quite ineffective at the jobs they purport to do. It is a topic well worthwhile discussing with your veterinary surgeon, but by and large liniments' most valuable function is to act as a lubricant during hand-rubbing. It is more often the hand-rubbing rather than the liniment itself which dissipates the swelling and encourages the circulation – the liniment simply lessens friction and prevents pull on the skin. Lard would be just as effective at this! In time there may be generally available on the market a liniment which really does penetrate the skin and have a medicinal effect on the injured area within the leg or, less likely, the joint. One is currently available in the USA, part of Epicoat-TGS' Therapeutic Grooming System. Negotiations have been going on with distributors in Britain and the product should be available in the UK by the time this book is published.

Liniments which give a cool feeling to the leg because of the spirit they contain may help radiate heart from the part more quickly but do not prevent the congestion of blood in the area which causes the heat in the first place.

Cold therapy is another topic which has two schools of thought. Some veterinary surgeons and physiotherapists agree with the time-honoured view that cold applications reduce the heat to the part, constrict the blood vessels and help reduce congestion in an injured area which can actually delay rather than speed healing. Others feel that cold simply constricts the blood vessels in the skin itself and that, because the skin forms such as effective temperature barrier anyway (that being one of its jobs, after all), the cold does not pass more deeply into the leg and therefore cold applications to the surface of the leg (skin) are a waste of time. In this case, time-consuming cold hosing and expensive chemical cold packs (even bags of frozen peas) are a waste of money.

The most logical form of treatment, to my mind, for injuries involving heat and swelling is that advocated by most of today's forward-thinking veterinary surgeons – anti-inflammatory drugs followed by physiotherapy and that highly unpopular and inconvenient treatment, rest, but perhaps with judicious exercise.

New techniques in the treatment of injury
by Gillian McCarthy

The rapidly expanding science of physiotherapy and related therapies means that the vet and horse owner have a wider range of options to consider when treating the injured horse. The treatment of injury includes *invasive* techniques (surgery, acupuncture) and *non-invasive* techniques (physiotherapy, clinical kinesiology (CK), osteopathy, chiropracty, acu*pressure* and acu-*laser* treatment).

Surgery may only be conducted by a recognised practitioner (i.e. a veterinary surgeon), whereas at present the *non-invasive techniques* are practised by a range of practitioners who may be more or less qualified in human technique, but for whom formal qualifications are not available for horse practice and, other than in the case of physiotherapy, are not recognised by the medical or veterinary profession. It does not, however, mean that these techniques do not work, and there are an increasing number of courses given for and by vets in such techniques as CK, osteopathy, and acupuncture, for animal practice. However, as there are no formal qualifications in some of these fields, it does leave the field open to quacks and charlatans to give very expensive and ineffective 'treatment' preying on the gullibility of desperate horse owners. Unfortunately however, it is certainly not unheard of for supposedly qualified practitioners at all levels to do the same, but at least one has some redress against their professional organisations.

In the case of injury, a competent horse keeper may well be able to deal perfectly adequately with minor cuts and bruises, but anything more than this should only be treated in consultation with your vet.

Heroic surgery should usually be considered as a *last* option as it involves not only the surgery itself, but the use of powerful drugs including anaesthetics and often antibiotics, that can have substantial side effects, and the surgery also leaves the site open to infection and possible further damage.

Whether or not surgery is undertaken, in the past the stock answer to many injuries has been, after initial treatment, to turn the horse away to rest. However, current thinking is that this is likely to lead to poorer healing, and the possible development of adhesions which can weaken the surrounding tissues and lead to a repeat of the injury as soon as work recommences, or other severe stress is incurred.

It is now generally accepted that the priorities should be to stabilise the condition, by controlling pain and swelling and if necessary bleeding, by the immediate use of cold bandages/packs to super-cool the area, although there is some argument about this as it is not necessarily desirable to restrict blood flow unduly as this is necessary for the healing process, and the cold does not reach the deeper tissues such as tendons. This procedure is followed by the use of anti-inflammatory drugs, along with pain killers if necessary, and then the introduction of appropriate physiotherapy techniques.

It is beyond the scope of this book to examine the so-called alternative therapy, or perhaps more appropriately complementary techniques. I will confine myself here to the already established physiotherapies.

Unfortunately at present any Tom, Dick or Harry can buy most of the machinery which is used in modern physiotherapy, and any Tom, Dick or Harry can do a lot of damage with it! Unless and until this iniquitous situation is changed, it is vital that you only proceed in using this equipment with the guidance of a trained and skilled (*not* one and the same thing) operator, in conjuction with your vet. A lot of this equipment can be leased, and I would suggest you lease it from one of the physiotherapy practices who will show you how to use it, specifically for whatever injury it is intended. Unfortunately, people who buy machinery may be shown how to use it for one injury, and then start applying it to every knock, bump and scratch in the yard, often quite inappropriately. It is worth remembering that while some of these machines can produce quite remarkable healing effects, such rapid growth and alteration in tissue could prove extremely harmful in the wrong situation.

Most good equine vets will now have a known and trusted therapist, sometimes within the practice, available for referrals, and if at all possible it is suggested that you use this route to obtain suitable therapy. Correctly used, many physiotherapy techniques will hasten and improve the quality of the healing of injury, ranging from simple massage, correctly done, through to sophisticated source stimulation and other techniques which should be considered whenever dealing with injury in the performance horse.

Horse owners who are interested in pursuing this area themselves are advised to combine suitable training, as suggested above, with a study of the basic science behind wound healing and a few hours spent reading *Equine Injury and Therapy* by Mary Bromiley *before* using it as an essential handy reference, and '*Physiotherapy in Veterinary Practice*, by the same author.

Whatever treatment regime is pursued, it is important to remember that without adequate and suitable nutrition the sick or injured horse is likely to experience a delayed recovery, and possible susceptibility to secondary problems.

It might be useful here to summarise the potential of some of the techniques available, but this information is given purely to illustrate the possibilities and is not in any way given as a recommendation. One important point is that, as Mary Bromiley points out, 'all machines have an analgesic, pain-killing effect. The absence of pain is *not* an indication of complete recovery' (my italics).

Hot and cold treatment

Two techniques of major importance, which do not involve the use of machines, are the use of hot and cold, often alternately, using water including jacuzzi boots, cold packs, crushed ice (applied through a wet towel), or cold bandages such as the Bonner bandage.

Massage and passive stretching

Hand massage and passive stretching by a skilled practitioner are also of major importance in obtaining normal movement in joints and reducing adhesions in muscle, and ensuring adequate circulation and lymph-drainage. The use of wet or dry compresses and of support bandages are also well tried and tested techniques.

Massage may also be useful as a warm-up technique for performance horses, and also after exercise; it is thought to help stimulate peripheral circulation and therefore drainage of metabolites such as lactic acid, a build-up of which leads to fatigue in muscles, and therefore aid more rapid recover with less stiffness incurred. It is often useful to use some form of lubricant such as an oil or gel when massaging.

Mechanical massage

The next step after hand massage is to use mechanical massagers which are available either as hand-held units, which are mains operated, or specialised pads which are attached to the surcingle. These may be used for up to 30 minutes at each session, although care should be taken that they are not stimulating the muscles to such an extent that they actually *cause* lactic acid build-up pre- and post-exercise.

Magnetic field therapy

Although there is still much research work to be done on this subject, it would certainly appear that in the case of soft tissue injuries at least, exposure to a magnetic field tends to enhance healing. The use of magnetic pads applied to the injured area for long periods is a technique which can be adopted by many horse owners, and should certainly do no harm. However, it is most important to obtain a correct diagnosis from your vet first, otherwise an injury which requires more positive treatment may be prolonged while you wait in vain for the magnetic pads to work. Having said this, there is probably a place in every competition yard for a set of magnetic shapes, to be applied routinely to small bumps and knocks. These will also then be available for use under veterinary guidance for more serious injuries.

The use of electrical magnetic field therapy for soft tissue injuries, including wounds, post-traumatic oedema, thoraco-lumbar (back) problems, tendon injuries, and also to improve the function of arthritic joints, and treatment of fractures, should only be conducted under expert supervision. A minimum of three weeks' treatment will be required even if clinical signs have disappeared. Magnetic field therapy should *not* be used where major damage to blood vessels has occurred.

Related therapies, which appear to act in a similar way, are Ionicare and Electrovet, both of which include similar applications to magnetic field therapy machines in their range of use.

Laser therapy

The term LASER stands for Light Amplification by Stimulated Emission of Radiation. The science of laser therapy in horses is still at an early stage of development, but quite dramatic healing effects can be obtained. However, in the wrong hands it is quite possible that the laser can produce considerable damage, and again it should not be used without proper training.

There are two types of laser: the high-power or 'hot' laser, unlikely to be used by the horse owner, and the low power or cold or soft lasers, which are available for stable use.

The most important aspect of laser use is that they lead to reduction in pain, especially if acupuncture points are stimulated, and when applied to the appropriate part of an injury they will accelerate healing, as they stimulate collagen synthesis. Laser acupuncture is an extremely useful technique, but a thorough knowledge of the acupuncture points is essential as the inadvertent use of the wrong points could cause considerable discomfort and imbalance in the system. The type of machine which has a sensor at the tip of the acupuncture probe to measure electrical skin resistance, will help you to find the acupuncture point, but will not tell you whether you have found the correct point! It may be necessary to treat up to 30 points in order to give pain relief, which may last for only a brief time or for as long as ten days. It may be necessary for both the operator and the horse's eyes to be protected while laser 'acupuncture' is being practised.

The use of the laser in soft tissue injuries, to stimulate the metabolism of the cells in the area, is still being developed but shows great promise. The technique may be used for tendon and ligament injuries, superficial joint and bone injuries, open wounds and after surgery, and also for old fibrous injuries. In particular, in the case of open wounds, the laser should be used as the first treatment, and the cold laser has certainly been found to accelerate wound healing without the development of granulation tissue (proud flesh). The laser reduces the rate of bacterial and fungal proliferation and thus helps to keep the wound sterile. Correct positioning of application is vital or the wound may heal in an abnormal fashion, and nothing will have been gained by using the treatment.

If you are purchasing the machine it is useful to obtain one which can alternate from pulse to continuous beam, as while the pulse laser helps to control pain, the continuous beam is more efficacious in healing.

As with most physiotherapy machines, over-use can cause as much damage as under-use, and in the case of the laser a two to four day interval between sessions is generally suggested.

Muscle stimulators

Electrical, including Faradic stimulation of muscles after injury, can help to prevent muscle wasting and degeneration (atrophy), and prevent the formation of adhesions and unnecessary scar tissue, both of which may affect muscle mobility. Such treatment can also improve venous and lymphatic drainage, and help to re-build and/or re-educate weakened muscles.

However, a number of competition horse owners have thought it might be rather a good idea to use such stimulators to 'warm-up' muscles prior to competitions. This is an extremely bad idea, as the stimulation is the equivalent of quite severe exercise of individual muscles and will lead to lactic acid build-up, which causes fatigue. Therefore, if you use this technique prior to competition you will have an already muscle-fatigued horse before it has even started. *Judicious* use of massage, especially hand massage and passive stretching, *suitable* warm-up exercises *and* warming-down exercises after competition, are obviously more desirable.

However, in skilled hands with a good knowledge of the anatomy of the musculature, combined later with correctly-designed exercise programmes, considerable benefits may be derived from the correct use of muscle stimulation, to ensure balanced recovery from an injury. If damaged muscle is not repaired and returned to its normal size and tone, it will *never* recover under normal exercise, which will tend to stimulate bi-laterally (both sides) and not unilaterally, and indeed as the horse is most likely to become more one-sided, the less than diligent rider may well allow a bad situation to become worse.

In the hands of a skilled therapist, the use of muscle stimulation is a useful diagnostic aid, as it can pinpoint precisely the location of damaged muscle.

Ultrasound

Ultrasound is the use of sound waves – in the veterinary field for both diagnosis (as they can be used to provide an image of internal structures) and treatment.

In *Equine Injury and Therapy*, Mary Bromiley points out that 'incorrectly used, it is probably the most dangerous piece of machinery on sale to the general public'. I have certainly seen a greyhound whose leg was broken by the over-use of ultrasound, on the principle that 'if a little does good, more must do more good', and I understand that post-treatment fractures (including sore shins or star fractures), arthritis, and death of deep tissue are commonly reported in animals after *un*suitable treatment using ultrasound equipment.

I strongly suggest that even if you have been shown in depth how to use such machinery for a specific injury, you do not even consider using it around the stable for other injuries until you have specifically consulted a suitable practitioner and your vet.

The effects of ultrasound include reduction of muscle spasm, increase in elasticity of scar tissue, stimulation of cell activity and blood flow, improvement in the structure of collagen tissue formation, improvement in quality of tendon repair, and improved bone healing after fracture, *provided* treatment is given within the first two weeks after injury.

Ultrasound is *not* normally used in combination with Faradism, and should *not* be used on a *treatment* setting, on areas such as the eyes, reproductive organs, the brain, tumours, thromboses, and in cases of heart disease, circulatory and intestinal disorders, haemarthrosis, and infection other than of the sinuses. Even when the correct technique and strength of treatment are used, treatment for excessive periods can cause severe damage and again should be avoided.

As was mentioned previously, simply turning your horse away to rest after an injury or even after physiotherapy, is unlikely to prove of much benefit unless efforts have been made to get the affected part working normally again. Apart from non-specific walking exercise in-hand, or on a horse walker, preferably of the loose-horse type (and if possible in both directions), other techniques include swimming – preferably in a straight pool and *always* in conjuction with a heart monitor to assess the level of stress or *dis*tress incurred – and treadmills. The water treadmill can be particularly useful for the injured horse, otherwise it is suggested that a treadmill with a level, not sloping, surface is used in the first instance, and that extreme care is taken not to jar the horse and incur further injuries to the limbs, particularly as the horse has become unfit. Too much fast work too soon can be very jarring indeed and the horse has no respite as he cannot stop.

After this stage specific ridden work may be carried out, having first ensured that the fit of the saddle is absolutely correct, again taking into account that the shape of the horse may have altered due to the injury or loss of fitness and condition, and that the rider is of such a standard to be capable of riding in an absolutely balanced fashion and to follow specific instructions which will exercise correctly the muscle groups which are to be addressed. The guidance of a trainer or instructor, with an in depth understanding of the musculature of the horse, and of the physiological effects of different types of exercise, in combination with your vet and or physiotherapist, is invaluable at this point.

As has been pointed out before, a unilateral injury (i.e. on one side only) will *not* correct itself and be restored under normal exercise regimes.

In conclusion, due to the new and exciting techniques now available in this field there is much that can be done to improve the recovery rates in equine sports injuries, to an extent that was undreamed of a few years ago when most of the horse management textbooks were written. It is therefore as well for the horse owner, vet and therapist alike to be open minded and, while avoiding too great a susceptibility to the unproven claims of unscrupulous manufacturers, to show a readiness to take expert advice on modern therapy techniques which may avoid the use of unnecessary and sometimes barbaric surgical techniques (such as tendon firing) when often more suitable and effective techniques may be available. The point in all our dealings with the horse is that it is *always* more beneficial to work *with* nature, rather than *against* it, so it makes sense to promote natural healing and assist it, rather than to follow the 'if in doubt cut it out' or 'turn it out' or 'shut it up for six weeks' school of treatment.

The foot and shoeing

The part of the horse which impacts with the ground and dictates the way in which force passes up the leg is, of course, the foot. In preventing lameness it cannot be stressed too strongly that the trimming of the feet is of paramount importance. An unfortunate fashion at the time of writing is to trim the feet with the toes too long and the heels too low. This significantly increases the strain on the tendons, soft tissues and bones of the feet and legs and positively invites lameness. Ensure that your horse's feet are trimmed as far as his natural conformation allows in accordance with the diagrams in Chapter 2. Basically the slope down the long pastern bone and toe of the front feet, at the toe, should be very near to 45° with the same slope

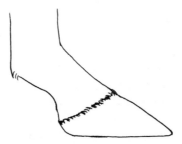

Fig. 10 The long toe and low heel type of conformation which unfortunately seems to be fairly prevalent in horses used for fast work, particularly flat racehorses. For such horses, fitting the shoe to just short of the extremity of the horn at the heels and sloping the heels of the shoe forward a little more than the angle of the hoof heel encourages speed and slows down the hoof as little as possible when it hits the ground. Unfortunately this can, particularly over a number of shoeings, lead to an over-exaggeration of this sort of fit, with the result that the heels do not have enough support and 'sink', the toe is allowed to grow too long (which, in fact, slows down the hoof breakover and, therefore, the pace) and incorrect stresses are inflicted on the leg. There is extra 'pull' on the tendons and ligaments at the back of the leg and a crushing force on the coronary band at the front which interferes with good horn production and can cause laminitis with the sensitive and insensitive laminae being forced apart.

at the heels (which should be strong and well-defined, as per the diagrams). The hind feet/pastern angle can be nearer 50°. From the front, the ends of the coronet should be the same height from the ground at each side of the foot. This constitutes correct foot balance.

There may be some horses whose natural conformation does not quite correlate with these criteria. In these cases, provided the horse does not hit himself and seems a sound character anyway, take the advice of an expert farrier and have the feet trimmed as near the ideal as possible, taking into account the horse's individual foot conformation.

Shoeing is also, obviously, important. The basic points of good shoeing should be known to readers of a book such as this. Generally, ensure that your horse is shod with the shoes well back to the heels, offering adequate support to this area. It seems to be very common these days to shoe short at the heels, which encourages the heels to weaken and drop with resultant stress and strain on the feet and legs, an accompanying lengthening of the toe and possibly mechanical laminitis due to incorrect forces on the soft tissues of the feet which weaken the normally strongly-interlocked sensitive and insensitive laminae. If, for some reason such as cold shoeing preventing a perfect fit or a precisely-fitting shoe not being available, it is necessary to fit a slightly too-short shoe, it is better to have it set back a little at the toe to ensure heel protection rather than leave the heels short.

Studs are very widely used for various ground conditions and are essential to prevent slipping and to give a good 'grip' on the ground, but it should be remembered that, especially if fitted in only one heel, they significantly upset the balance of the foot and, therefore, the direction of forces up the leg will be uneven, over-stressing the limb. Never leave studs in when the horse does not need them. Do not make the horse stand around, especially on hard ground, with studs in for the same reason, and use the smallest studs possible commensurate with the task in hand. Use also the lightest shoe you reasonably can to reduce drag and weight and consequent muscular effort during action, and concussion when the foot lands. All these measures add up to reduced stress on an already very hard-working component of the athletic horse, and can only assist the maintenance of soundness. In addition, give the horse as many periods as you can each year with no shoes (a properly balanced diet should ensure adequate hoof quality to stand up to working on soft surfaces without shoes until significant roadwork and fast work are needed) so that his feet and legs have the tremendous benefits of working naturally, with maximum blood circulation and all the benefits that brings. The feet can expand properly to suit the size and weight of the horse, as nature intended, and not be inevitably restricted by nailed-on metal shoes.

Metal-shoe substitutes of various types (such as nylon, plastic, polyurethane and paint-on 'bonding' substances) are all being tried, but at the time of writing have made virtually no inroads at all into the field of active competition or hard training. Research has shown that the stresses on a foot shod with a non-metal shoe are very similar to those on an unshod one and quite different from those experienced by a foot shod with nailed-on metal. As in all management matters, the further we get from nature the more problems we have, so it is to be hoped that further research and development of non-metal foot protection will eventually come up with a solution, maybe variable, that will protect the feet from excessive wear, provide 'grip' and support where necessary and also permit natural stresses on the foot.

One obvious way of preventing lameness, or rather more serious lameness, is not to work a horse that is already slightly injured. Not

Plate 21 Swimming can be a useful form of exercise, particularly for horses with limb injuries. It can help to maintain or increase the fitness of the heart, lungs and circulation but cannot be used as a replacement for road work and ridden exercise as it does nothing to enhance bone density. (Photograph supplied by Mr Ray Hutchinson, B.Vet.Med., MRCVS.)

many people would be foolish enough to do this but the danger is that those who habitually use anti-inflammatory drugs as a precaution (within permitted levels) may be masking very slight lameness or unlevelness. Continuing to work the horse in this condition will result in unremitting overstress on the injured part which will almost certainly be more seriously injured.

Those who regularly study their horses' action and have a very good picture of how they normally look and feel during work will be able to tell when something is not quite right, and modern technology can often confirm whether their hunch is correct. The racing world probably leads the field in installing such technology as force plates (popularly called 'testers') actually in a yard for fairly regular use, but money for such advances is more generally available in the racing industry than in other equestrian disciplines.

Force plates are special pads with electronic sensors over which the horse is walked or trotted. The pads sense the distribution of forces on the feet and legs and the results appear on a computer printout, for comparison against those for a sound horse. Although interpretation of the printout needs some expert knowledge and experience, the technique *can* be learned with some practice and initial help from a veterinary surgeon.

Using force plates can tell a trainer when the horse is very slightly injured, sore or 'feeling' so that further damaging work can be avoided and a valuable horse saved for another day – or several years. Every reasonable step should be taken to avoid aggravating an injury as healed tissue is never as strong as the original. Once a horse has had a serious tendon or ligament injury, for example, it is highly likely to break down again if returned to work at a similar level.

Other techniques of detecting, shall we say, pre-lameness injury include thermography and scintigraphy. Thermography measures the heat given off by a given part of the body such as a suspected injured tendon, and shows it on a special screen as a contour map. This is then compared with one of a sound limb and, in theory at least, the limb contaning a 'hot spot' is the lame one. Some practitioners, however, feel the technique is not wholly appropriate for early diagnosis of lameness as inflammation is not always present in such cases.

Scintigraphy is useful for diagnosing bone injuries caused by concussion or knocks, kicks etc. A sensitive instrument called a scintillation counter can detect and measure a slightly radioactive compound previously injected into the horse and absorbed by bone. Damaged bone will contain more of the compound than sound bone, and again by comparing a sound leg, the extent and site of a suspected injury can be detected.

More familiar techniques of diagnosing and detecting even slight injury include nerve blocking, X-raying, ultrasound scanning and Faradism. Another development is arthroscopy in which a probe called, predictably, an arthroscope can be inserted into a joint, and damage to soft tissues, joint cartilage and bone itself, if appropriate, can be seen.

Such techniques obviously have to be paid for and may involve transporting the horse to some establishment where the technology is available if the owner's usual vet does not possess it. However, when compared to the cost of the horse, its keep and training over the several years it takes to get a horse even on to a course let alone producing winning form, it is well worthwhile.

Respiratory problems

Thanks to the artificial way we keep most performance horses, denying them the undoubted benefits of significant periods of time (many hours) out in the fresh air, one of the major problems facing those involved in equestrian competition is respiratory disease and allergic condition. Many vets involved in research and in practices treating performance horses feel that in fact most horses today are in some way, even slightly, affected by some sort of respiratory disorder. The horse may appear to be perfectly fine but if he has been in such a condition for a long time, maybe since before his present owner acquired him, the owner will have no criterion by which to measure his present condition.

The horse's lung function compared to ours is absolutely superb, as may be expected from a creature evolved to run. That creature was also evolved to live in the open air, not surrounded by the stable dust and fodder and bedding moulds and spores which are present in most stable environments. These may begin by slightly irritating the mucous membranes of the lungs, causing slight inflammation and mucous production in the air spaces and reducing their volume and potential for oxygen uptake. It may go no further than this. Some individuals, however, will, as a result, succumb more easily to respiratory infection as bacteria and viruses find access to the body that much easier via damaged tissues. Not only can a disease itself put a horse off work for weeks or even months (as in the case of influenza or strangles) but also permanent further damage may occur to the lung tissue reducing still further the horse's ability to become fit.

In other horses, the familiar and distressing allergic condition popularly called broken wind may result. The body recognises the dust and spores as invading alien bodies and over-reacts, in some cases, by producing histamine which causes dilation and increased permeability of the capillaries (which may also make the horse a 'bleeder'). The inflammation which also results constricts the airways and, obviously, affects the horse's ability to breathe adequately.

Horses worked with any kind of respiratory disorder can also get heart strain, apart from permanently damaging their lungs, so the whole scenario of respiratory disorder can easily spell death to a competitive career and even to the horse himself.

Vaccines *are* available to protect against respiratory disease (although not, at the time of writing, against strangles in Britain) and horses with allergies can be kept on permanent medication which is effective if expensive. However, modern thinking on this whole topic is that management by means of a clean air regime is more than half the battle in preventing and lessening the effects of respiratory disorders. Most of our top eventers have taken this knowledge on board but other disciplines, including racing, seem slow to accept it. *Even if you think your horse has nothing wrong with his wind, you will probably find that after only a few weeks on a clean air regime his performance definitely improves.*

Basically, a clean air regime involves keeping the horse as far away from the things that cause the problems (dust and spores) as possible – or rather keeping them away from him. It is common knowledge that 'windy' horses improve greatly when turned out, except possibly on days with a high pollen count, only to revert to poor performance, gasping and wheezing and coughing, when stabled again. Most competition horses, certainly when in work, are denied significant periods out at grass often because of lack of understanding of their physiology by their connections, a lack of appreciation of the benefits of turning out, or misplaced or exaggerated fears of dangers lurking in the field.

In conversations with veterinary surgeons I have found that they usually find that far more injuries are caused in the stable itself or during work and transportation than in the field; on this basis, the least dangerous place for the horse to be is in the field! Turning out not only greatly benefits the lungs but the entire body as the horse is doing what nature meant it to do and what it is designed for – moving about most of the time continually and gently using its whole body, and also grazing and keeping its digestive system in good order. As many endurance competitors can confirm, grass of clean but low nutritional quality enhances well-being and fitness rather than hinders it. Instead of conventional stabling with short periods of half a day at the most in the field (and some horses do not even get that), a far more healthy method of accommodating horses would be to yard them, with or without access to pasture.

If stabling is the only form of accommodation available, far more attention should be paid to ventilation than is normal in my experience.

Leaving the top door open, plus a window on the same side, is *not* sufficient to ensure adequate air change. Stables should have installed every ventilation device possible, such as ridge-roof ventilators preferably running most of the whole length of the roof, gable-end louvres of significant size, and windows or ventilation holes or louvres opposite the normal window and door to create a high cross draught for removing carbon dioxide and generally stale air. On most days it should be possible to leave the bottom door open too, to create a ground-level inlet to help remove the ammonia which soon results from the decomposition of organic matter such as droppings and urine, particularly the latter. As it is common practice for some dirty bedding to be retained in the box as a base for new litter, normally only the worst being removed, there will always be some ammonia forming in most boxes. The only way round this is to remove *all* the used bedding every day, salvaging only the genuinely clean material. Stable Boy granules (Baystrait House, Station Road, Biggleswade, SG18 8AL) can be spread on the bare floor first and are claimed by the manufacturers and by many who use them to neutralise the harmful products of decomposing organic matter, so should significantly help maintain a healthy atmosphere. With the bottom door open, horses can obviously be kept in their boxes by means of a bar or chain across the doorway, or an American-style canvas webbing 'gate', commonly used in the USA.

If the loose box is a suitable size, all this ventilation will not result in draughts, and in any case the bottom door can be left shut on windy days. In roomy, lofty stables (minimum $3\frac{1}{2}$ m (12 ft) to the eaves) with the outlets described, and with well-kept bedding, ventilation is quite adequate.

Apart from general ventilation, the bedding material and type of forage fed to the horse are also important from a general management point of view. Only shredded paper or dust-extracted shavings should be used, although dust-extracted straw is also now becoming available. Sawdust is usually just that–dusty–and peat can be very dusty indeed yet is surprisingly often recommended as a dust-free bedding! You can actually see the dust in the horses' coats and smell it in the air, let alone find it on ledges. (Peat is also a cold, damp bedding, whether sedge or moss peat, and I personally have never found anything in it to recommend as a bedding material.) Full daily mucking out or semi-deep litter systems may be used, but research is showing that deep litter is not recommended, whatever the material used, for horses needing a clean air regime, as gas and spores do build up in the environment unless the drainage and ventilation are exceptional, particularly the latter as most urine will be taken up by the lower layers of the bedding no matter what the drainage is like.

As for forage, all hay should be soaked for 4 hours to swell the spores present on even a good sample to such a size that they cannot reach the tiny airways where much of the problem arises. Only excellent quality, clean hay should be used anyway, but even so, for this type of regime, it should be soaked. Alternatively, conserved forages of the hayage type should be fed as they are moist and nearer, in any case, to the natural food of the horse. If you find that your horse cleans up his ration too quickly, leaving him for a dangerously long period without food, simply feed a lower energy grade product and also give it in special hayage nets with small holes to force him to spin out his ration by only being able to fiddle out small amounts at once. For horses only used to hay, who sometimes refuse to eat hayage when first introduced, start by mixing a small amount of hayage with the normal hay ration, and gradually make a complete changeover to hayage over a period of four weeks. Silage can obviously be fed, but most owners of competition horses find it too inconvenient, messy, difficult to store and inconsistent in quality. There have also been problems with botulism in big-bale silage, plus difficulties in obtaining an accurate analysis of the nutritional content.

Slightly damping short feeds is good practice, of course, but if coarse mixes (sweet feeds in the USA) are fed, this is not necessary as they are slightly moist anyway.

The stable should not be mucked out while the horse is in as this inevitably raises the dust. All grooming should take place as far as possible out of doors (under cover if necessary) and the stable itself should be regularly brushed or preferably vacuumed from top to bottom, including all rafters and ledges, to remove build-up of dust. When any stable activity has taken place, time should be allowed for the dust to settle and for the atmosphere to clear again before the horse is put back into his box.

The same rules should be observed during transportation, where lack of ventilation is known to cause transport/shipping fever. It should be remembered that if you travel your horse in the same box as one who is not on a clean air regime and who, say, has straw in his compartment or unsoaked hay to eat en route, your own horse can, within a very short period of time, be affected and all your painstaking management at home put to nought. This can be a problem if you are staying away at a competition, too, so needs careful consideration as to who you stable your horse next to and in what type of stabling. Unless all boxes are completely cut off, with no shared air space, again your efforts will be wasted as dust and spores drifting in from neighbouring boxes will invade your horse's airspace. More and more competitors are realising the benefits of dust-free regimes, and organisers of competitions are having to cater for them to a greater extent, but 'dusty' management is still the norm and will only be changed at competition venues by increased pressure from competitors to provide or cater for better management practices, if only by providing all together stables for those wishing to keep their horses on a clean air regime.

Commercial companies usually catch on fairly quickly to trends in their field, and to assist those wishing to keep their animals in a dust-free environment Sedgemoor Developments plc of Mannaman House, Sealand Road, Chester, CH1 6BW have produced the Dust-Cure hay and straw cleaning machine, which they claim vacuum-cleans forage and bedding passed through it, almost completely cleaning it of dust and moulds (see Plate 22). Dust-free, cleaned forages and bedding materials are also gradually coming on to the general market for direct purchase.

At the time of writing a product has recently been made available consisting of an ozone-friendly spray-on liquid called Revestopur

Plate 22 The Dust-Cure hay and straw cleaning machine in use.

(marketed by Micro-Plus of Unit 8, Westover Industrial Estate, Ivybridge, Devon, PL21 9ES) which is sprayed on to shaken-out hay and straw and which, it is claimed, 'encapsulates the dust particles and micro-organisms and renders them harmless'. The idea, apparently, is to prevent them being inhaled. Provided people do not get the idea that this is a way of making mouldy hay fit for feeding, this product could well be worth investigating.

Air ionizers also have their advocates. They work by emitting negatively-charged ions (atoms) which are claimed to 'clean' the surrounding air by giving airborne particles of dust, mould, pollen, smoke etc. a negative electrical charge which pulls them towards the nearest earthed surface, usually the ground or floor. The effect seems to be to create fresh air, or an outdoor effect, indoors or in the stable. Many people report relief from hay fever, dust allergies, asthma, pollen, house-mite allergies and even migraine by means of ionizers, and owners of 'windy' horses report similar successes.

There are various herbal remedies for respiratory disorders, plus standard veterinary medications, but one practice which I read about in an old book and which certainly seems to work in my experience is to hang raw onions up in the stable (most easily in a tennis ball bag, the net type). For some unknown reason this definitely seems to keep respiratory 'lurgies' at bay. I tried to find out why some years ago by asking a veterinary professor I was interviewing, and he said he had known this practice keep free of foot and mouth disease a farm right in the middle of a seriously affected area. He also confirmed it definitely helps horses in such epidemics as strangles, influenza etc. although he could not tell me why. One thing is for sure, it cannot do any harm. If the horses try to eat the onions they soon stop! The onions must be changed at least once a week, as once they go soft their effectiveness ceases. Peel or cut them to let the fumes circulate.

Veterinary sports medicine

Apart from normal preventative and maintenance medicine which should be a normal part of the routine of any horse, competition horses and their owners can now call on substantial resources of knowledge in the field of sports medicine to check on health and performance, to monitor fitness, to spot sub-clinical disease and to generally produce an equine athlete in peak condition.

Because of the great interest in the phenomenon of the sports horse, research programmes in sports medicine exist all over the world and new knowledge is coming to light all the time. At present owners can expect to receive up-to-date knowledge and help on exercise physiology (how the horse functions during work); attaining, maintaining and assessing fitness; diet and metabolism, haematology and the role of blood in equine performance; the importance of bone, its growth, characteristics, modelling and remodelling, stresses and strains, injuries to bone and how all these affect training and performance; respiratory factors such as lung-function tests, ventilation-perfusion relationships, diffusion and the link between breathing rate and gait; the cardiovascular system and response to exercise; muscle conditioning and metabolism (energy production and utilisation); the role of the nervous system, the advantages and disadvantages of drugs; performance profiling; sports injuries (diagnosis and treatment); loss-of-performance syndrome and exercise intolerance and various other factors which are of acute interest and importance to competition horses.

If it was not obvious before, it should be obvious after reading the above list that it is essential for the serious competitor to have a veterinary surgeon who has an equally serious interest in equine performance and competition. Without such a person, the horse/rider team is at a serious disadvantage. Locally, riders will know of veterinary surgeons who *are* interested and word of mouth is still one of the best ways to find a suitable practitioner. Many competitors, however, 'import' vets from neighbouring districts to get who and what they want. However you go about it, the right vet is essential.

Health maintenance programmes

The competition horse obviously needs a basic health maintenance programme involving regular vaccinations, teeth checks and medical examinations, but in addition may also need various biological checks such as blood tests and profiles. These do cost money but are invaluable not only in monitoring and assessing fitness and condition but also in spotting disorders before they have become obvious enough even to suspect.

Competitors not working at top level often feel such expenditure is not necessary for them, and this may be true if they are happy enough with things as they are and have no ambition to rise up the ladder. If, however, you do aspire to greater things which will inevitably put greater stress on your horse, a more comprehensive maintenance programme is well worthwhile. Remember also that a less talented horse may well be competing at what is for him personally top level anyway, even lower down the competitive scale. If he is trying his heart out for you it is only fair to give him the benefits of modern sports medicine.

Drugs

Despite the fact that the drugs issue has been regularly aired for many years now and most sports are well covered by regulations stipulating what and how much horses in their disciplines may have administered, the topic continues to create considerable interest at world level. Opinions will always vary, with those in favour of 'precautionary' administration of drugs to sports horses believing they are just as right as those totally against the practice.

The undesirable face of competition always raises its ugly head when drugs are administered to affect performance in a dishonest way. While laboratories offering detection and analysis services are now capable of detecting the minutest trace of a drug, the disreputable competitors always seem to come up with a new one they have yet to detect. Masking agents which disguise the presence of a drug in the body are giving greatest cause for concern and, probably due to lack of funding, spot checks at home on competitors, which would seem to be an obvious course of action, are not being done.

Methods of detecting gingering substances applied to show jumpers' legs are also currently greatly in need of developing and refining. The Federation Equestre International is taking a close look at the whole problem of drug, and horse, abuse and it is hoped that tight regulations, and the means of policing them, will soon be in force.

Fitness

Interval training has now been on the competition horse scene for almost 20 years, yet still causes arguments as to its efficacy or otherwise. Some riders and trainers claim it is useless, while others swear by it. It is certainly true that it is not a panacea for *all* horses, and some do come to hand better and more quickly with traditional methods.

There are other methods of attaining fitness, too, which are covered in the already-mentioned book *Getting Horses Fit* by Sarah Pilliner.

The one point which is essential, and which applies whatever the actual method you use, is that it must work for the horse to which it is applied and you must have a method of fairly accurately assessing just how fit a horse is at any given time. Heart-rate monitors and other items of electronic equipment can be used, but by far the simplest and most immediate, practical test you can do is to check and faithfully record your horse's recovery rate after work. The rate at which his pulse/heartbeat returns to its pre-work rate will tell you for all practical purposes how fit he is.

Fitter horses usually have slower at-rest rates (at rest meaning quite

Plate 23 Heart rate monitors can give a useful on-board assessment of fitness and stress levels and are essential for a true interval training programme which should be based on heart recovery rates and not on timed periods of exercise alone. (Photograph by Gillian McCarthy.)

peaceful and relaxed in the stable before any work has been done) than unfit ones, and if you make a habit of checking the pulse daily or at least weekly during a fitness programme, you will notice over a period of time that the at-rest rate does decrease slightly. This is not, however, sufficient a criterion for fairly accurately assessing fitness.

After a normal warm-up period spent walking and trotting about in preparation for harder work, the horse's pulse/heart rate will be 60 to 80 beats per minute. Note it, mentally or otherwise, give the horse his intended work-out and at the end of it take his pulse again. Then re-check it again *10 minutes* later: it should now be noticeably slower and nearer to the pre-work rate than to that at which he finished work. If he has not recovered to his 60 or 80 beats per minute (or whatever) within 30 minutes he is still significantly unfit.

Another test is to use a heart-rate monitor and, keeping the horse's heart-rate at 200 or below, see how far he can travel in a set time of your choice, say 30 seconds. As he grows fitter he will be able to travel further in that time.

It should be remembered that weather, going and emotional factors such as excitement can all affect stress and, therefore, heart-rate, and

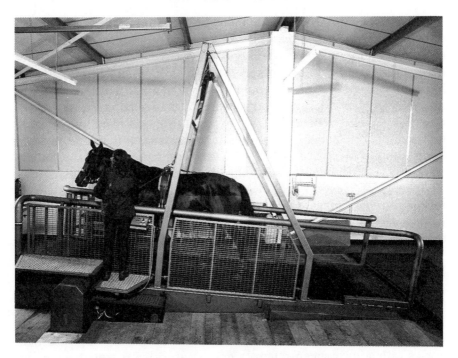

Plate 24 The treadmill is a useful means both of exercising the horse and of conducting standard exercise tests in order to assess the fitness of performance horses. It is also used extensively in exercise physiology research. (Photograph supplied by Dr David Snow.)

you should make allowances for this using your assessment of the particular horse's likes and dislikes and emotional tendencies.

Change of temperament

Most owners and managers of fit, athletic horses find that the horses' temperaments often change with increasing fitness, or when they have been in active work for some weeks or months. Normally these changes are for the worse. A fit, healthy, properly-managed horse who enjoys his work, however, should not become ratty. It is natural for high spirits to be felt and these can come out in playfulness, excuses to shy, squeal or become 'strong' during work. If the horse shows signs of actual bad temper, snapping and biting, pulling nasty faces, becoming restless in the box or even developing vices, these are signs of something wrong with the management rather than just feeling well. Feeling truly well does not result in bad temper, although this is often the excuse given.

Attention to the diet should comprise a reappraisal of the concentrate: bulk/roughage ratio as this can certainly be a source of feeling out of sorts. Some experts recommend only a 50:50 ratio in a very fit, hard-working horse but others advise reducing the bulk (normally the hay) portion even lower. It should be borne in mind that the horse was not evolved to exist on concentrates. Its digestion needs ample roughage to digest concentrates, this ability varying from individual to individual. A 50:50 ratio is pushing the horse's natural abilities to their limits, and a decrease below 50 per cent hay/hayage (by weight obviously) is calculated to make the horse feel uncomfortable and may well cause indigestion (colic), mild cases of which are not always recognised. Too many concentrates cause excess toxins which cause a feeling of being 'out of sorts' in mild cases and can create wood-chewing apart from general malaise.

There is a product called *Thrive*, marketed in Britain by Natural Animal Feeds, which is made of a mineral-containing clay and which Natural Animal Feeds claim helps neutralise the toxins present in a high-concentrate diet. Users certainly report excellent results but such products should not be used solely to enable managers to continue feeding a grossly unnatural diet to their horses, but simply to help horses with a low concentrate tolerance to absorb a reasonable amount of concentrates in their diets.

In many cases an increase in the *quality* and quantity of the hay, plus a slight decrease in the concentrate ration, will provide the nutrients required without the disadvantages of a too-high concentrate/too-low hay diet.

Frustration and boredom caused by over-confinement in stabled, fit animals are undoubtedly a cause of adverse temperament changes, plus the lack of natural social contact with other horses. It really is not enough for them merely to see other horses around or exercise with them for only a couple of hours a day, if that. Only a few competition yards seem to yard their horses rather than keep them stabled, but those that do report better balanced horses mentally, higher apparent levels of contentment, better commitment to work, better utilization of feed (probably due to the higher contentment levels) and, what is more, saved labour as individual stabling is certainly a labour intensive way of keeping horses.

It would be good to see more yards keeping their animals in this effective, more natural way, not least because the horses can take constant, gentle exercise as in nature with its consequent improvement in physical condition, but ordinary turning out for several hours a day in a paddock with another compatible animal (many stables keep a small, quiet pony for this purpose) would help greatly with temperament problems and is fairer on the horses. This daily turning out should be a regular, daily part of a horse's routine in addition to his work, and should not be regarded as simply a special treat when it is convenient to the owner or manager.

Poor, unnatural management practices stress horses unnecessarily and unreasonably. It is no wonder that so many of them vent their frustration and feelings of insecurity and, who is to say otherwise, sadness by means of a deteriorating temperament when in work.

Riding/work surfaces

The ideal conditions on which to work horses comprise well-drained, old (and therefore springy) turf with a fair covering of grass. Unfortunately, such conditions are very hard to come by and attempts to devise suitable artificial substitutes have so far failed. There are various sorts of artificial surfaces (artificial in terms of manufactured, as they mostly comprise natural materials) but none has, as yet, really provided all the essentials required of a suitable, safe surface for horses.

Horses need a surface with spring in it to help absorb concussion, one which is non-slip, which does not scatter in use (including when jumping and negotiating tight corners as on some racecourses), which neither clogs, floods, bakes nor freezes, which is not dusty and which has no appreciable kick-back when used in a racing situation. The problem of kick-back is not important in other disciplines, where horses usually compete singly. Kick-back, apart from being extremely unpleasant for riders and, especially, horses, also means the horse will get sand (or whatever the substance is) in his eyes, stinging his face and down his throat. Horses raced amid kick-back generally pull up coughing and this is something no conscientious owner or trainer should tolerate. Repeated discomfort can also soon put an animal off his job.

For training purposes, probably the best surface so far devised is 75 per cent hardwood, 25 per cent softwood and a sprinkling of rubber chips or shreds on the top. Such surfaces are in use and proving successful for training purposes (where horses do not work on each other's heels) in England and Ireland and some other countries, but are not felt suitable, for various reasons, for actual racing surfaces.

For non-racing disciplines natural turf is mostly used, with various wood and sand based arenas often being seen for show jumping and dressage. The types of grass mixtures best suited to equestrian competition are those used for football pitches and the like, comprising largely hard-wearing *agrostis* species.

10
Marketing

Much has been said in the equestrian press during recent years about the importance of marketing the competition horse. Certainly the European countries such as Germany, Denmark, Belgium and Holland, and also France, have been streets ahead of the UK on this score, but we are at last pulling ourselves together into a promisingly cohesive outfit and beginning to act seriously along more commercially effective lines.

Performance/progeny testing and associated sales

The continental Europeans have long had centres where uniform training procedures precede official, central sales of potential and specially-bred competition horses, usually, but not always, based on state-run lines. In America and some other countries, sales accompany special or designated shows, some studs have open days or viewing days for stallions and youngstock and sometimes sales are held on their own.

What really matters is that there should be some 'shop window' where potential performance horses can be seen in comparison with others, where, because of the occasion, real efforts have been made to have the horses trained to a reasonable standard, depending on their age, in good condition, preferably vetted and respectably turned out. In Britain now we have our annual high performance horse sales, preceded by a shortish training period undertaken by selected riders and instructors. These are, as already mentioned, improving each year and will, it is hoped, become a focal point of the equestrian year, a date for every breeder, rider, sponsor and purchaser to put in their diaries as not to be missed.

The advantages of similar sales-cum-displays are considerable, provided the young horses involved are not over-tired by continuously being pulled out of their boxes, shown, tried and assessed. Tiredness, especially in youngsters, not only prevents an animal being seen at its best but can sour an animal's temperament before its career even begins, particularly where they are also hauled around the country chasing qualifying classes for certain show-based championships, with the incessant standing around and travelling, the stress of strange places and water and maybe even food, the crowds, and the sense of always being under scrutiny, even in their boxes.

It is a great advantage to buyers to be able to see many horses at one venue. If the occasion is well-run and the standard of horse high, it also creates a tremendously good impression which puts buyers into a good mood and more inclined to buy! It is a prestige event for the nation or organisation concerned, be it a privately-run stud or competition stable or a formal, national sale, and breeders and producers can see the level of the competition. Buyers are more inclined to spend time and money going to one sale with a high reputation than to double or quadruple their expenditure of time and money travelling round to various establishments where maybe only one or two animals are available for viewing and trying.

The advantages of professional, and preferably uniform, training prior to the show and sale gives purchasers an idea of how well the animals concerned have responded to schooling, and purchasers can see by their attitudes how they are likely to progress and take to further training. At sales where grading takes place, the knowledge of an animal's grading status is a real help to buyers. It tells them roughly how much the animal will make during the actual sale and what its abilities are likely to be. Details in the sale catalogue of the animal's family history, as to performance, are invaluable and becoming essential in today's market. The time cannot be far off when stallions awarded prizes based on the old-fashioned British system of judging conformation and action alone will simply not be acceptable to serious buyers of competition youngstock. Mares, too, will have to prove themselves in competition a few years and attain a reasonable record before their offspring will be much in demand for attractive prices. The progeny of unproven animals will be regarded as too much of a gamble for the purchaser and, because they will not be such an attractive commodity, as hardly worth the production costs and effort for the breeder/producer. The only exceptions, in times to come, will be animals from parents known to consistently produce performers in the purchaser's desired discipline.

Other animals will find a market all right, but not in the higher echelons of the competition horse field. 'Fun' horses will always be needed for such activities as riding club events, local and regional shows, showing proper, hunting where applicable and so on. Even so, because breeding will always, for the forseeable future, contain some element of uncertainty, this market will probably be easily enough filled by properly performance-bred animals who have simply not made the grade at higher levels, either at a formal grading event or, later, in actual competition.

The way forward is undoubtedly largely by means of efficiently-run shows-cum-sales, combined with proper training and performance/progeny testing, although there will doubtless always be animals procured outside this system from reputable studs producing performance animals or dealers specialising in them.

Presentation and selling

From the seller's point of view, presentation is extremely important. A seller cannot expect a purchaser to be able to spot a potential champion in the rough (although some certainly can, of course) or to overlook, or forgive, the fact that the animal is just a touch 'not right at the moment', will not lead well in hand, is filthy dirty or, worse, too thin or too fat, both of which indicate lack of proper care and nutrition with a subsequent ill effect on the animal's physique. It also does not create a good impression if the animal's handlers are sloppy, untidily or inappropriately dressed, do not know how to present an animal properly or expect it to simply show itself. If the purchaser has visited the animal at home, he or she will not be put into a favourable frame of mind if the establishment is obviously untidy, run down, badly organised and with staff (and maybe even proprietors) inappropriately or even messily dressed. They will automatically expect to pay less for an animal from such a yard, if they buy it at all.

Vendors should remember that they never get a second chance to make a first impression – and first impressions *are* tremendously important when selling anything, not just horses. Make sure yours wins half your battle for you by having your establishment well-maintained and run at all times, you and your staff neatly and cleanly turned out (there is no reason to be dirty and scruffy just because you work with horses) and your animals well and properly trained up to a fair standard for the animal's age.

Proper handling should start from the foal's first day on earth and be progressively but imperceptibly carried on so that when the time comes to back the youngster and ride it away (I do detest the expression 'breaking in') it will be no big deal and nothing particularly new – simply one more strange thing these humans expect!

It is pointless presenting a horse for show, display or sale if it is not in perfect condition, perfectly sound, perfectly mannered for its age and perfectly able to carry out movements reasonably to be expected of an animal of its age. Anything less will not impress buyers and will reduce the selling price.

It is surprising how many people show and present animals, particularly in hand, obviously without having the slightest idea of the correct way to do this vitally important task. The purchaser, for a start, wants to actually *see* the animal, so do not get in the way, do not get yourself between the viewer/judges/spectators if you can possibly avoid it, and do not crowd or nag at the animal as this not only upsets it but indicates over-anxiety on your part (what are you trying to hide?). If walking the animal around in a circle such as an arena or show ring, walk on its outside nearest the fence so as to guide and balance it better but also so that you are on the far side when the animal is furthest away from the spectators and they can get a clear view from a distance of the whole animal.

Horses must be trained at home to lead up smartly, willingly and calmly in hand. They must not be seen to lag behind the leader or charge off in front. You should be at the horse's shoulder, not its head, and certainly not in front of it. When leading up in hand for individual inspection, proceed directly away from the viewer in a *straight* line; it helps to have your eye on a landmark ahead and make straight for that. Then turn slightly to your left (you being on the horse's nearside), and then right in almost a full circle, and proceed back (at walk or trot as the case may be) again in a straight line towards another landmark. Do not trot the horse round the circle, of course, and wait till he is on the straight line once more before trotting out again. Match your steps to his forelegs in trot, if you possibly can.

Above all, and this is important and most impressive to viewers, *trot the horse up on a loose leadrope or rein*; within reason, the longer the rope and the further you are away from the horse the better. This really gives the horse a chance to move freely and show his natural action unhindered by you. If the horse will not trot up well and calmly in hand without trying to charge off, he is not properly trained or is over-fresh. Youth is no excuse for this basic mistake.

Trotting up a horse on a tight rope, particularly with his head forced sideways towards the handler, looks very bad, hampers his action and can even make him seem to go unlevelly or even appear lame (bridle lameness, as it is termed). Of course, clever handlers can actually disguise faulty action or slight lameness by doing this, but this will out eventually!

When standing the horse up for inspection, his forelegs should be square and he must not rest a hind leg. He should be trained to stand with his head still in a natural position, on a loose rope, with you as far away from him as reasonably possible – and he must stand still and calmly yet, if possible, show an interest in his surroundings. Do not stand close to his head or at the side. Face him squarely, well away, and do not keep extending your arm and hand under his chin as if he is

Fig. 11 When running up a horse in hand for show, inspection or presentation always do so on a *loose* rein or rope so as not to hamper his natural action. Short, even tight, ropes inhibit the horse and can cause him to appear unlevel (in other words, lame) when he is not; they also shorten his stride and prevent his doing justice to his action. When inspecting a horse for purchase, insist that he is run up on a loose rope as a short, or tight, one can inhibit his action to the extent of disguising untrue action or lameness.

incapable of holding up his own head; do not keep bending down or moving about yourself, jiggling the leadrope, picking grass to interest him or generally acting like a rank amateur or mother hen. Stand still and calm, talk to him with recognised commands in a quiet, authoritative voice, give quiet clicks with your tongue if this will get him to prick his ears and, provided you have the right 'aura' to be presenting horses, he will take his cue from you (given adequate training at home) and will stand still, proud and calm.

I am not the only one who finds ludicrous and appalling the current fashion in some circles, notably Arabs in Britain at least, of training horses to stand with their heads right up, noses poked out and necks stretched unnaturally, with the leaders waving their hands above their heads like tic-tac men on a racecourse, clicking their fingers, dancing about or even whooping at the horses. The horses (not to mention the handlers) looks ridiculous and uncomfortable and this stance makes it very difficult for buyers and judges to see the horse as he really is. Arabs are superb performance horses in their own right but their credibility as a breed is suffering badly when seriously-interested purchasers see this sort of carry-on today.

If you have a good horse, let him appear to show himself with as little interference as possible from you. You are there to help him, not make him look foolish or below standard, and certainly not to draw attention to yourself.

Resist the other damaging current fashion of having your horse overtopped. Obesity worries purchasers, who rightly feel that those important legs, and the horse's other bodily systems, must have been overstressed by carrying around, and working with, all that excess weight. The horse should look covered but lean-ish, able to move with athleticism and spring with some sort of preview of what he will look like when mature and fit for real work. This is especially important if the horse is old enough to be shown under saddle or jumping loose or on the lunge.

Turnout depends not only on breed and classification of horse, and also nationality, but on the horse's individual make and shape and there is not space to go into all the ins and outs of turnout here. Mine may be a minority view, but personally I much prefer to see a horse presented *un*plaited, clean, well-groomed and discreetly trimmed and, horror of horrors, with his muzzle and eye 'antennae' feeler whiskers left *on*, which indicates a caring attitude on the part of his present owner. Nothing looks nicer than a natural-looking, well cared-for horse, smartly and carefully turned out without too much 'tarting up' having been done. This indicates supreme confidence in a top class animal, well looked after and with no need to gild the lily – very impressive!

By careful brushing it is still possible, if you feel the need, to exaggerate some parts of your horse and disguise others. Remember that to make a part look shallower or longer horizontally, brush the hair with a *slightly* damp body brush horizontally, and to make a part look narrower or deeper brush vertically. For example, if you feel your horse has rather short quarters brush the hair on the top and sides of the quarters directly back towards the tail horizontally. If you want to disguise a rather long back, brush the hair from behind the elbow to just in front of the stifles vertically downwards towards the ground. This 'deepens' the girth too.

If you do wish to plait up your horse and use quarter marks, sharks teeth and the like, make sure they are all really expertly done, otherwise don't bother. Quarter marks and sharks teeth draw attention to the part on which they are done, so use them to emphasise good points. Play down weaker areas by 'strategic brushing' as described above; decorating them with various marks will merely point them out.

Plaits should be correctly set for the shape and length of the neck. A rather thick, cresty neck needs the plaits set down on the side of the crest, whereas a straight neck should have the plaits, other than the two at the extreme ends of the neck, set up on the crest to give an illusion of a better shape. A shortish neck can be made to seem longer with an increased number (within reason) of smaller plaits, and vice versa. I feel a plaited tail looks much nicer than a pulled one, but this is a matter of personal perference. Normally the pulling or plaiting should be taken two-thirds of the way down the dock but this depends on the individual quarters. Appley quarters can be disguised by leaving a slightly fuller tail and not going too far down with the pulling/plaiting. On the other hand, the reverse is not always the case; weak, even cut-up quarters could do with tail hair to cover them up!

When plaiting the tail, if you take the locks of hair under each other rather than over, you get a raised braid all the way down which can look very attractive and give the appearance of a better tail carriage than the horse actually has. The important thing with tail plaits is that the top must not sag and the braid must be straight and central down the dock. If you cannot get this effect, either get someone else to do it or do not bother. So many good horses are spoiled by poor turnout. If turnout is not your speciality, get a good book on showing and study the tricks of the trade in the turnout/grooming chapter; also in equestrian magazines.

Do go easy on the baby oil, too, as horses with greasy faces look really awful. Just smear a little on an old silk scarf, evenly, place it over the body brush and go over the whole coat if you feel it lacks lustre. This gives a better effect than proprietary coat dressings. Use the oil to emphasise good points and thin-skinned areas such as round eyes and muzzle and between the buttocks, also muscled areas such as behind the shoulder, quarters, thighs and the top of the neck.

White chalk is universally used to emphasise white markings, but do carefully brush off the excess. Be careful which hoof dressing you use. So many are simply oils which sit on the surface of the hoof and pick up all the dust and dirt long before you enter the ring or arena. Varnish-type dressings are better for this purpose.

Knowledgeable buyers will not appreciate seeing well muscled-up youngsters as they will rightly be worried about all the work they have done to get them into that state at such a very young age. Youngsters should appear as previously described – well-covered but leanish, with athletic potential. Older horses, five and over, can be expected to be fit and muscled according to what work they have been doing.

I hope it is finally sinking in that to get an animal too fat and also to attempt to force its growth with excess concentrates, with a view to making it appear well grown, is one of the most dangerous things you can do to it from a management point of view. So-called contracted tendons (tendons which cannot keep up with unnaturally fast, 'forced' bone growth) have been familiar on Thoroughbred studs for years, for instance, but with our improved knowledge of equine nutrition these and other bone problems are considerably less common than formerly. It is to be hoped that the competition horse breeding industry does not take over similar problems in an effort to 'put up a good show' at progeny tests and the like, with so many buyers now demanding to see yearlings 'popped' over poles, even, to get some idea of potential. I really do hope that breeders and sellers will resist such trends and buyers will see sense and cease to push for unreasonable demands on the very horses upon whom the industry depends.

Schooling and presenting youngstock on the lunge should also be a minimal activity as circling places much more stress on the legs, back and general physique than working gently on large curves and straight lines. Long-reining is more appropriate for this reason, together with loose schooling, provided too much circling and also tight turns are avoided. There is nothing wrong with long-reining a youngster in moderation, any more than there is in teaching him to lead in hand and 'go walkies' about the place to become worldly-wise. It is when such schooling becomes drilling and over-demanding that trouble is likely to arise.

It is widely said and believed that Thoroughbreds mature earlier than other breeds, and this is why the industry is said to get away with racing two-year-olds which, it should be borne in mind, involves backing and riding the animals often at only *18 months of age* in real terms. They are galloping at home, so that their trainers can judge whether or not they have any potential, well before their actual second birthdays in many cases. Not surprisingly, a high percentage never even reach the racecourse due to stress injuries on immature bodies and general wear and tear.

I sincerely hope this type of thing is not going to start in the competition horse world as buyers and sellers seem, in many cases, to be pushing horses at a younger and younger age to show their potential if not to actually compete. The fact is that Thoroughbreds do not mature significantly earlier than other breeds. Competition horses contain a high percentage of Thoroughbred blood with various admixtures of other breeds and types too. I hope competition horse breeders, trainers, riders and managers can learn from the mistakes of the racing industry and safeguard the health and soundness of their animals by allowing them to mature before asking serious questions of them. We are constantly bemoaning the lack of top class animals. Let us not ruin those we have by working them too young.

Marketing aids

It is surprising how many studs can still only provide stud cards for their stallions to advertise their studs, and nothing else. Some of the more progressive ones do actually produce a stud brochure and some are now taking a leaf out of the Thoroughbred industry's book and producing videos of their stallions, broodmares and youngstock.

Some of the stud cards and brochures I have seen, from quite well-known studs producing successful animals, are appalling, with spelling mistakes, printing errors, plain grammatical mistakes, poorly-executed, badly-designed and with really down-market-looking presentation; all topped off with photographs bad enough to put any buyer off no matter how benevolent he or she may be feeling.

Your brochure/stud card is your public face and is just as important as the appearance of your establishment, horses and staff. It is not normally the sort of thing you need to change drastically every year, so it is well worth going to a professional design house in the first place to get a decent leaflet or booklet produced. This job should not just be left to the printer and, in any case, someone must check extremely carefully for spelling, printing and grammatical errors, preferably a professional editor who really understands the English language. Go for something classical, simple and tasteful. Don't use quaint or flashy typefaces such as mock gothic or Olde English. You do not need glossy art paper, but a good quality and weight of paper gives the look and feel you need to impress buyers. White or very pale grey or blue paper with, respectively, black, dark grey or dark blue printing are the most businesslike. Avoid green, brown and cream. Think in terms of the colours you would use for a man's business suit and you will not go far wrong.

Photographs

Photographs are vital and here it is important not only to have a session with a professional photographer or a genuinely good amateur, but also to have your horses immaculately turned out and *well-behaved* so that they know how to stand up for a photograph as opposed to in the show ring. You need a plain or natural background so as not to detract from the animals themselves.

Shots of horses galloping and playing at liberty are always appealing but you must have a top-class conformation shot of each important horse. The horse should be taken from the near side absolutely square on to the camera. The photographer must point the camera straight – not angled or sloped – at the horse's centre of gravity just behind and a little above the elbow. The horse must stand with his near foreleg absolutely straight, not leaning forward or back, with his off fore a little behind it showing from just below the knee down. The off hind leg should be straight and the near hind extended slightly behind it so that the off hind only shows from just below the hock down. Do not allow the tail to obscure the near hind leg. The horse should look straight ahead so that all his neck is visible, then just turn his *head only* towards the camera very slightly so the viewer is just starting to see his off side eye. If the neck bends towards the camera it will appear shortened, and is incorrect.

This may well sound pedantic but it is the time-honoured, and best, way to present a horse in a photograph. You do not want him to appear to have only two legs by standing him square, which looks really funny in a photograph. The other points have been proved time and time again to show the horse in his best light and really show off good conformation and type. It is impossible to judge conformation accurately with any other position, although other shots can, as I say, be included for effect, particularly shots of the horse working or competing.

It is essential to train the horse to stand like this on command and it is surprising how quickly they catch on to the different types of stance, particularly if, during training for photo sessions, you get someone to stand with a camera in the photographer's position. Horses used to being photographed will come out and stand correctly at once. In fact, it is better by far to get the whole thing over in less than a minute because some horses get bored with photo sessions very quickly – and it does show in the resulting shots.

That *doyenne* or Arab breeders, Lady Wentworth, used to hide a grey pony mare behind a bush near the chosen site for stallion photos. The horse would be brought out, stood up, and then the mare walked out from behind the bush so that the horse would positively radiate astonishment and alertness for the camera. A tip well worth passing on, I feel.

As for background, a brick wall (in reasonable condition) is ideal, or a stone one, but not horrendous, modern breeze blocks. Whitewashed walls are not a good idea as they play havoc with the camera's light meter. A beautiful, distant landscape or lawn with shrubbery are good but watch that you do not get trees growing out of the horse's head or a statue on his back! Avoid like the plague the following: people, hands poking into view, litter, busy backgrounds, sloping ground, grass which obscures the horse's hooves, windy days, poorly-maintained buildings, tools or other tack or equipment left lying around, taps sticking out of walls, clothes lines or telephone cables, electricity pylons, other than immaculate paintwork, children's toys, clutter behind windows, broken windows, patched-up windows or buildings, untidy grass in need of mowing, broken fencing, droppings, cars or other vehicles or farm machinery, stacked jumps or schooling fields in the distance, dead trees, notices; in short anything which looks grotty, mundane or which detracts from the horse. The list sounds daunting but you soon develop an eye for a site and a background, especially when you study objectively the resulting prints.

Do not let the photographer send you full-size proofs as this costs money. Instead ask for the contact sheet, a sheet of small prints which you study with the help of a magnifying glass. Then order your chosen shots or proofs from that. This is much cheaper and just as effective.

Videos

Videos are the coming thing, especially for the larger studs or for groups of small breeders to get together, perhaps through a breed society, and pool resources to get a good marketing video made. Most producers are well aware of the need to keep costs down and can do a very good job fairly reasonably. Your place must be in superb condition, as must your horses, as faults are magnified a hundred fold on film – and in stills come to that, hence the need to be so picky about poses and background. You will have wide scope to include what you want on a video, of course, and sequences of your horses competing and being presented with prizes are always good, as are 'at home' sequences showing good temperament and appealing idiosyncracies.

On film, trot up your horse for the camera just as you would for a judge or potential buyer – and *do* stand him up *as for a photograph* for ten seconds running time. This is not a waste of film. On the contrary, it allows viewers to get a good enough idea of conformation to decide whether or not your horse is worth a visit. They cannot judge conformation alone from moving shots. It also shows how well the horse is trained to stand up and still when required, so will emphasise your general handling and management.

Get the commentary done by someone *without* a pronounced accent and who is a proficient, preferably trained, speaker. As far as the UK goes, a gentle Irish, Scottish or Welsh accent is fine. If it is to be

English, unfortunately regional accents do not sound very professional. The speaker, or narrator to use the proper term, will have to speak *plain* BBC English if you wish to make a good impression, certainly not too far back or plummy.

The narrative or voice-over should be carefully written, with your advice on technical content, so that it does not sound amateurish, too chummy or over-formal and stilted, and should be carefully integrated with the visuals.

A good video production company should be able to arrange all this, but keep an eye on them as well as taking their advice, especially if they are not 'horsey', to ensure technical accuracy and that they use not only correct and traditional equestrian terms and jargon (which go completely unnoticed by horse people) but also that they do *not* use such hilariously un-horsey terms as 'horseback riding', 'mating', 'harness' (when they mean tack), 'going for a ride' (when they mean hacking) and so on, which, coversely, stick out like a sore thumb and show your enterprise in a bad light.

Buying

Sellers feel quite often that they and their animals are not appreciated and that the whole rigmarole is not worth the rewards. Conversely, buying a horse, too, can be a thoroughly soul-destroying experience, especially a competition horse carrying all your hopes and dreams on his back and demanding a relatively high price – when you are on the paying end, that is!

In the current performance horse climate, Papers, Registrations, Records etc. (note the capital letters) are essential if we are to build up any kind of international market-competitive performance horse industry and if our horses are to command and retain a significant monetary value. If you buy a horse of unknown breeding you may well get him cheaper as the seller has no history or potential to sell (although he or she may well do a good selling job on the conformation and action) but, with a few exceptions, he will never be worth as much as a documented animal from a performance-proven family. If the animal is a mare and she turns out to be able to 'do the business', she will be worth more as a proven performer herself with the potential of becoming a broodmare. Sent to a performance-proven stallion – one from a proven family or one known to produce performers – she and her offspring could be just what most of today's competition horse breeders and buyers are looking for, and willing to pay for.

Nowadays, papers are becoming essential for real credibility unless the animal has already proven itself as an individual. As a buyer, you also have much more chance of finding what you want if the history is there to back up your judgement of the conformation and action. When buying warmbloods, particularly on the continent of Europe, you can even be told just what your animal's behavioural quirks are likely to be, never mind his leanings towards a particular equestrian discipline, so finely tuned and minutely documented are their bloodlines.

Non-warmbloods, too, have been bred here in Britain by a select number of conscientious studs for a specific discipline or breed, and with these you can check on the performance records of many relatives and get a good idea of potential. By all means, if you wish, indulge in that seemingly peculiarly British and Irish trait of discovering a completely unknown quantity covered in mud in a remote field in some wild, inaccessible part of the country – if you like a real gamble and can risk the cash. Personally, I would prefer to cut the odds and buy something with some real promise to fulfil, regarding the extra money as an insurance against wasted years and dashed hopes.

There are umpteen sources for you to try in your search. There are the usual Horses For Sale columns, breeders if you want a youngster, yards which bring on carefully selected youngsters to a standard interesting enough to attract those buyers who want to be able to start on something immediately, specialist competition horse dealing yards, agencies, the grapevine, want advertisements so you can tell the world what you want (even though you may be offered anything but), For Sale and Wanted registers operated by some organisations and breed societies and, of course, 'abroad' which is a very big place.

You can also keep your eye on what animals are competing in your chosen discipline, which are being shown out hunting, those appearing in the now popular potential competition horse classes often held in conjunction with an event of your chosen discipline, ordinary show classes (if you can see through the fat) and the high performance sales (in Britain) and similar sales and occasions held in many countries. There are breed society shows, warmblood grading events, the National Light Horse Breeding Society (HIS) shows and, of course, any auction that takes your fancy (a long shot, this); and if you bought a racehorse out of a selling plate (selling race) it would not be the first time this had happened and the horse turned up trumps.

If you buy from a formal, well-run sale the procedure you follow will be previously laid down and you will get a copy of the sale conditions beforehand. If buying from other sources, you may consider it a good plan to send for a decent photograph of each horse which sounds good according to pedigree and history, and try on it the conformation criteria given elsewhere in this book. If the horse is hopelessly out of line go no further. However, a good rating at this stage may merit a trip to see the horse.

The action should be carefully assessed along the lines of the previously mentioned criteria. Do take serious account of your first impression of the horse. It will very often be correct and if you know at once that the horse is not for you, do tell the seller and do not waste any more time. To do otherwise is pointless and unfair.

It is a good plan to take an experienced friend or adviser with you if you are newish to the game, but certainly to act as a witness to any claims the seller may make and which may subsequently turn out to be untrue and result in your having to take steps to return the horse and obtain a refund, maybe through legal means.

It should be stressed here that most people have problems when buying from private sellers not fully in the business, who buy and sell a bit on the side or wish to change their present horse for another. It is often safer to buy from a reputable dealer or breeder with a good reputation to maintain. Not only will such an establishment have a good selection for you to choose from, they often allow trials at your home (you will have to arrange and pay for the insurance) and will normally take back animals which turn out to be unsuitable even after purchase, and not always at a reduced price either, provided of course they are in good condition and you have not turned the horse into a nervous wreck.

It is often recommended that you turn up early so you can check if the horse is being warmed up ready for your arrival, which may involve exercising off any lameness or stiffness, rapping it to 'get those feet up', putting it into a 'co-operative' frame of mind, or even co-ordinating a small army of helpers to catch it. A somewhat jaundiced view, perhaps, but one born of experience!

Always see the horse handled and ridden or driven by its present owner in its own familiar surroundings first. If they expect you to ride it because no one else is available, ask your companion to ride it first so you can judge and assess it. You should really see it do everything of which it is capable to get a good idea – but beware of three or four-year-olds who can already jump three feet, mounted or loose, do two-track work of any difficulty, lengthen and shorten stride and so on. The homework necessary to achieve this standard must be excessive and harmful to such a young body and mind, and sorry though you may feel for the animal, a year off in your field to recover and 'grow into himself' may come too late to repair the damage.

Prepare a list of questions to ask, such as is the horse easy to catch, shoe, box, clip, travel; is it safe in *all* traffic including trains, or with microlite aircraft, hang-gliders appearing from nowhere, helicopters, jets etc.; has it any vices (look at the stable for signs of crib-biting, box-walking and kicking, and if there are any check whether this is the horse's usual box); what quirks/likes and dislikes does he have; how often are the horses wormed (if not often enough there will probably be considerable internal damage by the time you see the horse); and anything else important and relevant to you.

Write down the answers on your list and make sure your companion is in on this part of the act. Some unscrupulous sellers do become wizards at lying while looking you innocently straight in the eye, but normally trying to make someone look at you while answering and noting not only their visual expression but their vocal tone and body language and gestures can give you a fair idea of whether or not they are telling the truth. I am sorry to sound cynical and distrustful, but an element of such qualities is essential – particularly when dealing with some small, private sellers who simply often wish to unload a horse, get some cash and have no good name to bother about.

If the initial stages have gone swimmingly it is your turn to try the horse and here personal 'feel' is something only you can decide. Remember that no horse is perfect and also that the horse does not know you or you him. Do not be afraid, however, after a gentle walk, trot and canter to introduce yourself, to really try the horse at what he is supposed to be able to do without being harsh or tiring him unduly. If you are at all undecided say so, and maybe ask if you can try him again a few days later.

Also, be careful of saying you will take the horse *without* adding the provisos that it is subject to veterinary inspection and all papers being available at time of hand-over, including vaccination certificates, any show entry receipts and freeze-mark papers, if applicable. A verbal 'yes' is a contract so add your provisos, too, or you could end up in the soup. Papers not handed over at the time of sale have a nasty habit of not turning up at all.

As a matter of interest, it is very helpful to see a horse running loose in his familiar field, at home and relaxed, and, if possible, working loose. You can really gauge his action and attitude this way. Also, when he is run up in hand for your preliminary look, specifically ask the handler to do this on a *loose* rope or rein. This is essential if you want to see free, natural action. Some presenters are expert at restricting a horse's head in such a way as to disguise faulty action. If they baulk at your request do politely insist – or be suspicious. It is also helpful to see the horse lunged at a steady trot in both directions on a hard surface, as this really shows up difficulties in action.

It is amazing the number of buyers who feel they can economise by dispensing with a veterinary examination without jeopordising their chances of getting a horse physically suitable for what they have in mind. If you have a horse on trial and it develops a disorder in your care which was probably simmering previously, you do not have a leg to stand on, nor may you have several months hence, if you have not taken the precaution of having it vetted. When buying the best you can afford, do not spoil the ship for a ha'porth of tar, in terms of competition horse prices.

When buying a horse for serious competition work, it is worth discussing with your vet the pros and cons of asking for blood tests (to detect drugs and general health plus sub-clinical disease) and X-rays of feet and legs – a whole vexed area of its own. Some vets even want to do lung function tests and other biological tests to get as precise an idea as possible of the horse's condition, and if the seller declines it may be understandable that he or she does not want these slightly stressful tests carrying out for every would-be purchaser who comes along. This is something you will have to discuss first with your vet and then with the owner.

However, a thorough veterinary inspection of some sort should be regarded as essential – and if the horse turns out not to be right remember that you have to be very knowledgeable indeed to buy a crock with any certainty of getting it right, even if it does come cheaper. Start sound and, with care and good management, you have a good chance of staying sound.

In conclusion

The continuing expansion, some would say explosion, in the competition horse market is one of the biggest changes to hit the horse world since the horse ceased to be of major importance in agriculture in the face of mechanisation. It will, it seems, continue to expand and certainly merits the interest and expenditure currently directed towards it on an international scale, both as a recreation which is slightly more exciting than tiddlywinks, to put it mildly, and which is a vast provider of jobs and revenue. The British horse world alone has been estimated to have a greater turnover than the record industry.

Warmbloods in general are currently having a big impact on the scene, but there are those who predict that this is just a fashion and that they will recede to smaller numbers in the future (although not for the next few decades, I would predict), retaining their enthusiasts as does any breed or type. In general, it is accepted that they do not usually possess the speed or fighting spirit for eventing. In this field, at least, Britain does still seem to lead the horseworld. Our mainly Thoroughbred eventers, with a dash of native blood (our own), so traditional here and in Ireland for hunting and competition work, are in demand world-wide, and we not uncommonly find ourselves being beaten by our 'own' horses ridden by foreign teams.

Like the French, but in a slightly different way, we too have a rather *laissez-faire* attitude, but when this applies to horse breeding it is to our detriment. Being of mixed Germanic and Latin stock we have some of the characteristics of both races, but probably more of the former; being an island race, however, for the whole of our formation into Britons (and I hope the Celts among us will be a little tolerant here), we are not used to being invaded or to regularly having our backs against the wall. This has led to the overriding British characteristic of independence and of not taking kindly to being told what to do or to excessive control from governments, our own or anyone else's.

As far as horse breeding is concerned, this has led to our breeding whatever we fancy, how we like, and waiting to see what the result will be, to our not keeping proper records of ancestors, of often having no clear aim as to what we want to produce, and generally failing to co-operate with each other and organise ourselves so as to be in a position to compete with other nations when it comes to producing horses for ourselves or selling them to others.

The Americans seem to be going along very much the same road with one important difference – they are much more keen to *learn* than the British. They are willing to sacrifice more for success than we are. They are more open to ideas from abroad and not only have official team trainers in the different disciplines but also have permanent training centres for their national teams, and the team members spend a great deal of time there. They also ride in a distinctive, uniform style which has proved extremely successful.

Our fragmented, individualistic approach seems to be insurmountable, and we also have great economic problems in the horse world due to our government of the day refusing to recognise the horse as an agricultural animal, as is done (at the time of writing) in all but one of the other EEC countries. This results in grossly unfair and punitive regulations regarding business rates, taxation and status, and also our VAT regulations positively punish breeders and sellers of horses. Faced with such gigantic handicaps before we even start, the success we do experience is all the more remarkable in the face of overseas competition and our nationalistic insistence on doing things 'my way'.

But the competition horse world is changing. The 'grandad syndrome' is no longer sufficient to ensure success in either horse breeding or riding/driving those horses. Other nations who are better organised, keep better records, are more willing and quicker to grasp the benefits of modern research and scientific findings are attaining more consistent success, and we can no longer take it for granted that we shall even be in the first three wherever we go and in whatever discipline.

Fortunately we and other countries such as America, Australia and New Zealand are finally setting ourselves up with a more organised approach and it is quite possible to do this without losing our national identities and individuality. The continental Europeans do have the vast benefit of government assistance, something which is unknown here in Britain, in the form not only of vast financial resources, superb premises fully staffed with paid employees and agricultural status for the horse, but also the recognition by governments of the tremendous financial and prestigious benefits accruing to their national purses and images from a successful and highly viable competition horse industry. They have always been much quicker than any of our governments to see the tremendous export value of such horses, the prices of which, at least when trained and tempered by experience and competition, come level with and past those hitherto only envisaged for Thoroughbred racing and breeding stock.

The competition horse industry will not go away. Economies will rise and fall and so will governments, but national preferences, leanings, recreational activities and a general will to keep horses on the scene will ensure that equestrianism as a whole will continue to flourish, particularly in those countries willing to develop, maintain and further refine and expand a logical, organised system of production and marketing, maybe tempered by national circumstances but all geared to one aim – the availability and effective production and management of high class competition horses.

Bibliography

Andrist, Friedrich *Mares, Foals and Foaling*. J A Allen, London.

Bromiley, Mary (1987) *Equine Injury and Therapy*. Blackwell Scientific Publications, Oxford. (Co-published in New York by Howell Book House.)

Bromiley, Mary (1990) *Physiotherapy in Veterinary Practice*. Blackwell Scientific Publications, Oxford.

Kiley-Worthington, Dr Marthe (1987) *The Behaviour of Horses in Relation to Management and Training*.

Lose, M. Phyllis (1978) *Blessed are the Brood Mares*. Macmillan, New York.

Lose, M. Phyllis (1987) *Blessed are the Foals*. Macmillan, New York.

McCarthy, Gillian (1987) *Pasture Management for Horses and Ponies*. Blackwell Scientific Publications, Oxford. (Co-published in New York by Howell Book House.)

Mills, Bruce and Barbara Carne (1988) *A Basic Guide to Horse Care and Management*. Howell Book House, New York.

Pavord, Tony and Marcy Drummond (1990) *Horse Breeding: A Practical Guide for Owners*. Howell Book House, New York.

Pilliner, Sarah (1986) *Getting Horses Fit*. Blackwell Scientific Publications, Oxford.

Rose, John and Sarah Pilliner (1989) *Practical Stud Management*. Blackwell Scientific Publications, Oxford. (Co-published in New York by Howell Book House.)

Tobin, Thomas (1981) *Drugs and the Performance Horse*. Charles C. Thomas.

Vogel, Colin (1989) *How to Keep Your Horse Healthy*. Blackwell Scientific Publications, Oxford. (Co-published in New York by Howell Book House.)

Wynmalen, Henry *Horse Breeding and Stud Management*. J A Allen, London.

Other books by Susan McBane

Keeping a Horse Outdoors
Your First Horse: A guide to buying and owning
Keeping Horses: How to save time and money
Behaviour Problems in Horses
Ponywise
The Horse and the Bit (editor)
The Horse in Winter
Effective Horse and Pony Management: A failsafe system
Horse Care and Riding: A Thinking Approach (Co-author)
A Natural Approach to Horse Management
Pony Problems: How to cope
Horse Facts (Co-author)
Understanding Your Horse
Know Your Pony
Turf International: A source book of racing round the world (Technical Editor)

Index

action, 1, 2, 4, 6, 8, 9, 10, 11, 12, 15,
    20, 21, 22, 24, 26, 32, 33, 38, 39, 40,
    42, 45, 46–58, 118, 199, 213, 223,
    224, 226
Akhal-Teke, 22–4, 26
American Performance Horse, 34
American Warmblood, 34
American Warmblood Society, 34
Andalusian, 29, 35
Anglo-Arab, 19, 21, 26, 30, 37, 38, 43,
    98
Appaloosa, 35–6
Arab, 9, 10, 11, 12, 13, 15, 16, 21, 22,
    23, 24, 25, 26, 27, 28, 29, 32, 33, 34,
    35, 36, 37, 38, 98, 185
artificial insemination, 69–71, 72, 73
Association of British Riding Schools,
    40

British Horse Project, 39, 43
British Horse Society, 40
British Show Jumping Association, 42
British Sports Horse Registry, 44
British Warmblood, 33
British Warmblood Society, 33, 41, 42,
    43, 44
Budyonny, 26

carriage driving, 4–5, 19, 21, 22, 27, 28,
    29, 31, 33, 49, 76, 187
Cleveland Bay, 19–20, 30, 33
conformation, 1, 2, 3, 4, 6, 7, 8, 10, 11,
    12, 13, 14, 16, 18, 20, 22, 24, 25, 32,
    33, 38, 39, 41, 42, 45, 46–58, 60, 62,

71, 114, 117, 118, 120, 196, 197, 213,
    222, 223, 224
Connemara, 22
constitution, 10, 11, 14, 19, 20, 21, 22,
    23, 24, 38, 46, 60, 65, 118
Criollo, 13

Danish, 25
Don, 26
dressage, 5–9, 18, 21, 24, 29, 32, 33, 34,
    35, 37, 39, 43, 76, 119, 167, 211
Dutch, 5, 33, 37

East Bulgarian, 27
East Prussian *see* Trakehner
Einsiedler, 29
embryo transfer, 69, 71–4
endurance riding, 9–11, 24, 35, 128,
    133, 134, 136, 139, 140, 159, 160,
    163, 168, 181, 187, 201
eventing, 2–3, 14, 16, 17, 18, 20, 34, 39,
    43, 47, 58, 76, 119, 129, 136, 139,
    140, 160, 175, 181, 187, 201, 227

Fédération Equestre International
    (FEI), 176, 177, 180, 181, 182, 207
feeding, 61, 76, 101, 103, 104, 105,
    119–74, 175, 176, 177, 178, 180, 182,
    183, 184–5, 186, 191, 201, 222, 203,
    206, 210, 213, 214, 219
feet, 55–8, 118, 196–200
Fell, 22
fencing, 95–8
French Trotter, 25, 26

Friesian, 29, 30
Furioso, 26, 28

Gelderland, 33
General Stud Book, 22
gene(s), 60, 110
genetic engineering, 73
genetic fingerprinting, 70
genetics see heredity
Gidran, 26
Groningen, 33

Hackney, 29
Hanoverian, 29, 30, 31, 32, 33
harness racing, 11–12, 24–5
heredity, 60–66, 112, 116, 120, 134
Highland, 22
HIS (Hunters Improvement Society), 42, 224
Holstein, 29, 31, 32–3
Hungarian, 26, 27, 28

inbreeding, 64, 70
inheritance see heredity
Irish Draught, 17, 20–21, 42, 44

Jockey Club, 42, 176, 177, 180
jumping, 24, 27, 49, 52–5, 76, see also show jumping

Limousin, 38
line breeding, 64
long distance riding see endurance riding
Lusitano, 35

Malapolski, 26
marketing, 14, 15, 212–29
Metis Trotter, 26
Morgan, 24, 34–5, 36

National Association of Trotting Horse Breeders, 25
National Light Horse Breeding Society (HIS) see HIS
National Pony Society, 40
National Trainers Federation, 182
Neapolitan, 30, 32
New Forest, 22

Nonius, 28
Norfolk Roadster see Norfolk Trotter
Norfolk Trotter, 24, 25, 26, 28, 37
Norman, 25, 28, 29, 30, 31, 37
nutrition see feeding

Oldenburg, 29–30
Orlov Trotter, 25, 26

parasites, 80, 84, 124
pasture, 79–90, 120, 134, 137, 138, 141, 146, 147, 153, 178, 201
pedigree(s), 63–4, 66, 110, 118
Percheron, 34
physiotherapy, 189–96
point-to-point, 14, 47, 51
polo, 12–13
prohibited substances, 155, 175–83, 207
psychology, 58–9

Quarter Horse, 13, 34

Saddlebred, 36
Schweiken, 32
Selle Francais, 37–8
Shagya, 23, 28
shelter, 90–95, 101
showing, 14–15, 167
show jumping, 1–2, 3, 20, 29, 32, 33, 34, 38, 39, 43, 48, 52–5, 76, 140, 181, 187, 207, 211
stabling, 91, 98–101, 103, 105, 106, 201, 202, 203, 204, 205, 210
Standardbred, 11, 24–5, 26, 36
stress, 101–2, 103, 104, 106, 113, 115, 118, 119, 120, 121, 123, 131, 133, 144, 150, 185, 187, 190, 195, 196, 197, 198, 199, 206, 208, 211, 213, 217, 219, 227
Swedish, 29
swimming, 198
Swiss, 29

Tarbes, 38
temperament, 1, 2, 5, 8, 10, 12, 13, 15, 16, 18, 20, 21, 24, 25, 26, 27, 28, 29, 30, 32, 33, 34, 38, 39, 41, 58–9, 60, 71, 111, 114, 118, 119, 120, 121, 132,

134, 138, 144, 153, 155, 159, 183, 209–11, 212, 222
Tersky, 26
Thoroughbred, 2, 3, 6, 9, 10, 11, 13, 15–18, 19, 20, 21, 22, 23, 24, 25, 26, 27, 28, 29, 30, 31, 32, 33, 34, 35, 36, 37, 38, 39, 42, 43, 44, 47, 51, 59, 61, 65, 68, 69, 70, 71, 75, 98, 185, 219, 220, 227, 229
Thoroughbred Breeders Association Equine Fertility Unit, 71
Trakehner, 29, 31–2, 33
Turcoman, 25, 38
Turk(mene) *see* Turcoman

ventilation, 98–101, 201
veterinary inspection, 117–18

watering, 127–9
weaning, 103–7, 121
Welsh Cob, 21–2, 34–5, 42
Westphalian, 29, 30
Wielkopolski, 26, 32
World Arab Horse Organization, 15
Wurttemberg, 29, 30

yarding, 102–3, 201
Yorkshire Coach Horse, 30